ANDREW JACKSON

ANDREW JACKSON

A RHETORICAL PORTRAYAL OF PRESIDENTIAL LEADERSHIP

AMOS KIEWE

THE UNIVERSITY OF TENNESSEE PRESS / KNOXVILLE

LIBRARY OF CONGRESS CATALOGING-IN-PUBLICATION DATA
Names: Kiewe, Amos, author.
Title: Andrew Jackson: a rhetorical portrayal of presidential leadership / Amos Kiewe.
Description: First edition. | Knoxville, TN: The University of Tennessee Press, [2019]
| Includes bibliographical references and index. |
Identifiers: LCCN 2018021890 (print) | LCCN 2018026674 (ebook)
| ISBN 9781621904489 (pdf) | ISBN 9781621904472 (hardcover)
Subjects: LCSH: Jackson, Andrew, 1767–1845—Oratory.
| Jackson, Andrew, 1767–1845—Relations with journalists.
| Press and politics—United States—History—19th century.
| Presidents—Press coverage—United States.
| Political oratory—United States—History—19th century.
| Rhetoric—Political aspects—United States—History—19th century.
| United States—Politics and government—1829–1837.
Classification: LCC E382 (ebook) | LCC E382.K54 2019 (print) | DDC 973.5/6092—dc23
LC record available at https://lccn.loc.gov/2018021890

CONTENTS

ILLUSTRATIONS

PREFACE

Writing about President Andrew Jackson in the postmodern era poses a challenge to any scholar seeking to balance political accomplishments with personal failings, especially those that could now be considered insensitive or even racist. Jackson experienced mostly hard-won political successes. Like most whites of the early republic, he was a product of his time with all its prejudices and stereotypes. He focused on the survival of the young democracy, worried about the porous borders, and was especially concerned with threats to the federal Union. Jackson also fought to take governing out of the hands of small elites and expand the democracy's reach. He ushered in an era of progressivism and added millions of new voters, proving that a political system whereby people govern themselves was not just an ideal.

Andrew Jackson was a true Democrat in the sense of abhorring "all privilege" or the existence of a better class, yet he was blind to the plight of slaves and Indians.[1] He was a plantation owner who treated his approximately 150 slaves like other masters did—sometimes kindly, other times harshly. Moreover, Jackson fought Indians throughout his military career. He sought their removal from the vicinity of whites who wanted to squash them, and he considered this removal plan benevolent. As a skilled politician, Jackson also knew how to maneuver wins in most of his political battles, and he won big. He had a knack for anticipating others' partisan moves and calculating his own actions accordingly. Additionally, he displayed a keen insight into the dynamic of politics, making astute domestic and international forecasts. Yet while Jackson stood at the outset of the abolitionist movement, he could not comprehend that slaves required the freedom he sought for others. Instead, the seventh president observed regional politics at its worst, a major threat to the Union.

Similarly, Danielle Allen confronts the contradiction between Jefferson's authoring the enduring Declaration of Independence and his keeping slaves and fathering their offspring. How might any scholar tackle such inconsistency? Allen confronts the principles of freedom and equality in the

Declaration of Independence, but she also sensitively addresses the text's omission of African slaves and Native Americans. She reconciles this tension by arguing that the declaration was part of a "script" that colonialists had lived by, then adding that every script requires application. Allen writes, "Truth be told, new scripts are invented only as people begin to undertake new actions. Spaces must be ripped open in the existing web of human habits, which invariably have a tightly adhesive grip on the human spirit."[2] She further elaborates on the tension between ideas and actions: "When we observe a person who says one thing and does another, we might be looking at a liar, but we might also be looking at a person who hasn't yet been able to turn her ideas into a script that is concrete enough to guide her actions."[3]

Jackson, too, had a "script," or what we would call a rhetorical vision of a popular democracy and government. But not all his actions caught up to his principles: he removed American Indians from Georgia, sustained slavery, and opposed abolitionists. Does this make Jackson's principles corrupt? Not wholly, one might argue, especially if the Jeffersonian principles he clearly espoused also paved the way for expansion of rights and ideas for governing. The very "script" of extending the number of voters, gradually removing landownership as a perquisite for voting, and opening government positions to able individuals and not only the privileged, commenced a trajectory that equalized more and more segments of society. Jackson grounded most of his rhetorical acts in a principled conviction about the supremacy of the Union. This belief would also be abolitionists' strongest one in the forthcoming years. One might even argue that had Jackson lived some thirty years later and seen how the fight over slavery was tearing apart the Union (just as South Carolina sought to do in the 1830s), he would have sided with the Union. To Jackson, the Union was sacred.

In the twenty-first century, when the term *imperial presidency* often describes executive authority, writing about Jackson's early nineteenth-century presidency is instructive precisely because his was the first to expand the power, authority, and reach of the executive. Jackson's relationship with Congress was difficult. He sought a different balance between the branches of government and formulated a system that was more amenable to an expanding nation and more responsive to the growing population. The present-day acrimoniousness between the executive and Congress has its roots in Jackson's presidency and the precedents it set. And though Jackson did not conquer all early evils, his presidency paved the way for and portended much of what would transpire in the proceeding decades, culminating in the Civil War.

ANDREW
JACKSON

ANDREW JACKSON

PRAGMATIC BUT PRINCIPLED RHETORIC

What makes the gentleman? The boy said, Education;
the uncle, Good Principles.
—Andrew Jackson recalling an exchange with his uncle[1]

The boy Jackson must have taken his uncle's advice to heart. More than anything else, principles would guide Jackson's political and rhetorical perspective during his eight years in the White House.

This book is a study in presidential public address. More specifically, this work seeks to give voice to the seventh president of the United States, Andrew Jackson (1829–37), who covered significant political and rhetorical terrain during his two terms in office and beyond. At the intersection of history, politics, and rhetoric, this is an analysis of words and their political impact. Then and now, words are a significant tool for politicians seeking to carve a rhetorical space, influence audiences, argue issues, and implement policies. Words reveal plans and attitudes, both stated and hidden. They shed light on strategies and calculations, as well as on a leader's cumulative strengths and weaknesses, proclivities, skills, and understanding. In studying Andrew Jackson's rhetoric over key issues and controversies of this presidency, I seek an account of major addresses' development, the reasoning and constraints behind them, and, ultimately, their impact on the polity. My primary argument here is that Jackson's public address (mostly in written form) constructed an image and framed issues in specific ways that influenced policy and the balance of power among the three branches of government. Thus, Jackson's public rhetoric also significantly changed the presidency. In assessing Jackson's public address, I treat specific rhetorical acts and speeches for their longitudinal evolution and not as stand-alone artifacts. In so doing, I wish to describe how the rhetorical and the political were conjoined and interdependent in forming an expanded space for the presidency.

The vast majority of studies on Jackson are historical and biographical, while rhetorical studies of him are rather few and quite limited. One particular study by Marvin Meyers[2] advocates the need to study Jackson's persuasion, which ought to include public appeals and messages as well as the function of language as a political tool. He adds that calling some public statements "propaganda" and considering them "as less significant intrinsically than the traffic in harder goods" is an erroneous perspective. Meyers calls for studying Jackson's political statements, which could provide insights into his policy, rhetoric, principles in use, and moral posturing, as well as a better understanding of the Jacksonian era.[3] I concur with this perspective whereby political rhetoric is of no lesser value than the policies themselves. To put it more succinctly, politics needs rhetorical legs to walk on. This study is pursued in this spirit and with a sharpened focus on the rhetorical as the manifestation and construction of the political.

This work also seeks to fill a void in studies of nineteenth-century presidential rhetoric. Presidential oratory has produced rich volumes of scholarship, especially since the 1980s. The majority of these studies cover twentieth-century presidents, and only few of them address presidencies of the previous century. The focus on Jackson's rhetoric is justified here on the grounds of the important development that his presidency brought to American politics. Until Jackson's election, presidential elections were designed to select "the office holder but not his policies."[4] In the early years of the republic, then, much was riding on the person voted into office, and less scrutiny was given to his policies or campaign promises. Jackson accomplished his significant changes to the presidency and the American polity with great rhetorical zeal.

The objective here is not a biographical account of Jackson per se but a keener view of the major issues, controversies, and crises his presidency confronted via the rhetorical. This focus is a window into a period that in hindsight would be significant in the nation's history. The general questions guiding this study are these: What was Jackson's rhetoric like, and what was its impact on contemporaries and beyond? Relatedly, was Jackson's rhetoric a significant component of his presidency?

✳✳✳✳✳

Andrew Jackson was a lawyer by profession. In addition, he was tantamount to the attorney general of Tennessee before Tennessee became a state and a congressman, senator, governor, and judge. Jackson was also a successful military general, becoming the Hero of New Orleans in 1815 and the champion of other battles. Thus Old Hickory, as he would affectionately be known, entered office tired but spirited. His character and convictions, developed primarily over years of military action and senatorial terms, brought a determined, skilled politician to the presidency. Jackson's "hero" image propelled him to the highest office more than anything else. Many considered him a larger-than-life figure, and he knew it. The Battle of New Orleans of January 8, 1815, would become mythic and grounds for his claim to the presidency. The account of bravery initially attached to the frontiersmen of Lexington and Concord was "crystalized," argues Ronald H. Carpenter, in the Battle of New Orleans, where ill-equipped, outnumbered US troops overcame an organized British army. Jackson gained quick popularity for his victory, which single-handedly made him a household name.[5] The image formed at the battlefield was attributed to his success despite the odds. Jackson and his disorganized, inexperienced men managed to overcome the army of one of England's best generals, Edward Pakenham. The result of some two thousand British soldiers killed or wounded to only eight American soldiers killed and thirteen wounded was an unimaginable feat.[6] Yet it is important to acknowledge that Jackson was involved with politics before investing in a military career. He served for a short time as a member of both the House and the Senate before the close of the eighteenth century, during which his key political principles were already in vogue. As early as 1801 Jackson asserted the popular belief that "the people were the sovereign." At the time, this was a relative change from privileged landowners being the primary individuals with voting rights.[7]

Jackson's military successes and the admiration of many did not blind him. He was a decent and moral person, but more significantly, he was a principled man. Jackson was not perfect—he had a temper, he was quick to duel, and he carried blind spots as to the plight of American Indians and slaves. He differed from his predecessors in the White House and altered much about presidential politics. In hindsight, he would serve as a model for future presidents. Jackson knew where he was going, believed in the greatness of his cause, and fought adversaries with great zeal and conviction. His causes were rather simple: justice and virtue imbedded in simple but foundational principles of democratic governance.[8] His early views on the presidency can be gleaned from his letter to James Monroe when Monroe assumed the office. Jackson suggested that the incoming president ought to be above partisanship and to select cabinet secretaries based on their capacity for the position. Additionally, Jackson asserted, the office must be seen as impartial to the entire nation and not obliged to any faction thereof.[9]

Though he was first and foremost a military hero, Jackson was early on portrayed as a brute, rough, savage, and backward. Yet his second senatorial stint in 1823–25, calculated in part to improve his image as necessary for a presidential contender, modified these prior perceptions. Daniel Webster commented in 1824, "General Jackson's manners are more presidential than those of any of the candidates." Indeed, Jackson's presence was impressive; tall and distinguished, he had "a natural grandeur which few could resist."[10] Perhaps more intuitively, Jackson would use his presence as a political asset, hence an advantageous materiality for public consumption. Those close to him knew that he was rather calm and controlled[11] and that his so-called fury was more strategic than habitual. Jackson's greatest strength was his natural intelligence and keen judgment of people and situations.

Though initially inexperienced, Jackson learned the role and functions of the president rather quickly and was aided by his common sense and his basic sense of right and wrong. He did not fully tap into the experience of his predecessors, and he quite actively sought a different presidential purview. Jackson understood the executive as a fluid institution. Though the role was constitutionally stipulated, its varied occupants could organically make and remake it. He was determined to exercise this freedom on his own terms. Jackson's overall take on the Constitution and the federation of states as an experiment that had to succeed supported his reasoning. His time in office was busy, and the crises he faced were detrimental to the nation's future. He was a new kind of president, chosen by the nation at large, putting to rest the Founders' cliquish, closed-door canvassing and political promotion. Ostensibly, he was "an authentic representative of this impulse of entrepreneurial democracy."[12] In sum, Jackson was an ambitious and quite astute politician who brought "natural instincts" to government.[13] His opponents often conditioned the rough politics of his presidential terms. They dismissed Jackson's innate political skills precisely because they judged him through the lens of "old" politics—those of the Founders. Nor did Jackson's detractors appreciate the democratic flavor and frontier logic he brought to the polity.

Jackson campaigned in 1824 by resorting to his strong administrative skills. He developed an organization that spread his name across the country and included an advance team to quickly refute unflattering information. Jackson did not specify a clear political agenda. He had a keen sense of the issues he wanted to address—in particular, ending corruption—but he remained vague on specifics. The old-fashioned and conventional political elite deemed Jackson's campaign unseemly. Early nineteenth-century candidates simply did not canvass on a large scale, at least not openly. Jackson and his aides changed all that realizing that winning elections would be "the business of professionals who managed powerful machines."[14]

Jackson lost the 1824 presidential election to John Quincy Adams in the House despite receiving the largest number of popular and Electoral College votes. The election, however, was decided by the House of Representatives (for only the second time, the first occurring in 1800-1801), since no candidate won the majority of the Electoral College. Remini argues that Jackson's outside credentials were the primary reason the House had opted for Adams despite Jackson winning the most votes. Many in the nation took the 1824 election loss as their own, supporting Jackson's contention that a "corrupt bargain" deprived him of the presidency. Given the number of candidates (initially five), it was quite unlikely that any of them could carry the Electoral College. But Jackson found in his defeat a popular appeal he translated into effective rhetorical lines. Rather quickly, the loss became the primary campaign material for the 1828 election. Jackson's supporters considered him the people's candidate. He was the Hero of New Orleans and perhaps the most popular person of his time. Jackson's detractors thought him nothing but a "military chieftain" and an Indian fighter, a man with neither political experience to become president nor a proper education.[15] His progressive political positions in state and federal posts were all discounted, allowing his military service to become a metonymy for unsuitability. Lurking behind opponents' criticism was the sheer fear of Jackson's popularity and its potential for remaking presidential elections that were previously the province of political elites. The fear was not unfounded.

Jackson was incensed by Henry Clay, who as Speaker of the House managed to secure the presidency for John Quincy Adams. As Jackson suggested, Clay then prearranged his own appointment as secretary of state in Adams's administration. Jackson expressed his views to the many who greeted him upon his return to Tennessee in early 1825. He began to describe his defeat with words such as *cheating*, *corruption*, and *bribery*. As these terms began resonating with the many he met, Jackson realized his popularity was his greatest asset. He intensified attacks on those who cost him the presidency, tailoring his criticism to popular appeal, telling audiences that "the people [had] been cheated," and that the "corruptions and intrigues at Washington . . . defeated the will of the people."[16] The presidential campaign of 1828 was under way.

Early nineteenth-century presidential candidates considered it unbecoming to solicit people's support. Thus, many people were surprised when Jackson did just that. Though he would often state that it was not his habit to seek an elected office, he also made it clear that he would not turn down the people's wishes that he run for office. His campaign operation brought the *Washington National Journal* to write on May 22, 1827, "[how surprising it is] that any man, representing himself to the nation as a candidate for the chief magistrate, should think it necessary to form so extraordinary an association for the purpose of promoting his views."[17] The nation had not seen the likes of Jackson's innovative campaign. He understood that his image carried rhetorical currency, especially since the presidential election was the interest of a growing nation and no longer in the hands of a few inside politicians. Jackson was a modern campaigner and ahead of his time.

Jackson's campaign rhetoric prompted a significant change in presidential politics. His initial image was that of "a savage armed with a tomahawk and with a scalping knife in his teeth," or so his opponents charged.[18] His supporters called him the "American Cincinnatus," a farmer who cultivated "with his own hand the soil that he defended from the grasp of a foreign foe."[19] This image perhaps borrowed liberally from George Washington, who was compared to Roman statesman Cincinnatus, who gave up power to return to his farm. Yet neither representation was correct.

Amos Kendall, Jackson's close aide and astute propagandist, called him "the farmer soldier." Others referred to him as the "Farmer of Tennessee."[20] However, Jackson was no farmer in the sense that his supporters encouraged, and he did not till the land with his own hands as some have suggested but he owned a large farm, raised cotton, tobacco, and other crops.[21] He worked with his campaign to tie his personal image to the pioneer spirit. The *Illinois Gazette* wrote in 1825 (before the House voted for Adams) that Jackson was gifted: "Endowed with the faculties to see the whole and grasp the most remote relations of vast and comprehensive designs, he is the most qualified to govern."[22] Jacksonians in New York City supported him for his "capacity," his "native strength of mind," and his "practical common sense," qualities which "are more valuable than all the acquired learning of the sages."[23] The *Ohio State Journal* opined that though Jackson did not acquire his knowledge from Voltaire, confidence in him owed to the fact that he was not "raised in the lap of luxury and wealth."[24] Against the learned Adams stood the farmer Jackson. Though from the backward hinterland, the latter was taken as a new creed of politician who possessed skills many considered necessary as the country expanded.

Jackson entered the presidency when the nation ended its youth—fifty-three years after the Declaration of Independence and only forty-two years after America became a democratic republic. The Founding Fathers were almost gone, and the nation was beginning to expand. Yet the United States' early battles lingered through 1815. Great Britain would try to punish the rebellious colonies one more time, ignoring the many changes since 1776 and the fact that America was becoming a great nation both territorially and politically. The democratic experiment was sustained. With Jackson's decisive presidential win in 1828, the country posed a challenge to the old world, proving that people can indeed govern themselves quite effectively. The United States also became a phenomenon in Europe, as evidenced by the arrival of various observers from the continent. Alexis de Tocqueville was the most famous among them, and he assessed the Jacksonian era in his tome *Democracy in America*. Yet what eluded many was the reality that the great democratic experiment was the cumulative effect of rhetorical battles in political speeches, letters, pamphlets, pub and town hall debates, and partisan presses. These clashes brought great oratory to the nation. But they also brought low and rough words, demagoguery, and pedestrian—if not altogether dirty—politics. Jackson in the White House epitomized the country's changes.

Common wisdom holds that nineteenth-century presidents engaged in limited public rhetoric relative to their twentieth- and twenty-first-century counterparts. Yet Jackson does not fully fit this comparison. A distinction is often made between the constitutional presidency of the eighteenth and nineteenth centuries and the rhetorical presidency ushered in during the first decade of the twentieth century. The first abided by more limited presidential reach, and the second is characterized by heavy reliance on rhetorical acts.[25] As this study reveals, Jackson was very much a rhetorical president, perhaps even ahead of his time. It was customary for presidents in the early republic to deliver few speeches—inaugural addresses and other selected statements. Even the State of the Union address was no longer delivered orally to Congress (George Washington and John Adams were the only presidents to do so, and the practice was abandoned until Woodrow Wilson reintroduced it). Instead, it was issued as a written report titled "An Annual Message to Congress." Still, the State of the Union was so rhetorically significant that it was among the most anticipated addresses and subject to extensive comments from politicians and the press.

Presidential speeches, then, were seldom directly addressed to the public. Others were read from written copies or excerpted in partisan newspapers for extensive distribution. The few directly orated presidential addresses allowed for a distance between the president and the people. This circumstance owed to habit and not necessarily to design; the presidential titles in use during the nation's early decades were *chief executive* or *chief magistrate*. Even so, the suasive function of the presidency was as essential then as it is now, despite different rhetorical opportunities and, by today's standards, limited rhetorical excesses. One hallmark of the early republic is presidents' indirect communication via the press. Journalists would cover private letters intended for wide dissemination, and Jackson utilized this rhetorical venue rather extensively. Jackson understood, perhaps intuitively, that, as Marvin Meyers suggests that "the appeals of the Democracy were carried by ideas and rhetoric by policies and public gestures."[26]

Despite many Americans' initial perception of him as a brute or even an illiterate (a likely stereotype of his western background his opponents encouraged), Jackson's letters and drafts of speeches and statements reveal a rather eloquent, skilled writer with a penchant for forceful, succinct language. Despite his reticence as a public orator, the seventh president was a deft expositor of sentiments, intent, and determination. Jackson was also helped by a cadre of key advisors, initially referred to as Amos Kendall and Company and later the Kitchen Cabinet. Those who lost favor with Jackson or thought several advisors held undue influence over him used the latter term disparagingly.[27] However, Kitchen Cabinet acquired a more neutral connotation. It referred to Jackson's White House staff that provided "the president a variety of services," including "policy advisors, lobbyists, liaison people, publicity experts, speech writers, and friends."[28] From a rhetorical perspective, the Kitchen Cabinet was an early version of the modern White House staff and a window into Jackson's administration. Policymaking and presentations were conjoined, extensively discussed, thought through, and strategized under Jackson's astute and careful oversight.

Jackson was a man of convictions and principles, and his rhetoric clearly illustrates these qualities, often relying on key principles to warrant his claims. His finalized public addresses are also quite reserved and even humble. They often contrast greatly with his letters concerning the same subjects. In a way, Jackson used contradictory rhetoric; it allowed a president with strong convictions and a reputation for bad temper (often unwarranted) to use generally restrained language consistent with his standing as the first "people's president." Yet Jackson's verbiage changed when sacred principles were challenged. South Carolina and the nullification crisis over Federally instituted tariffs resulted in a proclamation that was nothing like his other public addresses.

Jackson's rhetorical skills can be discerned from his first drafts of a number of speeches: his first inaugural address, his annual messages to Congress, his second inaugural address, several of his vetoes, his statement about removing deposits from the Bank of the United States, his proclamations, and the outline of his Farewell Address. As this volume will show, these remarks were mostly written by Jackson himself. His initial efforts demonstrate his great sense of clarity and focus, and they are in some cases superior to the final speeches incorporating speechwriters' input and modifications.

Jackson was also a prolific letter writer. He exchanged views with a vast network of friends and colleagues, rehearsing his public arguments, soliciting input while writing, testing issues and rhetorical strategies, and inquiring about their potential reception. Moreover, Jackson accepted others' advice with great care and sincerity. His status as a superb politician and a skilled reader of the political map of his time shaped his public arguments. He knew most political players and understood different statesmen's motives. He apprehended the entire gamut of the rhetorical process, including message construction, audience reception, constraints, and persuasive strategies. Additionally, Jackson's superb understanding of each issue's context helped with the "invention" of his rhetorical acts. All these skills allowed him to calibrate his rhetoric and calculate optimal positions. Rhetoric and politics were indistinguishable for him.

Jackson's rhetorical skills were also effective via the partisan press he formed as the mouthpiece for his administration's policies and views. Amos Kendall, Jackson's brilliant campaign strategist and advisor who ran a newspaper in Kentucky, conceived a national newspaper—the *Globe*—to be run by Francis Blair as the voice of the White House. Blair, Andrew Donelson, and Kendall were an effective team who quickly printed Jackson's formal messages and gained them wide and early circulation. The president's communications appealed directly to those whom he considered his

paramount stakeholders. Amos Kendall was a particularly effective aman-
uensis. According to one period account, Jackson often dictated ideas to
Kendall while lying down. Kendal would record the president's thoughts,
read them aloud, and, after several rounds of cooperative revisions, reach
the perfected version Jackson desired.[29] Additionally, with the skilled Martin
Van Buren, who transferred his support from William Crawford to Jackson
after the 1824 election, Jackson formed a political organization the nation
had never seen before. All these disparate efforts relied on Jackson's popularity as the compass for the new partisan coalition and the campaign
organization.[30]

Jackson's early career as a lawyer was instrumental to his rhetorical
education. Though not an orator, he was "an adequate speaker" with a
strong voice and "theatrical flair."[31] His many years in the military required
him to prepare documents and address his troops, tasks that were likewise
a stepping-stone in his rhetorical development. As the various speeches,
statements, and proclamations indicate, Jackson was an astute rhetorician.
His habit was to put initial thoughts on paper and give them to his aide and
nephew Andrew Donelson. Jackson would approach other advisors and key
cabinet secretaries such as the attorney general for additional input. Thereafter, he would write his own draft of a given address to be finalized by an
aide. At other times, he would edit his aides' drafts.[32] If not reclining on a
sofa, Jackson would pace the room while a staffer read a speech aloud; he
preferred to hear the text. The president strived for clear, succinct language
and forceful arguments while finalizing speeches.

Jackson's preparation for his Sixth Annual Message to Congress in 1834
captures his speechwriting process. He solicited input from department
heads and allowed closer officials like Vice President Van Buren and Atty.
Gen. Roger Taney greater authority in shaping the message. France's refusal
to pay agreed-upon indemnity angered Jackson greatly, and he felt that this
action necessitated strong language in his message. The president drafted
parts of the statement, including language related to France's behavior.
Without Jackson's knowledge, Secretary of State John Forsyth changed one
of these passages to make it more diplomatic. When the final draft was read
to him, Jackson stopped pacing in his office and declared, "That, sir, is not
my language . . . it has been changed, and I will have no other expression of
my own meaning than my own words."[33] Jackson controlled the rhetorical
process and weighted the importance of every word. He recalled what he
drafted and knew the phrasing he preferred. Most importantly, he held to
the desired effect he had in mind.

Jackson also displayed astute political skills, calculating and assessing each issue and timing his actions accordingly. His foes completely misunderstood his advanced rhetorical skills and found themselves defeated time and again. While Jackson was the people's president in the most active way, for the political elite, especially those residing in the nation's capital, his relationship with the masses was a sore and misunderstood point. Former House member John Sergeant well illustrates this point. He wrote to Henry Clay that Jackson's "administration [was] absolutely odious, and yet there [was] an adherence to the man."[34] While Jackson was "odious" to political insiders, his popularity nationwide was perplexing and its origin misunderstood by the political elite. Jackson's contemporaries had difficulty comprehending his administrative image and style, the serious reforms he brought to the presidency, and the persuasive methods he implemented in aiding his changes, authority, and reach.

Many considered Jackson an old man when he entered the presidency. Given his continuous health problems, the popular assumption was also that he would be a one-term president. His opponents were sure that he was on his deathbed on several occasions, and they waited in vain for his demise. Relatedly, for eight years, Jackson was surrounded by three individuals who actively desired the presidency: John C. Calhoun, Henry Clay, and Martin Van Buren. Every move these individuals made was calculated to advance their presidential prospects. Calhoun and Clay in particular would exploit every issue, controversy, or crisis. The often overconfident Clay wrote as follows to Thomas Speed: "Intelligence from all quarters through members of Congress, letters, travelers &c. is highly encouraging. The old buck [Andrew Jackson] is mortally wounded. He will run awhile, make a few shew of vigor and fall." Clay clearly underestimated Jackson and could not see beyond some superficial presence.[35] Van Buren, on the other hand, would ingratiate himself with Jackson to get closer to him. He eventually replaced Calhoun as vice president and realized his hopes of advancing to the highest office in the land.

Jackson's two terms in office coincided with several crucial issues, often reaching the level of national crises, that would determine the nation's fate for decades to come. Jackson was the first ex–military general after George Washington to assume the presidency. He was also the first popular person elected to the office after Washington. Jackson's election would transform the nature of presidential campaigns, giving Americans a decisive role in voicing their preferences and voting for their candidates. Jackson was also the first president who did not electorally represent one of the original thirteen colonies. He therefore represented the expanding nation and its growing confidence in the region and the world.

As the United States entered its sixth decade, James Madison was the only surviving Founding Father. The nation's early cracks were becoming serious. Political corruption was widespread, and the machinations of congressional politics made it quite visible, especially as related to the presidential elections. Early battles concerning the "principles of '98" and the interpretation of the Constitution thereof were still fresh in many politicians' minds. Tension was specifically apparent between states' right to determine the constitutionality of federal policies and the central government's opposing view on the matter. Jackson was attuned to the changing nature of the expanding nation. The growing conflict between the federal government and the states would precipitate one of the most serious crises and eventually lead to the Civil War some thirty years later. Yet the federal budget and the federal banking system would consume much of Jackson's time, as would the removal of Indian tribes farther west with untold suffering.

To a great degree, Jackson was unknown to most voters beyond his fame as a national hero. His constituents knew little or nothing about his political skills and views, and he preferred it that way. Jackson was a plantation owner who owned slaves, a southerner by birth, and a westerner by residence and temperament. Yet these characteristics did not necessarily condition a strict southern mind-set. To the contrary, Jackson was a staunch supporter and defender of the Union. Time and again, he would cite the Union as a necessity for the future of the United States and the key principle that would guide most of the crises he faced. Jackson also believed in limited federal government and states' right to engage in practices not assigned to the federal government. Nonetheless, his faith in the sanctity of the Union trumped all other competing interests. On that point Jackson was adamant—he would go to great lengths to advocate and implement his conviction.

His would be a presidency of breaking with traditions and, by implication, starting new ones. Jackson could afford to be different, to carve a new path for the presidency and the nation at large. He was confident, perhaps supremely so, and he held to strong principles. Such would be the case during his fight with the Bank of the United States, his quelling of secession-inclined South Carolina, and his decision to depart with a Farewell Address. At the time, this last act had been unique to the nation's founding president. Jackson's realism helped him with most issues, allowing him to accurately assess how far he could go and what risks he could take. And he did go far, and he did take risks his predecessors hesitated over. As most former presidents had suggested, Jackson concluded that Indian tribes had to be removed from their land. He reached this decision despite the pain and suffering that would ensue, and despite a Supreme Court that adjudicated otherwise. Jackson could rationalize anything, and he considered removal of the tribes the best solution for both whites and Indian tribes. His morality, he believed, did not have to be the morality of others as long as he believed that a given decision was right. And so he acted.

Upon reflection and the benefit of some two hundred years, Jackson stands among the great presidents but is controversial nonetheless. He brought both change and determination that are well reflected in his public addresses. He used rhetoric that was principled, even blunt when necessary. But Jackson also employed oratory that was eloquent and indicative of the sentiments of his time. The measure of his rhetorical successes is their influence on others, including future presidents. His presidency would later be described as an era. However, Jackson himself was indebted to the earlier Jeffersonian era, which espoused an egalitarian society cherishing freedom, equality, progress, and opportunity, and distrusted all things unnatural and artificial. Yet what was considered "natural" for Jackson included the westward migration of whites and the removal of the Indian tribes in the same direction, all in the name of a natural movement.[36]

His symbolic standing is equally impressive, ranging from a statue in front of the White House depicting him on horseback to the twenty-dollar bill bearing his image. The very metonymy of Jackson's famous toast "Our Federal Union: It Must be Preserved," which is carved on that statue in front of the White House, captures the essence of his two terms in office. The tribute stands for a principle and a guiding value for which the general, mounted on a horse, is ready to fight. Patriotism, battle, determination, and, above all else, the Union, were the essence of Jackson's presidential rhetoric.

Jackson was a rhetorical president to the degree that he valued the office's public functions in the forms of addresses, statements, proclamations, and vetoes as the embodiment of the nation. He understood that words and images would be in wide distribution, especially in the press. He paid close attention to the press, which was then in the service of a given political party and a self-serving public relations apparatus. The extensive volumes of Jackson's correspondence are rich with examples of his writing, his solicitation of opinions from across the nation, and his preparation of public pronouncements through outlines and drafts. Collectively, these documents reveal careful thought and planning that calculated how various important constituents would receive presidential messages. Jackson's popularity during and since his time in the White House is reflected in the era named after him—Jacksonian democracy. His impact on the country was profound, for he outmaneuvered political heavyweights such as Henry Clay, Daniel Webster, and John Calhoun. Jackson also extended his presidential influence beyond his presidency (1829-1837) all the way to 1849 by seeing candidates he supported, including Martin Van Buren and James Polk, win the office.

As presented and assessed here, Jackson's rhetoric primarily takes the forms of public addresses, statements, proclamations, and vetoes collectively covering the most important issues of his presidency. Though the focus is on public remarks, it is important to note that these were often informed by private correspondence. The two are accounted for here with the understanding that they are conjoined and interdependent. This book proceeds as follows: It begins with a discussion of the 1824 election with a specific focus on campaign material. Following this chapter are discussions of Jackson's First Inaugural Address, First Annual Message to Congress, Maysville Road Veto, Indian Removal Act, Bank Veto, Nullification Proclamation, Second Inaugural Address, statement on removal of deposits from the Bank of the United States, image construction, and Farewell Address. The volume concludes with a discussion of Jackson's public images and the rhetorical impacts thereof.

The general line pursued here is that the challenges and the crises Jackson confronted were, on balance, markers of the nation's growing pains. America sought to ameliorate acute problems such as the expanding territories, the rise of the working class, tensions between states and the federal government, the moneyed elite, the banking industry, and the treatment of Indian tribes, as well as the advent of abolitionism. The presidency as an institution would change significantly, primarily as a result of Jackson's rhetorical skill in expanding the executive's authority and overall reach.

1

A "MILITARY CHIEFTAIN" AND THE CAMPAIGN RHETORIC OF 1824

Presidential aspirants feared Jackson's popularity and chances of victory in the approaching election of 1824. Many Americans were looking for another George Washington, and the Hero of 1815 was a serious contender. The country was past its infancy. Territorial expansion and citizens' growing confidence brought changes to the polity, and more individuals sought to partake in national politics. The number of voters who resented the power of the political elite significantly increased. Calls for advancing the role of parties, thereby resuming the partisan politics of an earlier period, distinguished this era. Additionally, many considered the Battle of New Orleans the last challenge to the independent confederation of states. The nation now turned inward, focusing on westward expansion, internal improvements to roads, canals, and bridges, and a rising professional class that supported the entrepreneurial spirit. The political elite, often regarded as eastern in orientation, were no longer thought capable of handling these issues. Numerous

Americans looked for new faces unlike those of the Founding Fathers. The growing class of voters henceforth considered Jackson the ideal person for this new era of confidence and expansion.

As early as 1821, plans to promote Jackson for the presidency were under way, precipitated not insignificantly by the growing sense of corrupt politics, especially a corrupt executive. Like many others, Jackson was concerned over the general opinion that the presidency was compromised. This disquiet added to his own frustrations over Monroe's less-than-ethical practices, such as the suggestion that he altered documents related to Jackson's military expedition in Florida. Jackson did not appreciate such manipulation. In fact, it helped him seriously consider his presidential prospects.[1] Ambitious and confident, he was keen on entertaining his presidential chances under the banner of "Andrew Jackson and Reform." Jackson did not turn down efforts to recruit him.[2] Rather, he answered one inquiry about his candidacy by stating that his "undeviating rule of conduct through life . . . ha[d] been neither to seek, or decline public invitations to office."[3] Jackson's initial concerns about the recent Panic of 1819, the ensuing economic depression, and the revelations of corruption at the Bank of the United States bolstered his conviction that the nation might be ready for a reformer like him.

In 1822, Nashville political operatives and local newspapers began supporting Jackson for the presidency. This was mainly a matter of local politicians' self-promotion, and these advocates likely lacked serious conviction that Jackson could be nominated. But enthusiasm for Jackson was far greater than his early supporters realized.[4] He was even popular beyond the confines of his own state and the western region. Sensing the opportunity at hand, Jackson's team suggested a quick stint as a senator to elevate him nationally and transform his image from military general to statesman. From late 1823 until early 1825, Jackson would serve again as a senator from Tennessee, replacing early perceptions of him as a rough westerner with a more refined and cultivated image. His short time in the Senate was used strategically to mend fences with former opponents and present a new persona that could transcend his earlier military credentials.[5] In the context of a campaign against corruption, Jackson's refined image had to include a strong sense of his principles and ethics. These qualities were rather easy for Jackson to convey. He transformed himself quickly, building the character of a distinguished person who, as some noted, "commanded attention without uttering a word."[6]

Jackson also experimented with a new campaign strategy—writing letters to private individuals for public distribution. His letter to Dr. Littlejohn H.

Coleman of North Carolina presumably replied to questions about his views on "any political and national question pending before and about which the country [felt] an interest." With this correspondence, Jackson became the first presidential candidate to support the people's right to question contenders. Moreover, in publicly providing his views on various matters, he was able to set an agenda, discuss key issues, and construct an image.[7] Jackson subsequently framed his candidacy beyond the limitations of his military experience. Another innovation in the 1824 campaign, and a sign of the popular election's growing importance, was the campaign biography. This life story would be important in promoting Jackson's cause.

Initially, the leading candidate for the 1824 campaign was William H. Crawford, a former senator from Georgia, minister to France, secretary of war, and secretary of the Treasury. The other candidates were John Quincy Adams, John C. Calhoun, and Henry Clay. Jackson was not considered a viable contender for the presidency, but his prospects increased around February 1824.[8] With the exception of Adams, most candidates thought Jackson "unelectable."[9] That his standing increased in importance can be gleaned from an early test case regarding his vote on tariffs. During his senatorial stint, Jackson sided with northern interests, advocating high tariff rates as necessary protection from foreign imports. When southerners threatened to withdraw their support over this vote, Jackson wrote a letter to Dr. Coleman, a key supporter, and gave him permission to publish it in the North Carolina *Star* and the *Niles Weekly Register*.

Some considered the letter ambiguous. Others deemed it "superb electioneering propaganda."[10] In the missive, Jackson stated that he favored "a judicious examination and revision of [tariff rates]," and that "so far as the Tariff . . . embrace[d] the design of fostering, protecting, and preserving . . . the means of national defense and independence, particularly in a state of war, [he] would advocate and support it." He added, "I look at the Tariff with an eye to the proper distribution of labor and revenue; and with a view to discharge our national debt. I am one of those who do not believe that a national debt is a national blessing, but rather a curse to a republic; inasmuch as it is calculated to raise around the administration a moneyed aristocracy dangerous to the liberties of the country."[11]

In the brief, purposefully ambiguous letter meant for wide distribution, Jackson did more than answer concerns over his vote. He outlined key principles that would guide his future presidency, including a balanced approach to tariff rates, protection of US interests from foreign competition, emphasis on national defense, strong opposition to national debt, and acute displeasure with the moneyed elite. The argument in Jackson's measured reasoning rationalized what tariffs are all about—a policy for protecting the nation's interests. Jackson also included a statement that would guide him later during the Nullification Crisis: "This tariff—I mean a judicious one—possesses more fanciful than real dangers."[12] This prescient statement would prove time and again that Jackson possessed a superb political sense and a keen understanding of how various intricate issues came about. By noting that opposition to tariffs was the wrong issue to harp on, he indicated that he did not buy into the related polemics and would not be swayed by such tactics.

The opposition quickly attacked Jackson's use of the word "judicious." But his supporters saw something more sophisticated: a perspective on tariff rates that was connected to "strengthening the country from foreign danger, protecting labor, and reducing the debt."[13] This letter exemplifies Jackson's key campaign rhetoric and his favored tactic of strategically using personal letters as public addresses explaining his positions. He and his opponents resorted to this method time and again during presidential campaigns.

Individuals who did not know Jackson personally but were keen for him to be president also published letters or editorials. John Fitzgerald's case is instructive for a general understanding of campaign rhetoric in the early United States. As the editor of the Pensacola newspaper the *Floridian* and the author of articles written under the highly suggestive name PATRIA, Fitzgerald promoted Jackson's cause. He and other newspaper editors were uniquely positioned to voice and distribute their opinions. Thus Fitzgerald used his power to ask the question many were then contemplating: Who would be James Monroe's successor? Sensing that Jackson's outsider credentials and "temperament" were impediments, Fitzgerald was set to prove his fitness for office. The editor devoted several issues of the *Floridian* to advancing Jackson's cause.[14]

Fitzgerald strategically published an article about Jackson on the auspicious day of July 4, 1822, writing, "Andrew Jackson—has been surrounded by Judas and Peters, and an attempt has been made to crucify him; but the suffrages of a free people, freely given, will exalt him to the first office of the first nation on earth." Jackson, then, had been victimized, betrayed like Christ, and targeted precisely because he was the people's choice. The article's religious metaphors emphasize attempts to circumvent the people's wishes. Under the heading "Presidential Question," Fitzgerald also opined that Jackson, "unlike all the other presidential contenders in this new age of 'intrigue,' had not, and would not, scramble to get the office." After Monroe,

Jackson was "the last of the revolutionary stock." Fitzgerald noted, "[He] bears the scars which he received in the war of the revolution."

Moreover, Jackson was "a man of republican virtue who put aside the plow when the country called." Farmer Jackson, then, was like Washington—for many Americans "a second Washington." Fitzgerald declared, the "American people owe the General a debt of gratitude which can never be liquidated."[15] A popular myth was under way, one tying Jackson's success in battle to cherished narratives of the first president. As constructed, this image also argued the virtues of an outsider that insiders lacked due to their intrigues. It is noteworthy that Fitzgerald made this statement prior to the 1824 election. He was already drawing on the concept of corrupt individuals who wished to crucify an able and courageous hero. The religious metaphors were clearly meant to add an emotional depth to the charges. Finally, Jackson's potential candidacy was tied to the larger nation, the free people residing outside Washington, DC, whose opinion, Fitzgerald argued, ought to matter. A new era of political populism had begun, and this editor's advocacy reflected it. Jackson's primary support came from smaller states that deemed him their best defense against large states dominating the caucus process of presidential nominations.[16]

Other campaign publications shed important light on Jackson's candidacy and campaign rhetoric. The two prominent ones are *The Letters of Wyoming* and the Swartwout letter. In both instances, the letters are telling representations of Jackson's campaign and the various related charges and rebuttals. These documents constructed an image and an agenda for Jackson's run for office and later for his presidency. The missives are the closest one can get to raw materiality in assessing presidential candidates and their oratory. Taken together, these documents and other publicized letters and editorials are a window into the way America campaigned and debated issues in the 1820s. They provide insight into the political maneuvering and the rough-and-tumble rhetoric of the early nineteenth century.

THE LETTERS OF WYOMING

The Letters of Wyoming are likely a joint effort by Jackson and his close confidant John H. Eaton, the other senator from Tennessee. Biographer Robert V. Remini contends that, given their style, tone, and content, Jackson composed the letters while Eaton edited them. Written by a fictional Wyoming, the missives were published in the Philadelphia *Columbian Observer* in June and July 1823.[17] The complete title of the collected papers is *The Letters of Wyoming, to the People of the United States on the Presidential Election and in Favour of Andrew Jackson* (S. Simpson and J. Conrad published it as a booklet in 1824). Its title page also includes a short quote from the "*Life of Jackson*" and reads, "[m]idst the battle's commotion he rose on the view Of his Country—to shield her, or perish there too. . . . Jackson, all hail! Our Country's pride and boast, Whose mind's a Council, and whose arm a host. Welcome blest chief! Accept our grateful lays, Unbidden homage of our grateful praise. Remembrance long shall keep alive thy fame, And future ages venerate thy name."[18] Thus begins a 104-page collection of correspondence as campaign propaganda. The work praises heroic Jackson and expects a grateful nation to answer in kind via the election.

An introduction to the short volume acknowledges that the letters were published nationwide after their initial appearance in the *Columbian Observer*. The editor's note directly declares, "As the second Apostle of their Party, every Democrat must look up to Andrew Jackson, as the destined preserver of principles vitally necessary to the existence of those [text unclear] rights, to achieve which he bled in the Revolution, and to maintain which he saved his country in the late eventful contest with Britain."[19] This short advocacy highlights two themes: restoration of Jeffersonian democracy and Jackson's military heroism. *The Letters of Wyoming* pursue both concepts. The reasoning connecting them was that Jackson, who fought in the Revolutionary War and the War of 1812, belonged to the generation of the greats. He was linked to the country's founding and to the restoration of its lost values.

The theme of corruption runs throughout the *Letters* and sets the tone for the 1824 presidential campaign. In his correspondence, Wyoming depicted Jackson as a hero with pure motives facing intrigues and corruption in his quest.[20] As one letter states, "[The Constitution's designated right that] freemen of the nation should, by an unbiased vote, call some meritorious citizen to this high and distinguished post, is lost sight of, or buried in the corruption of the times. Intrigue passes for talent, and corruption has usurped the place of virtue."[21] Jackson became a presidential contender within this context. Wyoming asked voters to "look to the city of Washington, and let the virtuous patriots of the country weep at the spectacle."[22] He contended that the sour note of events in the nation's capital and the inside politics circumventing meritorious individuals' rise to the presidency could be remedied. Only Jackson, with "a soul that towers above intrigue," could do so, and this situation clearly signaled the other candidates' corruption.[23]

Responding to claims that Jackson's qualities "were not such, as that the high destinies of this nation should be confided" or that his speeches were not skillfully developed, Wyoming pointed to other candidates' speeches. Opponents delivered "speeches made to catch the popular ear; to swell the consequences of the speaker, without regard to the beneficial effect to be produced to the country. None of the *vox et preteriae nihil*; but productions of that kind and character, to have whelmed in them the glory, and happiness, and safety of a people."[24] Responding to criticism of Jackson's rhetorical skills, Wyoming highlighted the cheap rhetoric of challengers bent on self-promotion. In contrast, plenty of Jackson's well-written proclamations from his service as a general "prove the qualities of his mind, his warmth of feeling, and strong and bold conception." Finally, against accusations that Jackson lacked the ability "of tinkling brass, of high evanescent sound," Wyoming noted his "expression bold and commanding, and which looking to the important effect to be produced, tramples all foppery under foot."[25]

Wyoming considered Jackson's rhetoric substantive, courageous, and devoid of the other candidates' rhetorical flourishes. Therefore, Jackson was honest, and his opponents were not. Elaborating on this theme, Wyoming declared, "[What the country needs now] is a judgment matured, and active; conceptions clear and accurate, and a decision that dares to right in spite of selfish and designing advisers . . . , and such a man in truth is Andrew Jackson."[26] As an analogy, Wyoming argued that "[George] Washington, neither in the forum, nor the senate, had shown himself a dealer in words, and a maker of speeches; yet all eyes turned toward him."[27] The first president's lack of rhetorical excellence did little to diminish his leadership. The same would be true for Andrew Jackson, "the man who in the revolution bled, and who in our late struggle encountered every privation." As Wyoming concluded, "His is no lukewarm, fireside affection for his country, [but] the Champion, the Defender, the Deliverer of his Country."[28] Jackson's bold rhetoric contrasted with his opponents' flattery and foppery, and his actions spoke louder than others' patriotic talk.

Wyoming derogatorily termed Jackson's four opponents "the LEADING MEN of the COUNTRY." As the "ARISTOCRACY of the nation," Wyoming noted, "their decision of the Chief Magistrate will likely carry the day and . . . this is their main calculation."[29] He continued, "[It will ostensibly] come to pass that he who wishes to succeed to the first office in the government, will only have to caress and flatter those who by chance may constitute the LEADING MEN, and the people, kind, gentle souls, will be required to become the mere recorders of their edicts."[30] Critically and remarkably,

Wyoming's July 1823 argument that the political elite was corrupt anticipated what would be described a year hence as a "corrupt bargain." Under this deal, a few congressional insiders would disregard the popular vote and determine the presidency. Flattery and manipulation within the House would dictate the election. Wyoming grounded his popular appeal in two concepts: substance versus flattery and aristocracy versus common people.

Jackson would save the nation from such corruption.[31] Yet his outsider credentials, predicted Wyoming, would hurt him. For Jackson, being "reared in the interior and having never been to any of the European courts" prevented Jackson from learning "those rules of polite intercourse, which the head of a nation should be acquainted with." Yet "whether he may bow with right or left foot foremast. Upon this subject the constitution is silent."[32] Wyoming was clearly taking a jab at John Quincy Adams and his exposure to the European courts. But he was also expressing concern that the presidency would be decided by a few individuals citing Jackson's "disadvantages" relative to the refined, well-traveled Adams, who was the favored candidate in the House. Wyoming sarcastically reminded readers that the Constitution is mum about flattery and manners.

The *Letters of Wyoming* contain the author's critique of corrupt practices embodied in political preferences, adding how sad he was "to see my country manifest such fondness and partiality for exotics. In manners, dress, and language, we are imitators, and borrowers from a road; native genius sinks in comparison, with that which is foreign, and even our appetites mark the inferior flavour of our own, when contrasted with the products of a foreign soil. All that we have national, is our government, . . . witness for example those things called etiquette and courtly parade (and nonsense) so much in vogue at our metropolis. I want a man, my countrymen, at the head of this nation, who will throw such trifles off; one who may have character enough to induce a belief that it is right; one who has fought for his country, and defended her rights."[33]

In Wyoming's opinion, the country needed a person of character and conviction. He described the American reality as follows: "The other gentlemen who are before the country, may not be behind in their attachment to our republican principles, and may, whenever it shall be required of them, disclose a suitable and proper zeal in their support. It has been their misfortune, however, not to have been favoured with the same opportunities of manifesting their attachment, as have fallen to the lot of General Jackson." Jackson's unique military accomplishments raised him above all other candidates. Wyoming described yet another way in which Jackson outstripped his opponents: "He holds no office, he is where the chief magistrate of the nation should be always sought for, in private life. A private citizen, committed to no party, pledged to no system, allied to no intrigue, free of all prejudice, but coming directly from the people, and bearing with him an infinite acquaintance with their feeling, wishes, and wants."[34] Such was the author's view of Jackson's campaign. The president ought to come not from within the political elite but from the people. A private citizen promoted for performing outstanding deeds, and, as such, devoid of political ties and intrigues should hold the office. For such . . . individuals would value "virtue, integrity, and talent." Wyoming therefore concluded, "Jackson is the only man before the nation, who, resting on the shade of private life, is without patronage or favour, by which to win to him partisans and friends."[35]

Another letter analogizes Jackson's candidacy with George Washington's. Wyoming observed that Washington "was a 'man of home,' and without those polished refinements acquired at a foreign Court, and of late, considered material qualifications in the character of a Chief Magistrate."[36] As a soldier, Washington brought the nation to trust him like "the pilot who could guide his ship in safety through a perilous storm." Wyoming implied that Jackson could assume the same role: "Our second war has furnished us the same opportunity of deciding upon the qualities and pretensions of our leading men, as was afforded by the first."[37] With the nautical metaphor of an unpretentious pilot guiding the ship of state to safe harbor, Jackson was similar to Washington and completely unlike John Quincy Adams, the anticipated candidate. It was not expected for every presidential contender to have military experience. However, Wyoming maintained that Jackson's distinction in battle allowed him "superior claims" relative to his competitors.[38] Military success versus refined manners and, by implication, substance over style, remained the primary argument.

And what of the other candidates? asked Wyoming. He answered as follows: Adams "is indeed famed for his *belles lettres*, and classical acquirements"; Mr. Crawford has distinguished himself in the Treasury, in banking, "and in calculations of cents and dollars"; Mr. Calhoun "may know more of the details of his office; and Mr. Clay, on the floor of Congress, might much more readily swell the briny tear from his listener's eyes"; but "there are none of them with pretensions superior to Andrew Jackson."[39] By the process of elimination and with a dose of sarcasm, Wyoming determined that no candidate could compare to Jackson.

According to Wyoming, the congressional caucus that took over the election "was not resorted to, until who should be the next President, became a matter of management and intrigue." This was a process whereby "men of influence, undertook, and without authority, to say to the people, who the individual should be."[40] With this comment, Wyoming got to the heart of the national debate: whether Congress usurped the rights of the people to elect their president. A presidential election that turned to the House would allow larger states to dictate the presidential question. Subsequently, Wyoming stated, "it is folly to maintain that the people of the United States have a voice in the election of their Chief Magistrate."[41] According to the Constitution, he argued, "all power was, and should be, inherent in the people. Their object was to establish a Government purely Republican, and to make their Chief Magistrate to derive his power from, and be dependent on the people."[42] This was Jackson speaking, indicating early on what he would emphasize later as president—doing only what the Constitution allowed, knowing full well that given the transfer of the election to the House, that "under such an arrangement, dependence and responsibility is lost, and the people, stripped of all but constructive power, must abide the instruments of the Leading men—the men in office." The Jackson campaign could do nothing but "protest against a construction so hostile to all republican feeling."[43] The presidential contest, then, was between Jackson and the "Leading Men" accused of circumventing the people's wishes to elect one of their own.

In yet another letter, Wyoming characterized Jackson's superior candidacy in terms of his "talents of the first order": "His writings, actions, and above all, his military career, brilliant, all things considered, as that of any general of the age, proclaim him a man of high grade of talents, of firmness and devotion to the interest and cause of his country."[44] For his part, John Quincy Adams was "a gentleman of high literary attainments, a finished scholar" with particular skills in foreign relations. Yet, stated Wyoming, "he is a closet man, and from his books has acquired all that he has learned: and hence knows but little of man as he is." The letter goes on to call Adams "a blunt man, without address, or manners the least conciliating: extremely reserved, and always closely wrapped in thought." The correspondent further noted, "He [Adams] happens to be his *father's son*."[45] Adams, then, was a learned man who lacked the street smarts necessary for the high office, was not very approachable, and was elevated to high office primarily due to nepotism.

Adams was not the only opponent *The Letters of Wyoming* assessed. It described Calhoun as a "sprightly, smart young man: but wanting in age," further observing, "He is wanting in judgment and reflection. His quickness is an injury." Calling Calhoun someone who "always fires on the wing, and hence not unfrequently misses is mark," Wyoming nevertheless declared, "This gentleman has always been a correct Republican, and eight years hence his friends might venture to think of him."[46] In sum, Calhoun was young and impetuous, on the path to high office but not yet ready for it. Of Crawford a letter states, "[He] possesses a fine appearance, but in manner is rough and uncouth. His conversation is highly agreeable, and much more so than could be expected from one who talks so incessantly." At the same time, Wyoming deemed Crawford "a very maneuvering, artful, and intriguing man." Asserting, "Mr. Crawford's views of government and his radical notions are strong objections to him," the correspondent argued that Crawford's "doubtful character" should be a warning.[47] As for Henry Clay, Wyoming declared, "[He] is evidently a man of more genius than mind, more fancy than judgment." And like Calhoun, "he will be better of waiting eight years: and even then be young enough for so distinguished a trust."

Wyoming concluded his endorsement of Jackson in this manner: "All things considered, Andrew Jackson is the preferable candidate. In talents he is equal to any; in services performed, hardships and dangers encountered for his country, he is superior to them all. From his standing, and being unconnected with any of the intrigues of the day, he will at home be able to draw to his aid the best talents of this country, and abroad to extend and improve our respectability." The author continued, "[When foreign forces would try the country] and should come to our land with hostile feelings, we shall have a man at the head of affairs, who will not recline under the shade of the White House, and leave our bays, our shores, and cities, to be ravaged."[48] These were the stakes in the 1824 election. Wyoming hoped to persuade readers of Jackson's superior maturity, experience, and determination. However, the contention that Jackson was the only person who would defend the nation during hostilities sounded desperate. The correspondent may have realized that Jackson's chances were slim if the election was left to the House.

Wyoming summarized the primary issue in the 1824 election in this way: "*Who shall govern this nation, the People or the Leading Men*? Yeomanry of the country look to this, and think of this!! For 'that is the question.'"[49] The quandary as presented pitted the people against Congress and fairness against corruption. To cement the case for Jackson, Wyoming tackled every accusation against him including his temper, stating that the Tennessee senator's close associates and neighbors did not support such claims. The correspondent also addressed the issue of age. At fifty-six, Jackson "[was] yet in the prime and vigour of life," and when elected he would be younger than former presidents.[50]

For a final strategy, Wyoming related the now-famous anecdote of the fourteen-year-old Jackson refusing to brush a British officer's boots. "The officer, and a contemptible fellow he must have been, inasmuch as he should have commended rather than have censured his youthful pride of feeling, aimed a blow at him with his sword, by which his hand, thrown up for defence [sic], was well high severed."[51] Subsequently, Jackson and his older brother were thrown into prison "for no other crime than that he dared to be seen in *arms for his country*." Jackson "was alone of all his family permitted to survive the ravages of the Revolutionary war; yet he lived to avenge in the second, the wrongs and injuries and misfortunes, which had been produced to him by the first."[52] In his narrative of Jackson's illustrious biography, Wyoming zeroed in on the general's heroism and patriotism stretching from the Revolutionary War to the Battle of New Orleans. He surpassed all other candidates due to his bravery; his selfless and heroic acts are metonymy for his character.

Near the conclusion of the *Letters*, Wyoming preemptively explained his reasoning. He acknowledged his lack of sophistication in the art of argumentation, as well as his failure to resort to "the sort of logic, which can prove any thing [sic], even that a 'penny is better than heaven.'"[53] To explain this particular point, the *Letters'* publisher added a footnote. According to the note, Wyoming was critical of the syllogism the opposition used, "by which any thing [sic] and every thing [sic] may be proved—as, *er quo*, 'nothing is better than heaven, a cent is better than heaven.'" The publisher continued, "It is by this sort of argument, that Wyoming, and indeed some others better known, believe it alone possible to persuade this nation that Mr. Crawford or indeed any of the intriguers at Washington, is fit for the Presidency."[54] Rejecting such sophistication, Wyoming stated that unlike Jackson's opponents, he took "words and actions [by] their plain and simple import, and judge[d] of them accordingly." Based on this logic, he asserted, "Jackson is the friend of his country, that he has bled for her, suffered for her—a soldier of the Revolution and of the late war, therefore do I prefer him, desiring at the same time not to aid him by censuring others; he needs no such assistance."[55]

Notwithstanding Wyoming's declaration of resorting only to simple analysis of words and deeds, he employed in this tract the very syllogism he rejected. Even in his attempts at clarification, he achieved the same result. See, for his example, Wyoming's summary statement that Jackson ought to be the one elected president. This very explanation illuminates a theme running throughout the *Letters*, that of commentary on speechmaking and its persuasive qualities or lack thereof. These observations include comments on Jackson's rhetorical skills and preparation relative to his opponents, as well as the rhetorical strategy those opponents employed to deceive the nation.

Wyoming then took leave of his audience: "Indulgent Reader, adieu! You know me not; you may never know me. All I ask of you is to ascribe my labours and feeble exertions to some higher cause, than any thing which appertains to myself. . . . Democracy of the country, will again, by his election, rise into view, and be restored. Knaves will cease to fatten on the spoils of the people, and plain habits, and honest men, will once more rise into fashion."[56] The words "intrigue" and "corruption" run through the *Letters*. They are the theme of the final appeal, functioning as the agency for Jackson's pure and moral candidacy, the one that would restore democracy, humility, fairness, and honesty to the nation.[57] The *Letters of Wyoming* consistently promote Jackson's image and character, relying heavily on his military bravery and his unselfishness, devotion, and patriotism. The other presidential candidates lacked these qualities.

While the anonymous public address of yore would be greatly suspect today, it was often the voice of significance and credibility in the nineteenth century. In the early 1800s, this medium allowed candidates and their operatives to voice opinions via widely published pamphlets and letters. The heavy focus on character, heroism, and determination in the *Letters* is a window into the 1824 campaign's rhetoric justifying Jackson's superiority. Finally, the *Letters of Wyoming* spell out what it would take to resume democratic values and ensure liberty for all. As such, it is a retrospective tract examining the Revolutionary creed and seeking the restoration of its ideals, which corruption and intrigues had muddied. Whether the *Letters of Wyoming* brought additional support to Jackson is hard to measure. Even so, Jackson remained the leading candidate throughout the campaign.[58] To the surprise of many in Pennsylvania, Maryland, and North Carolina, Jackson's prospects improved quickly. The strength of the grassroots antiestablishment sentiment the retired general inspired alarmed seasoned politicians.[59]

The results of the 1824 race were predicted, but they were crushing nonetheless precisely because of the large number of voters that participated in the first popular presidential election. Jackson carried 99 of the 261 electoral votes. Adams came in second with 84 electoral votes, and

Crawford placed a distant third with 41 electoral votes. Jackson carried all the electoral votes in Alabama, Indiana, Mississippi, New Jersey, North Carolina, Pennsylvania, South Carolina, and Tennessee. He carried partial electoral votes in Illinois, Louisiana, and Maryland. Yet since no candidate won the majority of the Electoral College, Congress adjudicated the election. With Jackson winning the popular and Electoral College votes, failure to elect him risked affronting the multitudes of voters who cast their ballots for the first time.

Once inserted into the election, Congress followed the constitutional provision based on the Twelfth Amendment clause. Per this requirement, the House selected the president from the top three contenders when no candidate received a majority of the electoral votes. Clay's fourth-place finish was excluded from the House vote.[60] However, he would play a key role in the election to his personal benefit. The 1824 election ended on January 9, 1825, with Clay generating support for Adams in the House in exchange for becoming secretary of state (at that time, a position often calculated to promote a future presidential candidacy). Adams and Clay were suspected of reaching this arrangement in a private conversation.[61] Critically, once the election was turned over to the House, the House no longer had to abide by the electoral vote count. That very action would become a powerful issue for the next presidential election.

Still senator until early 1825, Jackson was in Washington, DC, when the vote was cast in Adams's favor. By all accounts—and many observed him closely after he lost the presidency—he was dignified and calm. Jackson's reaction generated the most favorable comments of his image and graceful manners, even when he attended Adams's inauguration. Onlookers were "awed by Jackson's 'manly style,' while Adams, likely sensing the ramifications of his scandalous election was 'truly an object of pity.'"[62] The political ramifications would be larger than those immediately related to the election of 1824; they would impact American politics and the needed reforms thereof.

THE SWARTWOUT LETTER

With the campaign of 1824 over, the anonymous Wyoming correspondence was followed by the publication of one letter, part of a series Jackson exchanged with Samuel Swartwout, a person of suspect character. The missive ended up in the press, though it is not clear if this happened with Jackson's knowledge or approval. Whatever the case, the letter's wide distribution in newspapers meant that Jackson's views of the recent election were now in the open.[63] The specific impetus for Jackson's initial communication to Swartwout was correspondence between Clay and Judge Francis J. Brooke of Virginia. Therein, Clay explained his decision not to support Jackson in the congressional proceedings despite his placing first in the popular vote. The letter came about after Clay suffered strong criticism for masterminding the election in the House and possibly securing his lucrative position of secretary of state. He argued, among other things, that "he feared to trust the execution of the laws in the hands of a 'Military Chieftain.'"[64] Clay sought to warn the nation about Jackson's proclivity for behaving like Napoleon Bonaparte (and other historical dictators).[65]

Reading the phrase "Military Chieftain," Swartwout, who had already exchanged several letters with Jackson, wrote the general on February 18, 1825, and urged him not to react to the attack. Speaking out could jeopardize his political standing.[66] Swartwout also offered his insight about Clay, who likely contacted Judge Brooke after realizing the damage his action in the presidential election had done to his character. Moreover, Clay probably intended his letter for widespread circulation to rectify the setback to his own ambitions. Swartwout wanted Jackson to stay above the fray, maintaining his dignified image and its material effect for the next contest. He told the general, "It is really a pity that the same scrupulous conscience had not admonished him [Clay] of his obligation to the constitution, whilst he was plotting the most deadly blow to the liberties of his country that it has ever rec'd, in the daring infraction of representative duty."[67] In short, Clay was late to claim that he voted his conscience. He did so following accusations of circumventing representative government, and only after he realized the power of public opinion.

Swartwout suggested, ever so cautiously, that if Jackson did respond that he do so in "mild & dignified language . . . which so conspicuously marked [his] other productions during the Presidential controversy."[68] In case Jackson had not realized the importance of responding, his correspondent imparted the following wisdom: "Intrigue & corruption have deprived the people of their President, but neither has been able to deprive the man of the people of his dignity, or of the fast hold he has in the affections of 10 millions [sic] of freemen."[69] But Swartwout was not done. He indicated to Jackson that "[his] silence & neglect of Henry Clay [would] mortify him more than volumes of reproaches," that "every man, excepting his coadjutors and followers, consider[ed] him as irrevocably lost," and that "he [had] fallen so low that he [could] never rise again except from personal contact with one greatly above him." Swartwout concluded, "I hope my dear Sir . . . I feel the importance of every act you do, however minute, upon the present welfare, perhaps the future destiny of our country. The eyes of the whole Union are upon you . . . Jackson, greater in adversity than in prosperity, is the only man who can rally the Nation & restore the Gov't to its primitive purity."[70]

Beyond this private solicitation, Jackson's remaining a presidential candidate was uppermost in the mind of several individuals ready to keep his name in public view for the next election. In his letter, Swartwout ostensibly asked Jackson to persist in his candidacy. He emphasized the general's great prospects and predicted that his election in 1828 he would redeem the nation after his loss in 1824. Jackson did not need Swartwout to convince him not to engage Clay, but he responded to his advice on February 22, 1825. That reply greatly impressed Swartwout, and a month later it was published in several newspapers. The possibility that this entire exchange was contrived cannot be ruled out; Jackson repeatedly attacked others anonymously and in press releases.

The introduction to the collection of letters states that Jackson consulted no one in writing Swartwout. Jackson indicated to Swartwout that he was aware of Clay's "Military Chieftain" remark as justification for not supporting his candidacy. Jackson resisted his initial impulse to react to the insult. He averred, "[The votes I received in the election are] enough to satisfy me, that the prejudice by them, sought to be produced availed but little. This is sufficient for me. I entertain a deep and heartfelt gratitude to my country, for the confidence & regard she has manifested toward me, leaving to prejudice minds whatever they can make of the epithet 'Military Chieftain.'"[71]

Jackson sarcastically countered the charge of "Military Chieftain." He assumed that his military record stood for itself and that appealing to the people and their sense of fairness would be sufficient to direct their anger over the election's outcome. Jackson's dignified assertion kept him above the fray:

> I contributed my mite to shake off the yoke of tyranny, and to build up
> the fabric of free government; and when lately our country was involved
> in war, having the commission of Major Gen'l of Militia in Tennessee,
> I made an appeal to the patriotism of the western [sic], when 3,000 of
> them went with me to the field, to support her Eagles. If this can consti-

tute me a "Military Chieftain" I am one. Aided by the patriotism of the western people, and an indulgent providence, it was my good fortune to protect our frontier border from the savages, & successfully to defend an important & vulnerable point of our Union. Our lives were risked, privations endured, sacrifices made, if Mr. Clay pleases, Martial law declared, not with any view of personal agrandisment [*sic*], but for the preservation of all and everything that was valuable, the honor safety & glory of our country. Does this constitute a "Military Chieftain"? . . . I have as you very well know, by some of the designing politicians of this country, been charged with taking bold & high-handed measures; but as they were not designed for any benefit to myself I should under similar circumstances not refrain from a course equally bold; that man who in time of difficulty & danger shall halt at any course, necessary to maintain the rights & privileges and independence of the country, is unsuited to authority; and if these opinions & sentiments shall entitle me to the name & character of a Military Chieftain, I am content so to be considered, satisfied too for Mr. Clay if he chooses to represent to the citizens of the West, that as the reason why in his opinion I merited not his & their confidence.[72]

Jackson then went for the rebuke, mocking Clay's "Chieftain" label and touting his own sacrifices to the nation. He confidently challenged Clay to explain his charge to western states, including his own state of Kentucky. Jackson knew full well how much inhabitants of the West appreciated his years of battling attacks on the frontier. Finally, Jackson questioned Clay's credibility and standing, stating,

Mr. Clay never yet has risked himself for his country, sacrificed his repose, or made an effort to repel an invading foe; of course his "conscience" assured him that it was altogether wrong in any other man to lead his countrymen to battle & victory. He who fights, and fights successfully must according to his standard be held up as a "Military Chieftain"; even Washington could he again appear among us might be so considered, because he dared to be a virtuous and successful soldier, an honest statesman & a correct man. It is only when overtaken by disaster & defeat that any man is to be considered a safe politician & correct statesman. Defeat might to be sure have brought with it one benefit, it might have enabled me to escape the notice and animadversions of Mr. Clay but considering that by an opposite result, my country has been somewhat benefitted, I rather prefer it even with the opprobrium & censure which he seems disposed to extend.[73]

Though Jackson was not going to challenge Clay after the election, he had to say something. He expressed himself in a forceful and stinging manner, achieving much more than a direct tit for tat. Jackson focused exclusively on the "Military Chieftain" censure, which he considered an insult but instead transformed into an affront to the country. He also turned the criticism on its head, by pointing out an irony: if winning militarily is a condition for political defeat, then a defeat, according to Clay's logic, should have forestalled the censure. There was simply no way for Clay to smoothly counter Jackson's rebuke. The ill-chosen attack on Jackson further damaged Clay.

Jackson's strategy is evidenced in his final words in the letter: "There is a purer tribunal to which in preference I would refer myself—to the judgment of an enlightened patriotic & uncorrupted people—to that tribunal I would rather appeal whence is derived whatever reputation either he [Clay] or I are possessed of." He appealed to the masses who voted for him and sought their continued support in the next election. Ever conscious of the people, Jackson reminded Swartwout of his reluctance to be a presidential candidate. He observed "I did not solicit the office of President, it was the frank & flattering call of the freeman of this country, not mine, which placed my name before the nation." The general continued, "When they failed in their colleges [Electoral College] to make a choice, no one beheld me seeking thro art or management to entice any Representative in Congress from a conscientious responsibility to his own, or the wishes of his constituents." Jackson's criticism was specific here. The people's representatives had to vote the wishes of their constituents, but they did not and thus acted in a corrupt and unrepresentative way. Finally, projecting his moderate tone, Jackson stated, "Demagogues I am persuaded have in times past, done more injury to the cause of freedom & the rights of man, than ever did a "Military Chieftain,"; and in our country, at least, in times of peace, should be more feared."[74] The "Military Chieftain," then, was not the true reason for Clay's vote. Rather, it was a cheap argument lacking substance and conviction. Jackson was consistent in his argument that a true representative government is foundational to the nation, and that any departure from this principle is tantamount to corruption.

Though the "Military Chieftain" remark stung, Jackson kept his public rhetoric measured and humble. There was nothing he could do following the House vote based on constitutional procedures. He limited his views to one ill-advised phrase Clay used against him and in so doing, he zeroed in on the very heart of Clay's concocted reasoning for not supporting a candidate who won the popular vote and most of the Electoral College. Clearly, Clay feared Jackson's popularity but could not say so. But Jackson could. In his retort, he time and again pointed to the factual evidence on hand: the popular support he received. The popular vote was the most appealing and righteous argument against Clay, and it was the primary issue that could keep Jackson in people's minds until the next election.

The Swartwout letter, functioning for all practical purposes as a public address, portrays Jackson as a reluctant but determined presidential candidate. Publishing the letter allowed Jackson a public voice and a vehicle to communicate his overall standing following the House vote for Adams. The missive exclusively addresses the Jackson-Clay tension and the latter man's alleged bargain with Adams. As a result, Jackson could focus on political corruption of the first order—the circumvention of popular will, the unpopular circumstances under which a president was elected, and an injured secretary of state—while his own popularity was at an all-time high.

A related and not insignificant variable in Jackson's rhetorical skills was his ability to tune to the press, to fully comprehend journalists' persuasiveness and critical role in the political arena. He indicated as much in comments to his friend General Coffee concerning the 1824 election's aftermath: "The poor Devil H. Clay, has come out with an address to his constituents, in a begging cringing tone, to clear himself from the corrupt intrigue and management to procure for himself the office of sec of state . . . The various papers are commenting on it, and will bring to his recollection before they are done the adage 'O that my enemy would write a book.' How little common sense this man displays in his course."[75] Jackson, then, used the press when he sought to disseminate a viewpoint or a position. But he also knew when to sit back and let the press work without any cajoling on his part. Jackson also engaged in extensive letter writing, assuming correctly that a rich correspondence, even when most letters were not published in the press, would disseminate his views among the country's political operatives.

President Adams himself provided an additional rhetorical incident that would prove beneficial to Jackson's presidential prospects. The new president ushered in an impressive program of public works, including the building of bridges and canals. Such large projects required Congress's assent for their payment. Yet Adams's public sentiments on the matter would be revealing if not altogether astonishing. In his First Annual Message to Congress, he declared "[We Americans must] not leave the impression that we prefer to slumber in indolence or fold up our arms and proclaim to the world that we are palsied by the will of our constituents."[76] This chastising statement, with its metaphor of disease, was not only foolish but ignorant of the events of the 1824 election. It was also a statement contradicting everything Jackson, his supporters, and his future supporters stood for. It proved Jackson's contention that an elite was running the country. In one stroke, Adams proved that he did not care much about the people, and that he was even arrogant about his public rhetoric.

Jackson saw something beyond the specific issue at hand. In a letter to Congressman James Buchanan (a future president himself), Jackson wrote, "I suspect that [the] administration begin[s] to perceive the necessity of public confidence without which it is an arduous undertaking to execute the solemn duties confided by the constitution to the chief magistrate."[77] "Public confidence" referred to an elusive form of rhetorical currency. The same term used during the Great Depression to represent the gap in popular support between Herbert Hoover and Franklin D. Roosevelt was in use a century earlier. In Jackson's time, "public confidence" was referred to with the same principal understanding that an executive's success depended on the public's faith in its president. Jackson's rhetoric would empower the people, while Adams's would chastise them.

With the 1828 presidential election under way, the charge of a "corrupt bargain" between Adams and Clay was resurrected to great effect. One Carter Beverley asked Jackson to respond to issues that arose during an early 1827 conversation at the Hermitage. In the course of this exchange, Jackson told a gathering that Clay's friends approached him during the House election with a bargain similar to the one they presumably offered Adams. Jackson replied to Beverley in a lengthy letter. A member of the House had indeed approached him concerning a "great intrigue"—making Henry Clay secretary of state in exchange for Clay urging his House supporters to vote for Jackson. Jackson told Beverley that he assigned "pure motives" to the House member and thus considered the communication credible. Still, the general rejected the offer, stating, "Before I would reach the presidential chair by such means of bargain and corruption, I would see the earth open and swallow both Mr. Clay and his friends, and myself with them: If they had not confidence in me to believe, if I were elected, that I would call to my aid in the Cabinet, men of the first virtue, talents and integrity, not to vote for me."[78] Jackson employed all the key words, "corruption," "bargain," "virtue," and "integrity," to emphasize his own impeccable character and his chief opponent's corruption.

The letter was published in *Niles' Register* in June 25, 1827, with Beverley forwarding gratitude to Jackson for clarifying matters and alleviating public anxiety over the last election. Beverley also published his correspondence with Jackson in the *U.S. Telegraph*, adding an exchange of letters with Clay's friend Noah Zane of Wheeling, Virginia. Zane's involvement in the letter was now used to further implicate Clay in scandal. While on his way from Kentucky to Washington, Beverley wanted to interview Clay and ask for his reaction to Jackson's charges. The appointment was set to take place in Wheeling, with Zane functioning as an intermediary. Before the meeting, Zane asked to see Jackson's letter. Though hesitant, Beverley gave him the missive but Zane later refused to return it. Beverley surmised that Zane rushed to make copies of the document for Clay, who then hurried out of town. Beverley did not get to see Clay, but Jackson's letter did the damage. Clay was forced to reply publicly in July 1827. It is quite plausible that Jackson was behind this letter to Beverley, seeking to cement his election with one more charge of a "corrupt bargain" and reminding many of what he was denied some three years earlier.

The quarrel between Jackson and Clay that began shortly after Jackson's invasion of Florida in 1818 intensified during the election of 1824. It continued in the years leading to the 1828 and 1832 elections and beyond. Clay was perhaps the best Speaker of the House and one the nation's greatest orators. Yet he would fail against Jackson's more strategic and calculated rhetoric. While Clay's sharp oratory aimed at immediate impact, Jackson's rhetoric was premeditated and aimed at long-range effects.

✳✳✳

The election loss of 1824 was described as an affront to popular sentiments. It brought Martin Van Buren, leader of the Radicals, into an alliance with Jackson. Van Buren was the conduit to the formation of the Democratic Party, which comprised of Jackson supporters who aligned with Calhoun after the 1824 election and Van Buren's own Radicals, who signed on in 1826. The new loose party brought together a western, a northern, and a southern faction, all united in opposition to Adams and formulated by Van Buren in particular. Van Buren advocated the revival of the two-party system and the tension therein as necessary for a successful democracy. Jackson was the glue of the tenuous coalition. The party included adherents to Jeffersonian principles, with their opposition to tariffs, internal improvements, and the Second Bank of the United States.[79] Jackson did not necessarily support all of these issues. Moreover, he was out of office and not connected to any political faction in Congress. But Jackson's symbolic popularity and rhetorical skill made him the ideal leader around which this coalition could rally and oppose the national Republican Party.[80] Ostensibly, he embodied the rhetorical currency and agency that masterful political operatives like Van Buren deemed necessary for the new party formation.

The public perception of the Adams-Clay alliance added to the wider perception that Jackson was deprived of his election win.[81] The "proof" of this perception lies in the quickness by which Jackson was described as being manipulated by political insiders, the rush to nominate him again for the presidency, and, ultimately, his successful election in 1828 as the head of a new partisan coalition. In calling Jackson nothing but a "Military Chieftain" and implying that this very quality was sufficient to elect another person, Clay epitomized the idea of an outsider not deserving the presidency. This derogatory label also ignored Jackson's extensive resume that included several appointed and elected positions. That Jackson won decisively in 1828 and carried the majority of the states except in New England, just as he did in 1824, points to his consistent popular appeal. Adams could not claim this accomplishment in 1824 or in 1828. In the end, rhetoric did matter in 1824, constructing an image of a "corrupt bargain" and adding significantly to the next election campaign. This circumstance proved Jackson's and his aides' rhetorical astuteness. In contrast, Adams displayed his limitations in this department in his Inaugural Address and First Annual Message to Congress.

The election of 1824 was crucial and transitory. It moved presidential candidacy outside Washington and transformed an internal political dance into the need for popular support.[82] Thus a new era was upon the nation. The Founders' aversion to partisan politics was pushed aside for two parties: Adams and Clay following Hamiltonian principles, and Jackson, Van Buren, and Calhoun following Jeffersonian principles.[83] Slogans such as "Let the cry be Jackson, Van Buren & Liberty," or "Jackson, Calhoun & Liberty" began to appear in newspapers, and in 1827 the newly formed Democratic Party won both houses of Congress.[84] Voters reacted to the debacle of 1824, and Jackson was on his way to winning the next election.

Ultimately, the end of the 1824 presidential election became the primary campaign material for the next race. Throughout 1827, the momentum was in Jackson's favor; key supporters predicted his victory. In February of that year, James Hamilton Jr. wrote Jackson, "Your cause is gaining ground rapidly, rather too fast for the time we have ahead." He also wrote, "[The]

Buck tail or Republican party are beginning to move in New York," and "[Van Buren is] *zealously cordially* and *entirely* with us."[85] In September, Van Buren himself informed Jackson, "I cannot be mistaken in believing, that we shall be able to give you a very decided majority of votes of this state." He further told the general, "[Many newspapers] have already come out in your favour, & the rest with at most three exceptions will do the same soon."[86] The rhetoric of populism that would elect Jackson president was under way.

2

THE FIRST INAUGURAL ADDRESS
PROJECTING THE AUDIENCE

Andrew Jackson's Inaugural Address came four years late. Once elected, Jackson would be the first "outsider" to come into the presidency with the strong public mandate his predecessors had lacked. Significantly, the election of 1824 would be the last decided by Congress, and in 1828 there was no way Jackson could be denied his win again.

Jackson would have been happier to give his Inaugural Address in 1825 with his wife, Rachel, at his side. The rough-and-tumble of the presidential campaign was unkind to both of them. Rachel Jackson had been viciously attacked by the opposition, and she died of a heart attack only days after her husband's victory. With the 1828 election, much changed in presidential politics. An insider unable to disassociate himself from the charge of a "corrupt bargain" failed against an outsider who presented himself as the nation's savior.

The campaign was vicious and the attacks on Jackson rather severe, focusing primarily on the danger that a "Military Chieftain" would become a dictator.[1] Some attempted to portray Jackson as a cruel general. Charles Hammond's *Liberty Hall & Cincinnati Gazette* charged Rachel Jackson with adultery in an attempt to provoke her husband's harsh response and prove his unsuitability to be president. Jackson's campaign committee urged to him to keep quiet. Aides told him, "Weigh & bale your cotton and sell it," and they suggested he burn any newspaper article that angered him.[2] Beyond the attacks, a new phenomenon was afoot: a "tidal wave of printed material which took the campaign to the people." Hammond's Cincinnati press added the *Truth's Advocate and Monthly Anti-Jackson Expositor, A Horn-book for the Jacksonians*, appearing in Dover, Delaware. At the same time, the pro-Jackson *Telegraph Extra* was issued as an extension of the Washington *United States Telegraph* to defend the general.[3] In all, the Adams campaign launched "a massive press assault on Jackson," while the Jackson camp sought to convince voters that "the real danger to the republic was located in the halls and corridors of the nation's capital."[4] Ostensibly, the election of 1828 was transitional. It wavered between charges of corruption and fitness for office, and, subsequently, between personality and character and the degree to which each man could save the country. While the Adams-Clay campaign depicted Jackson as Caesar, Jacksonites described him as Cincinnatus, "ready to answer the call of his country in its hour of peril."[5]

Jackson did not respond to the vicious personal attacks on his wife. More importantly, he did not take a public part in the campaign, preferring instead to be active behind the scenes.[6] Nonetheless, the 1828 presidential campaign focused on his biography, necessary political reforms, and military accomplishments, especially his success against Great Britain in the 1815 Battle of New Orleans. Jackson's campaign made the "corrupt bargain" that deprived him of the presidency in 1824 the primary issue. He outlined a reform agenda he would pursue once elected. Now, four years later, he would consider his election the result of the people's "own mere will" despite "all the torrents of slander that corruption & wickedness could invent, circulated thro subsidized presses."[7] Privately, Jackson was furious about the attacks on his character. But his public posture was to remain above such politics. Even with below-the-belt attacks on Rachel, accusing her of "adultery and bigamy," and claims that their marriage was a sham, Jackson only vented his anger in letters to close friends. He understood the opposition's intent to provoke him. The day would arrive, he wrote, when "retribution & vengeance must come, when the guilty will meet with their Just reward."[8]

One of the best ways to gauge a person's rhetorical skills is to assess his extemporaneous public speeches. Jackson used no notes while addressing those present at his wife's burial. After the interment, some of the mourners returned to the Hermitage, and there Jackson addressed them:

> [Thank you for] the honor you have done to the sainted one whose remains now repose in yonder grave. She is now in the bliss of heaven, and I know that she can suffer here no more on earth. That is enough for my consolation; my loss is her gain. But I am left without her to encounter the trials of life alone. I am now President elect of the United States, and in a short time must take my way to the metropolis of my country; and, if it had been God's will, I would have been grateful for the privilege of taking her to my post of honor and seating her by my side; but Providence knew what was best for her. For myself, I bow to God's will, and go alone to the place of new and arduous duties, and I shall not go without friends to reward, and I pray God that I may not be allowed to have enemies to punish. I can forgive all who have wronged me, but will have fervently to pray that I may have grace to enable me to forget or forgive any enemy who has ever maligned that blessed one who is now safe from all suffering and sorrow, whom they tried to put to shame for my sake![9]

Jackson's eloquence in a moment of utter sadness speaks to his rhetorical skills. Concise, articulate, and pinpointed, Jackson's eulogy exudes reserved anger. He used creative parallelism to describe the transition from a citizen to president. His unique phrasing allowed him to issue a veiled threat against those who maligned his wife and suggest that they may have caused her death. He did not wish to hide the pain of living without his beloved at this most critical juncture.

Jackson's journey from his home state of Tennessee to the nation's capital was most incongruous. The trip was difficult, if not utterly sad and depressing. Yet Jackson's popularity would precede him; joyful crowds watched him proceed to Washington. The same sentiments arose on Inauguration Day. Jackson would give his first address while still in mourning and uncertain of his course, but unprecedented numbers of people poured into the city to see him take the oath of office.[10]

With characteristic determination and zeal, Jackson embarked on a presidency that would last two controversial but historically significant terms. His inauguration was the culmination of years of American struggle, years that included his service in the American Revolution and the War of 1812, his two terms as senator from Tennessee, and his two presidential candidacies. Jackson would enter the White House as the most loved and adored president to date. That he was the first "people's president" became a cliché. Such a precedent and such a momentous inauguration would require a suitable address.

In a process that was perhaps analogous to his military preparation, Jackson took time crafting his Inaugural Address. He appreciated its importance, and he sought a speech that would reflect a new kind of president. Politics being a rather convoluted affair, however, Jackson's initial draft was revised into an iteration quite removed from his own wording and sentiments. Political reform would be the arch-metaphor for Jackson's entry to the White House.[11] However, Jackson's was a nuanced kind of reform whereby he looked back, seeking to restore American freedom—in light of what he and many saw as a corrupt deviation from the nation's founding ideals—by carving a new path. Indeed, many considered his election a dramatic change in the young nation. America was fifty years old yet adolescent enough for a restoration of morality to its polity. This would be Jackson's primary objective, but he had to be careful in crafting his official presidential address. He had to walk a fine line since his views on policy were not consistent. Jackson voted for the Tariff of 1824 and for internal improvement bills, and he was even supportive of Tennessee's pro–Bank of the United States faction. He opted, then, to say little; he did not want to be forced into stating his views on specific issues.[12]

Jackson understood the sentiments expressed in his election, stating, "The suffrages of a virtuous people have pronounced a verdict of condemnation against them [the opposition] and their slanders whilst it has justified my character and course." The new president was clearly happy as he wrote his long-standing confidant. However, he interpreted his victory narrowly, dwelling more on the vindication it provided than on its political significance.[13] This principle of "virtuous people" electing their president, however, would guide much of Jackson's presidency and develop as an important seed of his populist appeal. Most Democrats believed that in Jackson's election the people won over corruption and effected a radical change. Even the opposition noted, "A great revolution has taken place."[14] By all accounts, the inauguration of Andrew Jackson was a momentous event in the nation's history, drawing thousands of spectators to the nation's capital. An invitation-only event quickly transformed into a huge mob that descended on the White House the moment Jackson concluded his address.

The Inaugural Address as epideictic or ceremonial rhetoric is taken generically as "a rite of passage" and "a ritual of transition in which a newly elected president is invested with the office of the presidency."[15] As a unique speech type, the presidential Inaugural Address functions as a unifying opportunity whereby "the people" are reconstituted, national values are highlighted, links to the cherished past are emphasized, principles and philosophies of the new administration are outlined, and the institutional framework is emphasized.[16] In short, the Inaugural Address presents a presidential ethos linking the past to the future and instilling confidence in the people with the investiture of a new executive.

Before even drafting his Inaugural Address, Jackson outlined the principles that would guide his administration, principles that would significantly serve as an outline of his first presidential speech. The convergence of rhetoric and politics is revealing. Jackson considered the guidelines of his administration congruent with the framing of his speech and future statements. This outline also proved Jackson to be an able administrator who took time to plan policies and their public presentations. He also clarified objectives as necessary for policymaking and their expressive outlets. Jackson outlined his principles, requiring "[that a strong] constitutional attorney general [be appointed], that members of the House cannot be appointed the cabinet positions, that public debt must be paid off, that tariff rates be modified and that the federal government cannot finance internal improvement. Jackson also envisioned an enlightened administration, meaning that only qualified individuals would be appointed to government positions. These principles, Jackson promised, would "give a brilliant career to the administration."[17]

In short, Jackson would adhere to constitutional stipulations. Moreover, he was willing to dismiss politically appointed individuals and prohibit members of Congress from assuming cabinet positions (a jab at Henry Clay, who became secretary of state after promising to get his supporters to back John Quincy Adams for the presidency). Jackson also carved a middle course on the issue of tariffs. He sought to diffuse growing tension over their rates, and he hinted rather strongly that he would oppose state-based internal improvements. The new president remained silent on two other critical issues: the Bank of the United States and the removal of Indian tribes. Yet these issues would shortly appear front and center. In this outline Jackson hinted at a strategy he would use repeatedly; he would say little in public, and sometimes nothing at all, about the most controversial matters.

Assessing a speech relative to its projected reception is not too complicated a task. As a highly attended and anticipated speech, a presidential

Inaugural Address is often a good subject for such an assessment. However, what judgments can be rendered about a draft of a speech that was never given? Relatedly, what can be said about an undelivered speech that appears textually superior to the delivered version? This is the case of Jackson's First Inaugural Address.

Textual analysis of the initial version is limited because it cannot be assessed against its audience reception. Even if it could be evaluated in this way, Jackson's popularity suggests that the vast majority of his interlocutors would have reacted positively, if not enthusiastically, to any version of the address. The alternative approach is to assess the initial address's rhetorical and political quality relative to the final version. More specifically, as a highly anticipated address, it is generally written for an audience eager to hear the incoming president's plan, perspective, and political philosophy. The fusion of a presidential Inaugural Address as ceremonial in essence with deliberative qualities is audience centered through and through. Different constituencies are addressed, and specific policy frameworks are highlighted. Majority and minority views are often acknowledged, and issues or tensions of the day are covered. The way in which these complex issues are woven together can provide insight into how the president wished the American people to view his speech. Though differing in textual construction, Jackson's initial and final drafts were written for the same audience and situational variables. Thus the delivered speech is helpful in analyzing the undelivered one. Both are understood as seeking maximum effect—a proper, dignified entry into the new presidential role and a path for policy over the next four years.

The three versions of Jackson's First Inaugural Address speak, then, to two differing perspectives on what the president and his aides thought the American people should hear and read. The significant gap between these drafts presents a unique opportunity to gauge intent, projection, and audience reception relative to each version.

JACKSON'S FIRST DRAFT OF THE INAUGURAL ADDRESS

In Jackson's own first draft, he projected humility and appreciation for the "distinguished favor" in becoming president, noting "the circumstances which [had] marked the recent contest of opinion to administer the affairs of a government."[18] He was intent on highlighting "the right of the people to control its measures, and whose only object and glory are the equal happiness and freedom of all the members of the confederacy." In light of this succinct statement of democratic philosophy in which the people control the polity, Jackson positioned himself as awed by such an ominous scene. He acknowledged his "solemn apprehensions for the safety of the great and important interests committed to [his] charge," declaring, "I confess, fellow citizens, that I approach it [the presidency] with trembling reluctance." Jackson's principal thought about the people governing themselves—the only principle that could secure a happy confederation—would guide his presidency and anchor every measure he would undertake thereafter.

Jackson further demonstrated humility with his reference to divine power in the nation's doings. He thanked "the smiles of that overruling Providence, 'in the hollow of whose hand' is the destiny of nations," who "[should] enable us to steer, the Bark of liberty, through every difficulty." The opening signals rhetorical subtlety and an economic style. Jackson explicated the rule of American governance in clear, elegant principles: "The achievements of our fathers, our subsequent intercourse with each other, the various relations we have sustained with the other powers of the world, and our present attitude at home, exhibits the practical operations of these principles, all of which are comprised in the sovereignty of the people. This is the basis of our system, and to its security from violation and innovation must our practice and experience as a government be dedicated." With powerful phrasing, Jackson further elaborated on his political philosophy of the United States as a nation unique in its construction, grateful to its founders, and based on the sovereignty of the people, the government's ultimate responsibility. This passage clearly echoes his popular election.

With his political philosophy in vogue, Jackson talked humbly about being called to the "voluntary suffrages of [his] country." He called for a government abiding by the principle that the people control its measures, a government committed to "equal happiness and freedom of all the members of the confederacy." Looking back at his predecessors, Jackson declared he would consider them "as mirrors, not so much for the measures which m[a]y be demanded by the present state of the country, but as applications of the same principles to the various exigencies which have occurred in our history, and as shedding light upon those which may hereafter arise." He saw his term in office as "useful to that which follows," and a guide "on that sacred fountain to which we must often go for the refreshment of our laws, and the invigoration of the public morals." Jackson projected his entry to the presidency as transitional and transformational. In assuming leadership, he connected a past taken as a sacred fountain to a future that might necessitate his own time in office as a guide for future presidents.

Jackson devoted about half of his Inaugural Address to the expression of gratitude, eloquently and subtly transitioning into the unique features of the American polity. The practical part, wherein he more explicitly stated specific measures and policies, occupies only a small part of the speech. Thus the remarks are largely ceremonial and to a lesser degree deliberative or policy oriented. The ceremonial part is rich with references to liberty and its manifestation in limited government and a happy populace. This empowering address gave Jackson's audience reasons to celebrate the inauguration and acknowledged the people's role and duty in choosing their government. Jackson read the sentiments of his election correctly, and he gave Americans their due thanks. His draft is temporal to the extent that it marked his inauguration as special and allowed the many people who stood with him to be part of *his* and, ostensibly, *their* day.

Even in outlining the "duties that are confided to the President," Jackson remained humble and limited. He addressed the duties of his role, which included executing laws, preserving foreign relations, and selecting "individuals fitting as far as possible the qualifications of the head and the heart," emphasizing that "in a free government the demand for moral qualities should be made superior to that of talent." His reforms would be dictated by the moral character and qualifications of individuals hired for government posts; his administration would restore ethics to government. Jackson elaborated on this point by noting the gap between American democracy and monarchial governments where "the safeguard of the empire consists chiefly in the will by which the monarch can wield the bigoted acquiescence of his Subjects," he observed, "But it is different with us. Here the will of the people, prescribed in the constitution of their own choice, controuls [*sic*] the service of the public functionaries, and is interested more deeply in the preservation of those qualities which ensures fidelity and honest devotion to their interests."

At each point in the draft, Jackson paid tribute to the unique makeup of the American democracy "sanctioned by the constitution, as lawful and just." He especially emphasized the role of the federal government and its constitutional foundation. Consider this astute phrasing: "The general safety was the great motive for the confederation of the states, and never could have been effected without conferring on the Federal Government the power to provide those internal supplies which constitute the means of war, and which if left to the ordinary operations of commerce, might be withheld at a time when we most needed them."

Jackson argued that the federal government was created for general safety and that the confederation of states would fail without such a central power. With this significant point, he stressed the primacy of the federal government. Jackson was attuned to growing regional tensions and the ways in which a potential break could be argued. Thus, his statement here was preemptive, seeking to quell any such talk with the view that the "confederation of states" was superior to any alternative in time of peace or war. Jackson crafted his next point about tariffs to leave no doubt that he considered them the issue of contention. He iterated his "hearty cooperation" in imposing rates "high enough to insure us against . . . calamity." If Jackson anticipated the eruption of a major emergency over tariffs, he did not say. Yet his incorporating the operative principles of the federal government suggests he was quite aware that a tariffs crisis could quickly turn into a constitutional crisis over the makeup of the Union itself. Jackson's reference to rates that were just "high enough" was strategic and accommodating. With this reference, he also looked back to his point some five years earlier about his "judicial" approach to tariffs. Jackson's positioning the issue of tariffs adjacent to the principle of a limited but able central government strongly indicated that he also saw the local perspective. He hinted that he would be sympathetic on the issue of tariffs but that he would also maintain a principled view of the federal government's role.

Though early in his presidency, Jackson was cognizant of the strong link between tariffs and the thorny issue of states' rights. He devoted a full paragraph to the relationship between the states and the federal government, but here he did not focus exclusively on tariffs. Jackson outlined the principle that "all the states are equal in sovereignty, and in claims to the benefits accruing from the confederation," therefore, he observed, states must support the national debt to ensure "the support of the Government, and safety of the Union." Jackson acknowledged some states' dissatisfaction over a less-than-equitable basis of debt and revenues, and he professed his desire to "secure harmony by removing the grounds of Jealousy [sic]" among states.

The growing tension between states and the "general government" clearly concerned Jackson. He publicly mused, "It is to be regretted that no line can be so obviously drawn as that all shall understand alike its boundaries." The Constitution was constructed on the "sentiment of conciliation, and spirit of compromise." As such, he asserted, "[I] shall be the last to cry out treason against those who interpret [the Constitution] differently from myself the policy, or powers of the government [as described in the Constitution]." Jackson went out of his way to show understanding, even compassion, over tensions among the states and between states and the federal government. Only a strong central government and the spirit of compromise could keep the Union safe, he stated. Yet if a state would argue otherwise, Jackson vowed not to deem it disloyal for an opposing view of the Constitution. He spoke as a father figure allowing a young nation to debate issues yet to be firmly settled. But such phrasing also reveals that Jackson understood the volatility of the situation. Tensions were close to the surface. Even a cursory assessment of this statement would render it too risky despite its benevolent intent, and so it unsurprisingly was omitted from the final speech. Only time would prove how risky such a promise might have been. In the end, Jackson would do exactly what he promised not to do: level treason charges at those supporting secession from the Union.

Though purposefully vague, only Jackson's final paragraph turns to what he called "some of the Topics which shall engage my earliest attention." He addressed subjects including eliminating the national debt, supporting the economy of revenue disbursements, implementing a judicious tariff, regulating commerce and agriculture, and respecting states' rights. Jackson opted for a minimalist approach to his Inaugural Address. He preferred to highlight the key issues of the day and, with the utmost subtlety, the growing need for a strong central government and the tensions it caused with the states. Indeed, subtlety is the speech's principal theme.

ANDREW JACKSON DONELSON'S DRAFT

After consulting with aides, Andrew Jackson Donelson, Jackson's nephew and private secretary, penned a shorter second draft with an eye to improving its overall direction. The second version of the speech is more concise, having Jackson state, "No thanks can be adequate to the honor they [the free people] confer, it admonishes me that the best return I can make, is a zealous dedication of my humble abilities to their service, and their good."[19] While Jackson began his draft with a condensed philosophy of government deriving its power from the people, Donelson used his first paragraph to express limited humble gratitude for the honor of being elected president. Jackson's second paragraph testifies to his humility and trepidation at the task ahead of him. Donelson's draft avoids these sentiments altogether, instead devoting two paragraphs to Jackson's readiness to abide by constitutional directives in executing his responsibilities.[20]

Donelson also omitted Jackson's lengthy tribute to his predecessors as guides to "various exigencies" and "those which may hereafter arise," all emanating from the principle of "the sovereignty of the people." Rather, Jackson's secretary delved into a statement about "the rights of the separate states," which were "animated by a respect for these sovereign members of our union; taking care not to confound the powers they have reserved to themselves with those they have granted to the Confederacy." This was a political move; Jackson was cognizant of growing tensions between the federal government and the states. He spelled out his awareness more specifically and artfully in his own draft, identifying tariffs as the issue of contention. Jackson wrote, "General & state governments when understood to embrace the protection of our own labour, merit the most serious consideration."[21] Yet Donelson addressed tariffs only vaguely, preferring instead the euphemistic term "public revenue," and he urged considering this revenue relative to the objective of extinguishing the national debt.[22]

The following paragraph in the second draft elaborates further that for "a proper protection of the subjects of impost with a view to the collection of the revenue, it would seem . . . that the spirit of equity, caution and compromise" necessitated a balanced approach considering the interests of commerce, agriculture, and manufacturers.[23] Jackson had the federal government standing above the states and advocating the proportional distribution of surpluses to the states after paying the national debt. Yet in this version of the speech, the issue of "improvement" is subordinate to federal needs. Additionally, the term is devoid of the qualifier "internal." In Donelson's draft, the phrase "internal improvements" conditions the entire paragraph, and it does so with the same sentiments of first "liquidating the national debt" prior to using such funds for other purposes. Again, Jackson used subtler phrasing. In his version, he first presented the principle of federal government operations and then subjected the issue of internal improvements to it. Donelson placed internal improvements front and center with any explanation appearing more as a justification thereof. Jackson let principles appear first, guiding his views and his perspective on issues that followed. Jackson also carved a clear demarcation between the "powers granted to the general government, and those reserved to the states and the people." He devoted a full paragraph to this principle, perhaps seeking to calm those states already embroiled in the tariff quandary and fearful of an intrusive federal government. This point is not present in Donelson's draft.[24]

Finally, while Jackson avoided any reference to the Indian tribes, Donelson covered the issue with a brief statement about treating the tribes "consistent with habits of our government, and the feelings of our people," and promising "[a] just and liberal policy," that "due to their dependent situation, and to our national character."[25] Though generalized and vague, these instructive statements nonetheless indicate the new administration's intent to comply with the federal government's wishes for a just solution.

The second draft ends with a call to select individuals of talent and integrity for public office, advocating "the advancement of the public service, more on the ability and virtue of the public officers, than on their numbers." The advocate of reforms left few references to this objective to the end of the address. This version of the speech ties needed reforms to public virtue, connected to divine protection in Jackson's execution of his duties.

THE FINAL AND FORMAL VERSION OF THE FIRST INAUGURAL ADDRESS

Jackson's First Inaugural Address (March 4, 1829), the first to be delivered from the west portico of the United States Capitol, lasted some ten minutes, making it among the shortest such speeches to date. Upon its publication in print, the address received strong approval. To a great extent, Donelson's draft was kept intact, though several modifications are instructive nonetheless. Jackson's opening paragraph is reminiscent of Thomas Jefferson's opening paragraph of his First Inaugural Address, with its phrases "duties that I have been appointed to perform," "I avail myself," and "express the gratitude." The eloquent and even touching first paragraph of Jackson's version of his remarks did not survive. As delivered, his speech omitted the sentimental phrases "solemn apprehensions for the safety of the great and important interests committed to my charge" and "I confess, fellow citizens, that I approach it [the presidency] with trembling reluctance." These ideas were instead reduced to "the best return I can make is the zealous dedication of my humble abilities." Rather than "I have been called by voluntary suffrages of my country," in Jackson's initial draft, the second draft includes, "I have been appointed to perform by the choice of a free people."[26] Such changes indicate a clear shift from personal sentiments to a generic and more formal style. It was important for Jackson to follow the tradition of the genre of Inaugural Addresses. So, too, was the implied continuity of presidential enactment, perhaps precisely because many expected Jackson to commence a new chapter in American history.

In the second paragraph of the final address, Jackson summarized the principles he outlined prior to composition. These doctrines summarized his philosophy of the role of the president and the federal government as stipulated in the Constitution. Jackson considered the presidency "an instrument of the Federal Constitution," one that existed to administer the foreign policy of the United States, to manage the nation's revenue, and to command its military. Here, too, Jackson followed the structure of inaugural remarks delivered by his immediate predecessors, John Quincy Adams and James Monroe. In elaborating on these points, the new president espoused a clear view of the limited role of the federal government, including the office of the executive. He stated his aim "to preserve peace and to cultivate friendship," as well as to manage foreign relations in "fair and honorable terms." Jackson also included a short statement of significant foresight. He spoke of the United States "becoming a powerful nation," hinting that this role might require a different approach to foreign relations. The nation was changing as its territory and influence increased. Jackson sought to make this point, perhaps for posterity and in recognition of the nation's new responsibilities.

Jackson stated his belief in maintaining "the rights of the separate States," respecting the "sovereign members of our Union," and "taking care not to confound the powers they have reserved to themselves with those they have granted the Confederacy." A limited federal government and a clear separation between its rights and the states' would be Jackson's overall approach to government. Significantly, however, Jackson stated that both powers were granted by the states. One can interpret this statement not so much as his constitutional perspective, though it was, but as his realization that specific looming issues, such as the concern over tariffs and related regional tensions, would be difficult to solve. Perhaps an early preemptive statement about the rights of states relative to those of the federal government would diffuse further strife. That the states gave power to the confederacy would be a crucial legal point serving Jackson well in the future. In any event, the new president did not say that the states could reclaim the power they gave to the federal government and hence disrupt the Union. This point, too, would be crucial later on. Yet the first draft makes the same overall argument much more eloquently.

Jackson acknowledged that the issue of "public revenue" would require "no inconsiderable share of [his] official solicitude." While this was a general, vaguely phrased principle, his principal operative approach would be that of "a strict and faithful economy." To that extent, Jackson made it clear that he would extinguish the national debt. He considered such a burden "incompatible with real independence." For Jackson, federal debt had a corrupting effect on the nation, and his task was to minimize this tendency and require accountability from the officers of the federal government. Strategically and subtly, Jackson tied the issue of public revenue to his concern over the tariff issue. He stated that a "spirit of equity, caution, and compromise" was required, that the "great interests of agriculture, commerce, and manufactures should be equally favored, and that perhaps the only exception to this rule should consist in the peculiar encouragement of any products of either of them that may be found essential to our national independence." Jackson sought to mollify those concerned with the tariff issue and regional calculations. He asked that these concerns be balanced with other important issues, but he afforded these issues legitimacy as long as they were rationalized in terms of the nation's independence.

On several important issues Jackson said very little. Regarding internal improvement or the diffusion of knowledge, he stated, "So far as they can be promoted by the constitutional acts of the Federal Government," they "are of high importance." Donelson's drafted statement on internal improvements was further truncated to be guided principally by constitutional acts. Jackson's elaboration on the importance of these matters is surprisingly short and constrained. Vague statements carry the day without dwelling too much on specifics. Similarly, on the issue of the Indian nation, a topic inserted in Donelson's draft, Jackson remained reticent. He stated his desire to observe "a just and liberal policy, and to give that humane and considerable attention to their [American Indians'] rights and their wants which is consistent with the habits of our Government and the feelings of our people." In this seemingly balanced approach, Jackson hinted that any solution to the tribal issue would be in accordance with *our* government and *our* people. Yet a "just and liberal policy" may very well have been the cover for anything but. As John Quincy Adams and James Monroe included statements about Indian tribes in their Inaugural Addresses, Jackson's aides may have advised him that excluding such a reference was unwise.[27]

The largest portion of the Inaugural Address, a topic completely absent from Jackson's draft but fully developed and intact in Donelson's, concerns the issue of a standing army. Jackson considered this force "as dangerous to free governments in time of peace." He did not plan to enlarge the army, and he intended to keep it subordinate to the nation's civil authorities. Jackson acknowledged the gradual growth of the navy and its enlarged responsibilities "in distant climes," as well as improvements in the army's facilities and science. His primary focus, though, was on national militia as "the bulwark of our defense, which in the present state of our intelligence and population must render us invincible." Here, Jackson would use the most supportive language, calling the militia an integral part of the American experience where "our Government is administered for the good of the people, and is regulated by their will." The president continued, "As long as it secures to us the rights of person and of property, liberty of conscience and of the press, it will be worth defending; and so long as it is worth defending a patriotic militia will cover it with an impenetrable aegis." Such a militia composed of "a million of armed freemen," he assured his listeners, could guarantee that the country would "never be conquered by a foreign foe." Jackson therefore concluded, "I shall cheerfully lend all the aid in my power."

The popular general understood from experience the advantages of a large regular militia balanced by a limited army. Yet the inclusion of this significant and lengthiest point only in the final draft deserves explanation. Perhaps Jackson's aides felt that focusing on states' militias provided a tangible example of his pro-state sentiments. The new president's view of the economy and his strong interest in curtailing federal expenditures may have also played a role in his preference for state militias over a standing army supported by the federal government. Jackson's earlier point about potentially reassessing foreign policy may have been strategic, tempering any perception of a more militaristic United States. Especially under a highly respected general, local and state militias would be taken for their defensive plans rather than any offensive ones. Finally, presenting militias as the cornerstone of the nation's defense allowed Jackson to dwell on his favorite topics of patriotism and liberty.

The last point of the Inaugural Address is devoted to reforms. Jackson indicated that he would focus on this issue, and though the language in the address is tempered, his intention is rather clear. Jackson spoke of abuses that have brought "patronage of the Federal Government into conflict with the freedom of elections," "[had] disturbed the rightful course of appointment and have placed or continued power in unfaithful or incompetent hands." Jackson's strong words reflected his outrage and dismay at corruption in the federal government, as well as his insistence that the people's representatives be ethical (echoes of 1824 are well reflected here). Indeed, in the name of reform, Jackson would usher in the dismissal of many government officials, and the backlash would be intense. Yet he would do what he thought necessary to appoint those "whose diligence and talents [would] insure their respective stations able and faithful cooperation, depending for the advancement of the public service more on the integrity and zeal of the public officers than on their numbers."

Jackson concluded his Inaugural Address with a pledge to, in his words, "look with reverence to the examples of public virtue left by my predecessors." He put his trust in his fellow citizens, as well as in "the Power whose providence mercifully protected our national infancy, and has since upheld our liberties in various vicissitudes." This paragraph, too, was taken directly from Donelson's draft.

COMPARING THE THREE VERSIONS

The differences between the first and second drafts of Jackson's Inaugural Address are rather striking. In the final version, Donelson's rendering remains largely intact. Jackson made the initial address mostly ceremonial, personal, and eloquent with concise prose, but he outlined a more specific agenda in the final draft. Additionally, he focused his draft on the audience, recognizing "the will of the people" and the "sovereignty of the people." The president avoided these rather new terms in the final draft, focusing on policy and a more conventional entry into office.[28] Jackson wrote the address with full recognition of the changes his popular election symbolized. He understood what his presidency would bring to the many first-time voters, and he thus devoted an ample portion of his remarks to the people as the holders of the young republic's power. The final draft is more in line with previous Inaugural Addresses, presenting a smooth, if not altogether routine, entry into office and minimizing the significant changes the election of 1828 presented.

Jackson's draft is more tuned to the people's sentiments, while the final draft takes notice of specific issues he would seek to implement. Jackson looked to the past in his version of the speech, and he noted the transition and potential implications his ascendancy heralded. He also sought a return to the spirit and morality of the republic's beginning. Jackson's draft is subtle, addressing the issues of the day without specifics and reiterating basic principles he assumed all would agree with. The final draft, with its clusters of active verbs, is exactly that—an active address emphasizing the future. The final address is forward-looking and political in essence. Finally, while the initial draft is richly descriptive, the ultimate speech is more direct and specific. The latter iteration lacks the subtlety, eloquence, and rhetorical economy of Jackson's draft.

The gap between the primary two versions of the address lies largely in the treatment of the primary issue of the day—the nation's economy—yet the true issue of the day was not visible to all. On the surface, the growing tension was between the states and the federal government, manifested primarily in economic terms. One side of the debate supported the Union's westward expansion. The other advocated internal improvements in the existing (and mostly original) states of the Union. Internal improvements necessitated financial investments in roads, bridges, and related transportation and communications infrastructure. Such investments would clearly hamper the federal budget required for expansion, especially with a budget deficit. Financial gaps between US states and regions would further exacerbate the situation. This issue would become clearer some ten to fifteen years hence and stretch all the way to the Civil War. But Jackson discerned the seeds for conflict as he entered the presidency, and he tried to preemptively handle thorny issues.

For now, the issue of tariff rates would be the focal point of the growing economic rift between the North and South. But sooner rather than later, it would be clear to many that slavery was the larger issue. What was glaringly absent from the First Inaugural Address was any mention of the Bank of the United States, an institution Jackson had opposed for quite some time. But, as he would state later, "he had wished to speak out against it so early as his Inaugural but had been dissuaded: everyone knew, he said, that he always had been opposed to the Bank of the United States, 'nay all banks.'"[29]

In his initial draft, more than his final address, Jackson recognized the nation's concerns. He preferred a subtle approach relying on unifying, relatable founding principles. The final draft is direct and principled, the sort that at least his advisors thought necessary under these constraints. Two different conceptions of audience are inherent in the gap between Jackson's draft of the First Inaugural Address and the final version. The president understood the tension between specific states and the federal government. Though he supported a strong yet limited federal administration, he sought to present a balanced viewpoint that was rhetorically more accommodating to the states. Jackson did not see the need to over argue this point upon entering the White House, preferring restraint to diffuse tension. He even stated that this was not the time to detail policies. The president conceived of the nation as happy in his speech, and he wanted to go no further.

Taking the multitude in Washington for his inauguration as evidence of the significant transition his ascendancy marked, Jackson used his address to emphasize the nation's values, uniqueness, and greatness. He clearly minimized all detailed discussion about specific issues, presenting them at the value level most people could share and approve. Jackson avoided particulars not only for the sake of diffusing tension but also as a measure of strategic silence. He did not want to tip his hand regarding worries over such matters as tariff rates and their related state–federal government concerns. Nor were Jackson's views one-sided. Though he favored a strong, constitutionally warranted federal government, he significantly considered that government a means of maximizing efficiency and balancing competing interests, primarily economic interests.

In the final version of the Inaugural Address, the primary feature and hence the most significant difference from Jackson's draft, is its topicality. The speech jumps quickly into explicating the presidency and following the constitutional stipulations "as the instrument of the Federal Government." Jackson stated that the executive's task was "to execute the laws of the United States, to superintend their foreign and their confederate relations, to manage their revenue, [and] to command their forces." After listing his primary duties, he briefly spelled out his political philosophy: "[I] keep steadily in view the limitations as well as the extent of the Executive power, trusting thereby to discharge the functions of my office without transcending its authority." These two passages present Jackson's objective of stating the role of the federal government vis-à-vis the Constitution while dwelling on its limitations. The tension between the federal government and the states was clear to him, and he intended to convince the states of his measured, tempered view.

A comparison of the two versions of Jackson's speech reveals this balancing act, which was important precisely because the issues of the day made a strong central government a practical necessity. The nation was growing. More states were joining the Union, and more territories were waiting to be explored and acquired. These circumstances would present a more complex confederation with a growing need for a strong central governing body, the kind that no ideology could counter. Jackson's final version of the Inaugural Address was written with a realism that was only subtly evident in the initial draft. Jackson's aides sought greater clarity in order to manage these developing complex issues. By temperament and practice, the seventh president opted for subtle rhetoric. He knew that in action he would be more resolute than anyone else in the nation.

✳✳✳✳

With thousands on hand to see their hero installed as president, Jackson delivered an address befitting the occasion. He enacted the people's responsibility for the nation. Americans were powerful in their ability to demand changes and seek reforms that corresponded with a progressive country drawing its support from the voters. The inauguration was a popular event, and if any proof of Jackson's enactment was needed, it could be found in the mob descending on the White House. Indeed, the event's aftermath was a public celebration bordering on sheer chaos that Washington had never seen. At a reception open to anyone, enthusiastic supporters ransacked the White House. One person reported that Jackson himself was "nearly pressed to death and almost suffocated and torn to pieces" by well-wishers.[30] At four o'clock in the afternoon, the president had to be rescued and moved to another location.

Lest the chaos and distraction in the White House seem regrettable, it is important to realize that this inaugural event was many people's first. The people's excessive enthusiasm was an authentic reflection of how much Jackson's presidency meant to them. As biographer Remini states, "Andrew Jackson was the people's own President—the first such—and that was something wonderful and exciting. Seeing the crowds and hearing them cheer a government that they themselves had called into existence augured well for the future of a democratic society."[31]

With such an enthusiastic, affectionate audience on hand, it is likely that any version of Jackson's Inaugural Address would have succeeded. Donelson believed the political platform for Jackson's term was central to his speech. For his part, Jackson considered the address a ceremonial marking of significant change in American history. The president's insight was richer and deeper than that of his aide, who focused on the remarks' limited reach. Yet Jackson adopted the advice given to him, and this step, too, was significant in the operation and administration of the country's new chief magistrate. Jackson was a team player, and he would function like one during his entire administration. The speechwriting process in particular was collaborative. Even so, Jackson would not always accept editorial changes. One decision

Jackson made concerning his First Inaugural Address—and this choice remained intact—was to keep it very short. He delivered remarks roughly one-third the length of the previous three inaugural speeches, respectively given by John Quincy Adams and James Monroe. In contrast to former presidents' more deliberative approach, Jackson crafted an Inaugural Address that was short, thematically tight, and ceremonial in essence.

THE FIRST ANNUAL
MESSAGE TO CONGRESS
A BLUEPRINT FOR AN AMBITIOUS AGENDA

On December 8, 1829, some eight months after delivering his short Inaugural Address, Jackson sent federal legislators his First Annual Message to Congress, one of the greatest documents of his presidency. Therein, Jackson included one of the most impressive agendas that any executive has introduced at the outset of an administration. In his yearly dispatches, the precursor to later State of the Union Addresses, Jackson would carefully explain his government's plans and philosophy.

More than two centuries of presidents have delivered a State of the Union Address. The speeches vary so greatly that Karlyn K. Campbell and Kathleen H. Jamieson hesitate to even classify them as a genre.[1] However, Campbell and Jamieson identify the State of the Union's three general characteristics: the discussion of national values, the highlighting of relevant information and issues, and the generation of policy recommendations.[2] In his First Annual Message, Jackson both abided by these generic stipulations and projected his intention to be different from his predecessors. The memorandum covers both conventional and unconventional items. Therein, the president outlined an ambitious plan for the government and Congress, and he impressed the nation with an activist administration reflecting popular sentiments. Jackson followed the custom of the time, whereby a new president's first message to Congress was highly anticipated. Given Jackson's unique path to the presidency, this address would be of the utmost importance.

There are several reasons why Jackson unveiled a forceful agenda at the outset of his presidency. He said little about his programs while campaigning, and he restricted his Inaugural Address to a few key issues without much explication. Perhaps he wished to contrast his First Annual Message with the rhetorically awkward remarks of his predecessor. Disorganized and intellectually puzzling, Adams's initial speech to Congress was ridiculed for contrasting America's complete lack of observatories for astronomical research with the 130 such observatories in Europe. Adams engaged in comparisons with European countries as befitted a former diplomat to European court. But in so doing, he appeared detached and arrogant.[3]

Jackson, in contrast, had to impress the nation that his position resulted from direct election by the people. Though his elevation differed from his predecessors', he was as able as those men if not more so. He entered the presidency sensing that the nation had reached a crossroads and that important decisions had to be made on several fronts. The time in which Jackson lived also factored in his activist path to presidential politics. The nation was still young enough to carve a new course of action. At the same time, America was mature enough to accept such changes, especially those borne of corruption. Jackson saw himself as an activist and a transformative president, a conduit to changes the nation had to undergo. Now, his plans had to be translated into rhetorical acts

Jackson was already thinking about his agenda in the late summer of 1829, but this advance planning did not mean that he would spell out every issue. He demonstrated his administrative skills while preparing the address, drafting the initial version, and soliciting additional drafts from aides and cabinet secretaries. His would be a strategic plan and, subsequently, a strategic address. Jackson made inquiries regarding the Bank of the United States and jotted notes for future consideration. It remained to be seen whether this matter would be raised in the formal report to Congress. When preparing key documents, Jackson customarily took notes to serve as outlines for later drafts. On the matter of Texas, a crucial issue throughout his two terms, he advised the government's representative to Mexico, "Let a listening ear, a silent tongue, and a stedfast [sic] heart, the three jewels of wisdom, guard every advance which you make on the subject of Texas. The acquisition of that territory is becoming every day an object of more importance which they already ascribe to us."[4]

In a November 26, 1829, letter to Jackson, Secretary Ingham directly referred to the upcoming speech to Congress. One can infer from the exchange that Jackson solicited cabinet secretaries' opinions about what to include in the message. Ingham apologized for having little time to focus on the Bank of the United States, as he was busy instead with the examination of the Treasury balance. Both issues greatly interested Jackson. Ingham urged the president to be careful with any statement about the bank, stating, "Whatever may be said in a Message to congress, will be difficult to change and if it should not prove acceptable to public opinion it will increase instead of diminish the power of the present institution."[5]

A letter form Atty. Gen. John M. Berrien confirms that Jackson requested his opinion on the constitutional authority of Congress "to establish a corporation for banking purposes."[6] Citing the Bank of the United States' existence and the long controversy over its establishment, including its constitutional grounding, Berrien suggested that Jackson let the issue rest: "It does not seem to me to be expedient, by anticipating the agitation of the subject, to communicate at this early day those exciting discussion, which unless they eventuate in the renewal of the charter, will without doubt be revived at each successive session, until some substitute institution exclusive in its character, shall be established."[7] Such were the early plans for the First Annual Message to Congress.

DRAFTING THE FIRST ANNUAL MESSAGE TO CONGRESS

Jackson was the first to put his stamp on this crucial address. Though others submitted multiple drafts for his consideration, the president retained the substance and phrasing of many points from his initial effort in the finalized Annual Message.[8] He set his agenda and primary arguments therein, often exhibiting lawyerlike contemplation of issues.

Jackson commenced his draft with a tribute to the Almighty for the nation's peace and prosperity, as well as for "united harmony to enact all laws that may tend to promote the prosperity of his Kingdom, and the best interests of the union."[9] He made God and Union strong features in his opening. For Jackson, what happened on Earth was divinely inspired, and the Almighty wielded the Union, which should not be trampled. With this phrasing, the president expressed concern over regional issues and their impact on the Union. Given the growing tension between the federal government and the states, he may have figured that tackling this issue early on with a transcendent vision of the Deity's role in the nation's welfare would suffice.

Jackson first highlighted America's strong relations with foreign nations. He stated that negotiations with France and England, which he did not detail, "[might] eventuate in a manner satisfactory to all." The president similarly noted, "At home, there has been nothing to produce disquiet: every where [sic] peace & harmony has prevailed." Referencing his constitutional requirement to advise Congress "from time to time of the state of the Union," Jackson stressed the need to amend the Constitution regarding the election of "the chief magistrate of the country" such that it "[should] in no wise or in any event devolve upon the House of Representatives."[10] He thus straightforwardly repudiated Congress's role in selecting a president. The government of the United States, explained Jackson, was inherently "one of experiment" whereby "untried principles" entered into practice with the recognition that they were not perfect and thus in need of modifications. Jackson opined that the election of the president was one of the most crucial issues, and one which put the nation most at risk. The provision for presidential elections needed the strongest guard, which he explained as follows: "Jealous of their [the people's] rights, as they ever should be, they will never be satisfied with any ruler who is not the selection & choice of themselves; and he will never fail to have an unpleasant administration, who may obtain the direction of our national affairs, by any other means, than the free, unbiased opinions of the people."[11]

Jackson placed the election of 1824 front and center in this speech; he was determined to reform presidential elections such that the people's vote would be the sole adjudicator. To this end, he articulated his guiding principle: "For a single individual of the House of Representatives to give a decision in [sic] behalf of a million of people . . . can seldom fail to excite suspicion jealousy, & the distrust in the minds of a people vigilant and attentive to the maintainance [sic] of their own rights."[12] The potential for corruption in the standard of political representation had to be corrected. With it must come a profound transformation and enactment of the people as a responsible community.

Jackson also called for a constitutional amendment "securing to the people the priviledge [sic] of voting immediately & by name, for the person preferred for chief magistrate."[13] As he could proudly consider his the first popular election, the general sought to enshrine this form of voting in the law and in so doing significantly reform Americans' representatives. Jackson's primary justification for his argument was that a "fair expression of the public will, free from management," a euphemism for political manipulation, "[was] of the highest importance in popular elections." He added this principal thought: "Elections loose [sic] their value & purity, if by intrigue & fraud, the priviledge [sic] of voting may be so affected as by possibility to change the result, & impair thereby the choice of the elector." As far as Jackson was concerned, Congress had no role in electing the president. He further posited that any member of the House running for president should not hold any position in the incoming administration. This was a clear reference to Clay, who masterminded the House selection of John Quincy Adams as president in 1824.[14]

Jackson also raised the related issue of the length of the presidential term, suggesting that executives' service be limited to a single term (be it for four or six years). His rationale, often phrased as a principle, was that with one term in office, "the chief magistrate of a free people, should never be found seeking & manoevoring [sic] to possess himself of the office."[15] Jackson sought to free the presidency from any gamesmanship over reelection—such practices were most corrupting. With this wise idea, Jackson sought to unshackle the president from political bargaining and subsequent intrigues, keep the position pure, and abide by constitutional principles. This idea would also free the president to act as necessary without political calculations and unnecessary compromises.

Jackson did not limit the single term in office to the president, instead recommending it for any public office holders. Since "no man was made for office; & offices created for no one," Jackson disapproved of individuals holding political positions for life. He considered such employment "contrary to our free institutions."[16] Jackson intended "to declare that the [government] offices [should] become vacant at stated periods, whereby the dishonest faithless & undeserving might quietly retire, and the honest meritorious & well qualified, be retained by reappointment."[17] A thinking administrator, he wanted to end corruption in government, increase efficiency, and instill a healthy "rotation in office" that would promote qualified individuals who lacked powerful connections and prevent the elite from holding public positions for themselves. Jackson also sought political pressure via the encouragement of public sentiments. Here he displayed rhetorical acumen, professing the executive's right to select accomplished people for high office. Declaring "that no restriction should be imposed," Jackson argued "that the Executive should have afforded to him the widest range for the selection of talents."[18] An egalitarian era was under way, and Jackson's reforms endorsed "the people" as meritorious for any high office.

Jackson added a significant note about his personal convictions: "Being without any thing of motive or self to serve, I shall omit no occasion to declare candidly & freely whatsoever views & opinions I may entertain calculated to afford security to those high privileges of government we enjoy."[19] Jackson knew he outlined major if not altogether radical reforms that would be questioned and challenged. His desire for a constitutional amendment regarding presidential elections was clearly conditioned by his own loss in 1824. No doubt many would see his proposed reforms as vindication thereof. He may have felt compelled to explain that he had no personal stakes but only national objectives in suggesting these changes. Jackson's motives, then, were pure, while others' motives were not. He was directing a rather strong hint at congressmen who would allow holding offices "within the gift of the President." Such a possibility, repeated Jackson, would be denied if "deciding the presidential election in future be taken [he struck through "away"] from the House of Representatives."[20] To strengthen this point, Jackson added that presidents, too, should be restricted from appointing members of the House to office. As he noted, such "inducements may be offered to swerve them from a faithful performance of duty to their constituents, and their country."[21]

Jackson consistently presented the same principles as grounds for his opinion on specific matters: honesty, fairness, and propriety consistent with the Constitution of a free people. Above all else, Jackson wanted "the legislative hall of the country, [to] be maintained pure, and ever free from temptation."[22] He was convinced that the nation ought to fear politicians' motives and selfishness, which were "extending their corrupting influence to the people."[23] To this point about corruption, Jackson added an observation about his advanced age. He intimated that, though he was a father only by adoption, his sole motive in instituting these changes was to leave to his children and country "prosperous & happy," and with "liberties unimpaired forever."[24] Twice in the draft, Jackson spoke of his pure motives. A psychologist might suggest that Jackson had an opposing motive or perhaps suspected the effect of his reforms could impinge upon his character. The paternal point and the reference to his advanced age were to be considered proof of Jackson's disinterestedness. Experience and patriotic devotion were his sole motives. Metaphorically considering the nation his extended family was a theme dear to Jackson; he often fretted about his extended family. Thus his public rhetoric often projected a paternalistic view of politics.

On the issue of the 1828 tariff ruling, Jackson again proved his political skills. He acknowledged the difficulties that tariff rates had imposed on some, stating his wish that there were no import duties between nations. He preferred only a fair exchange of goods and fair competition. But such could not be the case in international commerce. Jackson also stated that tariff legislation "[gave] rise to speculations and produce [sic] to some class of our citizens injury." Yet, he contended, anger or hurt feelings should not be the approach. Jackson instead asked for an understanding of the larger context whereby "the mutual benefits of the whole united states [sic]" ought to be the guiding principle.[25] In short, the sole concern with regard to tariffs should be what "the general good require[s]." Regional tensions over this issue were simmering before Jackson took office. He now sought to nip them in the bud with an altruism befitting the nation, an altruism that respected harmoniousness and made the Union its primary focus.[26]

As regards financial matters, Jackson highlighted America's prosperity and the spirit of free enterprise a progressive populace exhibited. The increase in population and subsequent increase in commerce, Jackson forecasted, would add to the nation's prosperity. He continued, "[This is a circumstance] which leaves the Citizen untrammeled & free to pursue his interest, where his enterprise may open the way." In a few years, he predicted, "we shall present this marvelous picture to the world, a nation free from debt, and capable of applying all its resources to the great end and purpose."[27] These were Jackson's progressive ideals: a nation unique in its political experimentation and economic success, and, importantly, a nation enjoying peace and prosperity and relieved of debt as a means for greater enterprises. Jackson also gave these ideals an international dimension. In his view, other nations were waiting anxiously to see how the American experiment in self-governance would unfold. Jackson's principal idea of a democratic, progressive nation ostensibly relied on implementing an efficient economy. This was his master plan.

With the discharge of the public debt, Jackson predicted, in his words, plans for "great national works of internal improvements in which the whole nation are [sic] interested & which may be considered entirely national and of first importance to its prosperity."[28] He acknowledged different opinions on the matter; some had expedient objectives, and others did not consider internal improvements within Congress's jurisdiction. Jackson offered a solution, asking rhetorically, "Would it not be salutary to make such apportionment of the surplus revenue amongst the states, for the purpose of internal improvement as may be found to be, a fair, federal, and [he struck through "useful"] Just disposition of it?"[29] The financing of internal improvements was at issue, with Jackson seeking to abide by constitutional constraints, believing in the overall objective of limiting such expenditures to national projects and therefore eliminating jealousy and complaints among the states.

On the matter of the Indian tribes, Jackson voiced sympathy for their condition and outlined a plan to improve it. Up to this point, he stated, the government's policy had been "gradually to open to them the ways of civilization; and from their wandering habits, to [striking out "draw"] entice them to a course of life calculated to present fairer prospects of comfort and happiness."[30] Yet civilizing the tribes failed. Jackson rejected the recent proposal for autonomous enclaves in existing states, arguing, "No people were ever free, or capable of forming & [he struck through "putting"] carrying into execution a social compact for themselves until education and intelligence was first introduced."[31] For Jackson, the gist of the issue was the tribes' lack of education and their ignorance of civilized ways. He thought southern tribes in particular "erratic in their habits" and thus incapable of self-governance producing happiness and prosperity.[32] The government, averred Jackson, could not secure the tribes' independence within a given state. The president held the following prejudicial attitudes toward American Indians: a benevolent government could go only so far in helping uneducated and erratic tribes, and, by implication, tribes could not continue to live among educated and cultured people. Jackson could not go beyond the civilized/uncivilized dichotomy as the justification for their removal. His would be a progressive nation, and those unprepared for it or unable to adapt to its new ways had to leave.

Jackson's draft of the First Annual Message to Congress ends with an unfinished sentence about the future of Indian tribes removed beyond the Mississippi (he would add the missing portion of the draft later). As he left it, the president's statement is a clear rejection of any autonomous regions within the limits of any state. Its overall sentiments tend toward separating the tribes from whites. The passage here does not include the constitutional argument resembling Jackson's thinking about rejecting a state within a state. He either strategically limited his view of the issue or left it incomplete.

Amos Kendall worked from Jackson's and Donelson's drafts and submitted his own version of the address. Van Buren, Eaton, and two scribers further developed Kendall's composition. This lengthy draft covers all the topics Jackson outlined except the Indian nations, and it remains within his framework while employing a more flattering but economical style. In his short draft, Van Buren focused exclusively on the tariff issue, warning of "deleterious consequences" and "insatiate avarice" caused by political economy and partisan sentiments.[33] He asserted that the tariff issue was subjected to "sinister" motives and "political & party contests of the day," both of which were forgetting the interests of the country and "fomenting pretensions upon this subject." Though vague in his references, Van Buren chided those "unworthy of a public trust who can be induced by any consideration to minister to unjust pretensions whether the result of ambitious personal design or of overweaning [sic] avarice."[34] The secretary of state did not say whether he meant Calhoun. But the implication is rather obvious. If Van Buren alluded to some inside discussion in this ad hominem attack, Jackson in his final message presented this critical issue in a more tempered manner that was devoid of personal references.

Jackson's papers include drafts of a variety of documents: Jackson's statement on debt collection and the reorganization of the navy; Kendall's version of a statement on Treasury frauds; Jackson's reference to the Seneca annuity and Eaton's draft on "Indian removal," a continuation of Jackson's incomplete composition; Hamilton's and Donelson's statements on the Bank of the United States, and Jackson's introduction and conclusion of the First Annual Message. Eaton's draft on Indian removal did not make it into the final message, but it is instructive for a later discussion of Jackson's approach to the subject.[35]

Hamilton's draft statement to Congress about the Bank of the United States is significant. The bank's charter would not expire until 1836, and in light of this fact Hamilton wrote, "In order to avoid the evil resulting from precipitancy in a measure involving such important principles and such deep pecuniary interests, I feel that I cannot in justice to our constituents and to the parties interested too soon present it to the deliberative consideration of the Legislature and the people."[36] With this clever statement, he put the bank on notice but said nothing more. Hamilton also raised the issue of the bank's constitutionality. The institution potentially infringed on states' rights, and it also gave stockholders exclusive privileges "of a dangerous tendency."[37] While nothing else in the draft elaborates on them, these points are sufficient indicators of how Jackson would approach his aversion to the Bank of the United States.

In all, the drafts of the First Annual Message to Congress had several iterations and involved input from most of Jackson's top aides. The document's composition process was an early indication of the mechanisms of speechwriting and preparation for major addresses. Significantly, Jackson wrote the first and lengthiest draft, setting the address's agenda, overall tone, and rhetorical framing. The final address was a cumulative effort drafted in the same manner as contemporary State of the Union Addresses, but with one distinct caveat. Jackson crafted the first iteration and ensured that it dominated the final product.

THE FIRST ANNUAL MESSAGE TO CONGRESS, DECEMBER 8, 1829

Jackson opened by greeting the representatives of twelve million "happy people" and thanking a "benign Providence" for the conditions of peace and "progressive improvement." A reference to God had been replaced with an ambiguous reference to Providence. Mention of the Union had been pushed to the end of the introductory paragraph and modified such that Jackson now called "to promote the objects of our union."[38] Jackson's straightforward references in the draft are superior to the cautious phrasing here. In this version, the reference to the Union in particular is tenuous. Jackson described the Union as a given in his draft, but he characterized it as "work in progress" in the final document. Jackson was continuously concerned about the Union's strength. Regional encroachment caused him angst, and he likely considered it better to present the Union as a matter of fact. In this iteration of the message, the president took a moderate tone, implying a more patient perspective to the gradual strengthening of the Union and likely hoping to assuage states' rights advocates.

Turning to foreign relations, Jackson called the nation's international network "pacific and friendly." Despite challenges, he anticipated positive results. The president highlighted the nation's strengths as "fully adequate to the maintenance of all her interests," further noting that "under the protection of Providence," they would "cause all our just rights to be respected" by other nations.[39] Over pending issues with France, England, and Spain, Jackson voiced his belief that the nation's just causes would end satisfactorily.

Thereafter, Jackson detailed the issue with each of the three main European powers, beginning with Great Britain and looking "forward to years of peaceful, honorable, and elevated competition." He discussed "mutual respect" and preserving "cordial relations" so that the United States could anticipate "with confidence . . . a speedy and acceptable adjustment of our affairs." Jackson used vague terms to describe negotiations with Great Britain, referencing the "friendly disposition" of their sovereign and the recognition of "the justice of our cause."[40] Given the two wars he fought with this nation, Jackson's overall approach to Great Britain was mild and accommodating. He was no longer a military general. Rather, he was a statesman whose overall attitude was that of a confident power willing to pursue peaceful relations despite some lingering issues.

With France, the main issue was reparations owed over seized properties; Jackson termed the lack of progress on this front "irrefutable justice."[41] Similarly, the issues with Spain were indemnity and commercial relations, especially those based on navigation. Negotiations were underway with this country. Jackson also included statements about Russia, Turkey, Austria, Portugal, and the Barbary powers, stressing trade and commerce as the underpinning and overlapping issues.[42] In essence, the commercial networks of the United States were increasing, and he was eager to expand such ties. He believed they befitted the nation's growing reputation in the world and its emphasis on commerce and trade.

In the section devoted to foreign relations, Jackson also referred to the Southern Hemisphere. He hoped to see internal peace and quiet restored to this region, and he anticipated improved commercial relations. As for Mexico, Jackson was concerned over some of its countrymen's negative attitudes toward the United States. The recall of the American minister, Mr. Poinsett, was an added concern. Jackson stated, "Our conduct toward that Republic has been uniformly of the most friendly character," and he hoped that the minister's removal would set a positive course between the two nations.[43] Jackson stated that though he complied with Mexico's request of the envoy's removal, he had full confidence in Mr. Poinsett's talent and integrity. The president's earlier confidential letter to Colonel Butler found no echo in this address. Nor did Jackson reference Mexico's growing significance to the United States and his concern that Great Britain was interfering with this matter.

On the domestic front, Jackson turned to administrative reforms, starting with the need to amend the constitutional procedures for electing the president and vice president. He announced that, as America's system of government was deemed an experiment, now was the time for "remedying its defects." Jackson forwarded the principal idea that "to the people belongs the right of electing their Chief Magistrate; it was never designed that their choice should in any case be defeated, either by the intervention of electoral colleges or by the agency confided under certain contingencies, to the House of Representatives." As in the draft, the presidential election of 1824 was reflected throughout this statement. Jackson had a penchant for using principled thoughts to warrant a given case, and he succinctly summarized his position about the abuses of power by a few and the disregard of the people's votes. He simply did not entrust the selection of a president to the people's representatives. Even "without corruption," the president argued, a representative might be "liable to be misrepresented," he might perhaps "err from ignorance of the wishes of his constituents," or he might ignore the constituents altogether and make his own judgment about the best person to be president.[44] This is a clever line and a milder criticism. Jackson hinted at corruption but set the topic aside, and he challenged the practice without assigning insidious motives. Those who knew better could not miss Jackson's implied charge of corruption.

Jackson proposed a constitutional amendment to "remove all intermediate agency in the election of the President and Vice-President," and he suggested that a proportional weight be given to each state in this selection. He also proposed limiting the president's service to a single four- or six-year term and demanding that members of Congress not be appointed to cabinet positions as "the gift of the President." With this last point, Jackson again referred to Clay's reward in the Adams administration.[45] The reforms he outlined also included a term limit of four years for all governmental appointments as a means to greater integrity and equal opportunity to enter such high-level positions. Jackson's egalitarian view called for significant election reforms that would allow voters to choose the president and vice president. Significantly, the election would be by the candidates' names, thus disallowing Congress from making its own selection that ignored citizens' votes.

Being from a western state, Jackson was attuned to the growing wave of populism wherein electors were selected directly by votes and ownership of property was eliminated as a requirement for voting. He well understood the rise of "a mass electorate," but Adams and Clay missed this development altogether.[46] Subsequently, Jackson called for opening governmental positions to the wider population and for ending the notion that only landowners could apply for government positions. The Jacksonian era was proceeding with forceful policy proposals designed to advance popular appeals.

Jackson strategically addressed the significant issue of tariffs within the larger consideration of agriculture and commerce as more crucial to the nation's economy. He offered that, thus far, tariffs had not proven so injurious to agriculture and commerce, imports had not suffered, and domestic competition had not been limited due to tariff rates. What had transpired was an increase in production of certain goods that exceeded domestic demands. Subsequently, prices were lowered, and losses were incurred. In other words, tariffs were the wrong cause as advocated by some. Furthermore, Jackson stated, "We must ever expect selfish legislation in other nations, and are therefore compelled to adapt our own to their regulations in the manner best calculated to avoid serious injury and to harmonize the conflicting interests of our agriculture, our commerce, and our manufactures." This more palpable argument is based primarily on economic reasoning and the interdependence of the nation's key economic forces.

Jackson next delivered his initial draft argument. He hoped that "feelings and prejudices [over tariffs] should be merged in the patriotic determination to promote the great interests of the whole," and he sought to transcend regional sentiments with "higher and purer motives" and appeals to "our political compact."[47] With this careful phrasing, Jackson asked that the Union as a whole be considered more important than its regional parts. The president also suggested that the tariff issue be revisited and that a rate reduction be implemented gradually. He addressed any tensions over states' rights and the federal government with an ambiguous, brief mention of "feelings and prejudices." At the outset of his administration, Jackson hoped to convince those advocating strife to transcend local interests with national ones. Downplaying the stated concerns over tariffs and providing a reasonable economic explanation, he sought to obviate early on what could be a thorny issue.

As for the public debt, Jackson provided figures to show an overall positive but shrinking surplus. The public debt necessitated a "sudden withdrawal of so large a sum from the banks in which it was deposited" that serious concerns arose about the stability of the money market. Yet, Jackson stated, "this evil was wholly averted by an early anticipation of it at the Treasury, aided by the judicious arrangement of the officers of the Bank of the United States."[48] He offered a strategic tribute to the institution whose merits he questioned. The phrasing could have been meant to counter already-suspect sentiments or, at the minimum, to balance Jackson's negative statements about the bank. Either way, Jackson was not yet ready to tackle the bank.

On the matter of internal improvements, Jackson called for a systematic policy that would "reconcile the diversified interests of the States and strengthen the bonds which unite them." Jackson lamented that funding for such internal improvements to date was accomplished with expedient interests and as "an infraction of the Constitution," was both unwelcomed and "employed at the expense of harmony in the legislative councils." Jackson opposed any circumventing of the Constitution. He proposed that federal surpluses, once incurred, be used for those projects the Constitution allowed, and clearly not those that infringed on individual states. He also suggested that surpluses be distributed relative to the "ratio of representation" of each state. On this front Jackson was adamant, stating, "The great mass of legislation relating to our internal affairs was intended to be left where the Federal Convention found it—in the state governments. Nothing is clearer in my view," and "This is not the reflection of a day, but belongs to the most deeply rooted convictions of my mind."

Finally, Jackson firmly declared, "For my own sense of its importance, [I] warn you against all encroachments upon the legitimate sphere of State sovereignty."[49] Jackson's emphasis on this point is telling. He wanted to convince Congress that his views on the Constitution were neither capricious nor momentary assessments but rather long-held convictions. Yet he presented his credentials as a supporter of states' rights vis-à-vis internal improvements while the tariff issue was getting tangled over the federal government's perceived infringements. Jackson's strong and even adamant language hints that he knew of but would not approve certain improvement plans in progress. He sought to preempt them early on, and his warning rhetoric would prove prescient.

On the matters of the federal budget, Jackson noted that he was "forcibly struck with the large amount of public money which appears to be outstanding." The government was owed huge sums that "[might] yet be recovered," but most of it was lost due to inefficient collection of debt. To remedy the problem, Jackson proposed that responsibility for recouping debt be transferred from the Treasury to the US attorney general's office, since the issues therein were primarily legal. Jackson also called for benevolent reforms of debt laws. As he asserted, "Experience proves that oppressive debt is the bane of enterprise, and it should be the care of a republic not to exert a grinding power over misfortune and poverty." On the matter of fraud, Jackson took the opposite view. Criminals had been able to subvert laws with a two-year statute of limitations on fraud. Jackson opined that "the statute ought not to run in favor of any man while he retains all the evidences of his crime." Instead, he proposed that the government have up to two years after "disclosure of the fraud or after the accused is out of office to commence their persecution."[50] Efficiency, benevolence, and fairness were key principles close to Jackson's heart. Now he sought them as staples of an efficient government.

Jackson also proposed standardizing military salaries and extending pension law to Revolutionary War veterans, who "[had] strong claims upon their country's gratitude and bounty."[51] Moreover, he touched on the issue of money held in trust for the Seneca tribe. The funds had diminished in value, and Jackson advised better investment and returns to secure them. His discussion of the Seneca tribe functions as a transitional paragraph of goodwill leading to a longer section devoted to Indian affairs. Here, Jackson addressed the many efforts to acculturate the various tribes in the "arts of civilization" and to end their "wandering life." He noted that whites' purchase of tribal lands pushed American Indians farther into the wilderness, thus bringing them more misery. This description of the tribes' lot is more complex and accurate than the narrow, ethnocentric depiction in the draft. Attempts in Georgia and Alabama "to erect an independent government within the limits" of these two states, continued Jackson, further complicated things. Refused an independent nation, the tribes called on the government for protection.[52]

Jackson resorted to the Constitution for clarity on this issue, restating this clause therein: "'No new state shall be formed or erected within the jurisdiction of any other state' without consent of its legislature." He indicated that he had informed the tribes of his decision and advised them "to emigrate beyond the Mississippi or submit to the laws of those states [Georgia and Alabama]." Jackson did not leave this section on a cold note. He presented at some length the history of the once-powerful tribes in other parts of the nation who had gradually disappeared due to the progress of whites and "their arts of civilization." Now Jackson wanted "to avert so great a calamity," wondering "whether something [could not] be done, consistently with the rights of the states, to preserve this much-injured race." That "something" meant "setting apart an ample district west of the Mississippi . . . to be guaranteed to the Indian tribes as long as they [should] occupy it." Jackson stated, however, that the emigration ought to be voluntary. It would be cruel and unjust to compel the tribes to do so.[53]

The final portion of the First Annual Message to Congress covers issues related to administrative reforms, extending an already impressive approach to organizational matters. However, Jackson primarily focused this section on the navy and its important role as the "best standing security of this country against foreign aggression." The president's penchant for efficiency and thrift prompted him to note that ships decayed over time—such was the case with several "of our finest vessels." He proposed not building new ships in peacetime and instead depositing timber and related material at shipyards so that new vessels could be constructed quickly when needed. Jackson also suggested doing away with the Navy Board and putting its functions under the existing War Department. In addition, he advocated merging the Marine Corps with the unit responsible for artillery or infantry, purely for "curing the many defects in its organization."[54] Jackson conceived two primary units of defense, the army and the navy, and he sought increased efficiency through organizational and financial reforms.

In the Annual Message, Jackson also covered proposed reforms in various governmental offices, beginning with the office of the postmaster general and its crucial "means of diffusing knowledge." He considered this agency "the veins and arteries" of the "body politic" and "free press."[55] The president's progressive agenda included specific measures to increase access to information and knowledge, thereby spreading education to larger segments of society. Jackson happily reported on implementing greater efficiency and eliminating abuse to generate better revenues. Next, he discussed the deficient judiciary, whose branches were located in only fifteen states. Three other states had only circuit courts, and six states had no branches of the federal judiciary. This "state of things," declared Jackson, "ought to be remedied," and the entire system ought to be streamlined and equalized among all the states.[56] As for the Department of State, Jackson believed that, given the "large addition that [had] been made to the family of independent nations" and the subsequent increased need of American representation abroad, a new home department needed to be created. The two units could split foreign and domestic responsibilities between them, allowing the State Department to focus solely on foreign relations.[57]

Finally, Jackson contended that it was not too early to consider the future of the Bank of the United States. The institution's charter would expire in 1836. Taking Hamilton's paragraph almost in its entirety, Jackson stated, "The constitutionality and the expediency of the law creating this bank are well questioned by a large portion of our fellow-citizens, and it must be admitted by all that it has failed in the great end of establishing a uniform and sound currency." He thus offered more than a strong hint of his disfavor for the bank and any attempt to recharter it. Then the president went even further: "If such an institution is deemed essential to the fiscal operations of the Government, I submit to the wisdom of the Legislature whether a national one, founded upon the credit of the Government and its revenues, might not be devised which would avoid all constitutional difficulties and at the same time secure all the advantages to the Government and country that were expected to result from the present bank."[58] Jackson left the most volatile issue to the end of the Annual Message.

FROM DRAFTS TO THE OFFICIAL VERSION

Jackson's First Annual Message to Congress is an impressive document for ushering in a comprehensive activist agenda. Thematically, it pursues reforms aimed at curtailing corruption and increasing efficiency in governmental operations, covering foreign and domestic issues, and explicating an impressive presidential agenda. The First Annual Message has an administrative flavor, and it reflects the overall reach of a new government seeking a radical change from previous administrations and practices. The document is also strategic. In it, Jackson calculated advantages and disadvantages of specific issues, assessed their reception, and calibrated his approach and rhetoric for maximum effect. Jackson tackled issues he knew the public would support, but he did not shy away from advancing proposals on controversial matters. Even so, he addressed more difficult issues such as tariffs and the Bank of the United States quite carefully.

Jackson's initial draft carries more forceful language and more pin-pointed phrasing, while the final version is more subtle, measured, and eloquent. Jackson left his initial draft incomplete. Just as department heads have done before and since when crafting State of the Union Addresses, members of Jackson's administration wrote specific portions of his message addressing narrow issues. The generally personal wording and the two statements about his pure motives in pursuing specific agenda items were removed from Jackson's initial draft. His Annual Message was refined for a more formal presentation, and in so doing it became more generic and less individual. On the issue of tariffs, Jackson's transcendent argument about the importance of the Union over its parts remains unfinished. The final draft forwards more solid reasoning, arguing that tensions over tariffs were overblown and that noneconomic causes intensified them.

Jackson's First Annual Message to Congress is unique for the range of issues it covers. The president promoted a large and ambitious agenda: economic and political reforms; improved operation of governmental offices; election reforms, including the presidential election; foreign relations; regional tensions; Indian tribes; and judicial and bank reforms. The most striking feature of the Annual Message is its insightfulness and overall prescience. Jackson covered every major issue that would come to the fore during his two terms, rather accurately anticipating how events would unfold and how he would respond. On the issues of tariffs, the Bank of the United States, the Indian tribes, and internal improvements, Jackson outlined his views, the principles he would use to assess them, and the solutions he would pursue. Though he remained vaguer on some issues than others, he provided sufficient information for all to discern just how he would proceed. He would later respond to each of the primary matters addressed in the message just as he outlined. Ostensibly, Jackson entered the White House with a solid understanding of most issues at hand. In his first few months as president, he established his thoughts as to how he would deal with them. He would not divert from his initial plans. The First Annual Message is remarkable for its exposition of Jackson's grasp of and approach to the challenges he faced.

✳✳✳✳

The First Annual Message's overall character lies in its reflection of Jackson's 1824 presidential loss, the issues that loss raised, and, relatedly, his successful campaign to become the people's choice for president in 1828. In this address, Jackson gave back to the people what they gave him. He planned to change the course of the nation through various reforms. Jackson's First Annual Message to Congress is more than an Annual Message; it is a statement of principles about converting the republic into a democracy whereby the government is responsible to the people. Yet the notion of the people is generic. When it came to specific points of contention, Jackson drew clear distinctions between himself and a host of opposing groups, such as congressmen, senators, the Bank of the United States, government officeholders, nullifiers, and Indian tribes. Lines were drawn and issues identified as the Jackson presidency began in earnest.

The sheer volume of reforms and issues the First Annual Message tackles has a rhetorical impact. Jackson impressed an activist discourse and, by implication, an active administration on Congress and the nation. The message outlined not only an impressive agenda but also a powerful executive. Jackson's determined stance in seeking to implement his agenda made his entry into the office dramatically different from that of his predecessors. It would not take long for the polity to appreciate just how much Jackson would change the presidency, and that he would do so rhetorically and strategically.

THE MAYSVILLE ROAD BILL VETO
AN EARLY WARNING

The Maysville Road Bill Veto came early in the Jackson administration. On first glance, it was an issue of minor importance. Jackson, however, objected to Congress's authorization of "a subscription of stock in the Maysville, Washington, Paris, and Lexington Turnpike Road Company."[1] House members passed the bill by a vote of 102 to 85, and the Senate approved it by a vote of 24 to 18. The veto's ramifications were significant and far reaching. The road improvement in question was within the state of Kentucky along the Ohio River, roughly sixty miles in length. Its objective was improving a section of the longer Cumberland Road connecting Maysville to Lexington. In the early nineteenth century, people traveling between the eastern states and the western parts of the country, to and from the frontier states of Ohio, Kentucky, Tennessee, and beyond, faced arduous and lengthy journeys. Any improvement would be welcomed. Connecting remote parts of the expanding nation would contribute significantly to commerce, communication, and industry. The Cumberland Road, also known as the National Road, was the first interstate highway. Many pioneers navigated it on their way to western regions. Jackson himself frequently traveled between Tennessee and Washington, and he often commented on the arduous, tiring journey involving rough roads and river crossings. Bad weather and muddy roads made the experience especially difficult. The nation's road arteries clearly needed improvement, but their financing was the crux of the matter.

Jackson opposed state-based improvement financed by the federal government because eliminating the deficit was his principal objective. As revenues were generated primarily from tariffs (pressure was mounting on that front as well), adding to the government's debt was simply the wrong move. Martin Van Buren (secretary of state from 1829 to 1831) in particular opposed this practice and convinced the president to end it. That the Maysville Road was in Henry Clay's state did not endear the project to Jackson. Clay, after all, was the father of the American system, which advocated the necessity of major projects including roads, canals, and bridges for connecting the growing nation's regions. Jackson selected this specific project for strong opposition primarily because it concerned a pet project and, by default, a policy on state-based projects. Jackson may also have suspected that Clay was behind the Maysville Road plan, and that the road and tariffs would be major issues during the next presidential campaign. Moreover, the president calculated, Clay expected to prevail on this issue. Indeed, Clay assumed that a veto would turn many against Jackson.[2] Yet as many would learn early on, this was no deterrent to the general.

Jackson was quite concerned about the nation's finances, and in his First Annual Message to Congress he promised to pay down the deficit as soon as possible. Added expenditures were not the direction he sought, especially not at the outset of his administration. If the Maysville Road project was intended to test the new president—a likely plausibility—those behind it would soon discover their error. But Jackson, too, early on sought a test case that he could veto and use to assert his authority as a powerful president.[3] In short, Jackson and Congress were testing each other. The Maysville Road was the first important issue the seventh president faced, and his way of handling it would carry larger implications. It had to be done right.

JACKSON'S NOTES FOR THE MAYSVILLE ROAD VETO

Around May 19 and May 26, 1830, Jackson outlined rough notes for the Maysville Road Veto. His handwritten draft differs from the final and official order. Jackson's papers also include versions of the veto by Van Buren and James K. Polk. Comparing the drafts and the final document clearly shows that Van Buren's lengthy work is the closest to the ultimate veto. A note in Jackson's correspondence suggests that Van Buren was the first to convince him to reject the Maysville Road project.[4] Jackson's draft, then, more than the final veto, offers an accurate window into his thinking, style, and arguments in their raw form. A comparison of the various drafts also affords a rare opportunity to discern Jackson's and his aides' rhetorical inclinations and political calculations. The veto's evolution provides a sense of how the president and his staff conceived its reception and assessed its potential effects.

At the outset, Jackson wrote "1rst. Its constitutionality," suggesting that the framers gave "Congress the power of Legislation over all exterior and interior national matters reserving to the states exclusively the sovereign power of regulating on all their local concerns." Congress's responsibility for foreign and defense issues did not include constructing post roads.[5] More than once in his draft, Jackson called the government created by sages a "government of experiment." He said of the Founders, "[They] granted all powers thought necessary for national purposes, never expecting that congress [sic] would attempt to Legislate and appropriate money only where the powers granted gave them jurisdiction over the subject—and certainly it will not be contended where congress have no juris[diction] over the subject that it can appropriate money to that object."[6]

In other words, Jackson argued, Congress had no jurisdiction over state issues. The Constitution did not grant Congress such a right, and neither did it grant Congress the right "to become a member of [a] corporation created by the states."[7] Congress entering areas not designated to itself was unethical, added Jackson, because it "must destroy the purity of our govt. it [sic] must lead to consolidation and the destruction of state rights."[8] The president could envision the federal government owning shares in state corporations and thus beginning to influence local politics. Such measures would "destroy the purity of our govt." as well as "destroying the morals of [our] people."[9] Such corrupting practices would be worse than the behavior of the Bank of the United States, he declared, rather explicitly introducing an issue he had thus far addressed measuredly.[10] Jackson argued that constitutional principles must be adhered to. If changes to the Constitution were warranted and the people wished them, a clear process existed for making them. Until that process had been followed, the Constitution's principles had to be respected.

Jackson repeated the argument that the Maysville corporation plan jeopardized the states' independence. The project, he stated, "at once destroys that harmony that by the framers of the constitution was intended to exist between the two govts. [*sic*] and which has for years destroyed that harmony of the union."[11] Jackson considered comity between states and the federal government central. He would not deviate from the way the Constitution established the relationship between the two. Calling for a constitutional amendment was the only measure Jackson could offer those behind the Maysville Road improvement, and he knew full well how remote its chances were. Addressing harmony was Jackson's strategic way of voicing his concern about growing challenges to the federal government's role, especially from regional interests. Weakening the federal government would weaken the Union as well.

The urgent matter of paying down the public debt and distributing revenues to the states was the only policy Jackson supported. He found any other scheme involving a federal government deal with a state unacceptable. If such a practice were to be implemented, he asked rhetorically, "Where would you stop?" The government would become a stockholder in many petty state corporations and, he declared, wield "its power in your elections and all the interior concerns of the state."[12] Jackson also averred that he could see how quickly taxes, with all their dangers to the nation's liberty, would be imposed. The "you" and "your" references to the states and their representatives increase the rhetorical distance Jackson sought to insert between the federal government he represented and the state representatives he was lecturing. Ultimately, Jackson opposed taxes and would proudly declare that United States, unlike many other nations, did not impose them.

Jackson stated that he could find no provision giving Congress the power "to appropriate money to objects where the constitution had not given jurisdiction over the subject, or where the object was not clearly national."[13] And if Congress now entered such a relationship with a state, he asked, "What power cannot congress exercise over & within a state?"[14] Jackson followed this principle: "Powers of Congress in Legislation under the granted powers of the constitution are entirely national—all local matters being reserved as appropriate objects of the States."[15] With this succinct statement, he rejected the Maysville Road Bill. If given to the states, he contended, federal government money could be appropriated only in the form of revenue distribution and only after paying down the nation's debt.

The final note in the draft, titled "The expediency," precedes the following remark: "voice of the people from Main [*sic*] to Louisiana during the last canvass for the presidency has answered this in the negative—they have cried aloud for reform, retrenchment for the public expenditures, & economy in the expenditures of the Government—they expect the public debt to be speedily paid, not increased by appropriations for local not national concerns."[16] In short, the last presidential campaign carried a clear referendum about addressing several key national issues. Jackson stated his objective to abide by the will of the people with the Constitution as the ultimate guide. Though the president indulged in some hyperbole, since New England states did not vote for him, he elected to present a united American front on key issues. Reforms and economy were the two issues Jackson stated he would pursue. This was the case even if he read the public mandate as wider than demonstrated during the presidential campaign.

Antebellum veto messages, taken primarily "as protection against congressional encroachment on executive power," were often argued under the phrase of "necessary and proper" stipulated in article 1, section 8 of the Constitution. As Campbell and Jamieson note, Jackson expanded the use of veto messages relative to his predecessors. He also assigned Van Buren "to watch Congress and bring to the White House the first vulnerable bill to meet his eye."[17] The Maysville Veto, then, was a test case Jackson sought as he faced increased pressure from Congress to expand "mounting enthusiasm for public spending."[18]

It is in this context that Jackson asserted the following: "[Given the national budget deficit whereby] appropriations have exceeded the whole expenditures of the year 1829 by [blank] and the bills reported to the House if acted upon & passed will far exceed by many millions the amount available in the Treasury for the year 1830—is it not then inexpedient & unjust at this time if the constitutional power existed to exhaust your Treasury on local improvements."[19] His omission of the sum for expenditures and his repetitive emphasis on erasing the deficit aside, Jackson stuck to his principle.[20] His argument preceded the evidence therein; monetary details such as an accurate gap between spending and income were not critical to the president. Subsequently, Jackson rejected the Maysville Road Bill on straightforward grounds—constitutional reasoning and the simple fact that national expenditures had exceeded revenues. He saw no reason to increase the national debt by committing to local improvements.

Jackson's papers also include a draft by Tennessee congressman James Polk, a family friend. Polk's version of the veto is notable for its formality and distinct administrative style. Its author wrote therein, "I have looked to the Constitution, to experience and to reason for lights to direct me in the best course to promote the permanent prosperity of our country." Tenuous references and instances of the passive voice appear throughout Polk's draft. This veto mentions "contested" interpretations of the Constitution and what the "Government may or may not do in particular circumstances."[21] Polk took his time reaching the gist of his argument, even then declaring, "Having anxiously sought in the Constitution the grounds on which this power rests, I am brought to the conclusion upon a full review of the whole grounds, that the existence of the power is too questionable to justify its exercise."[22] This indirect and convoluted style is quite dissimilar to Jackson's active and direct approach. Thus Polk's contributions did not appear in the final veto.

THE MAYSVILLE ROAD BILL VETO, MAY 27, 1830

With minor stylistic modifications and one significant change in reasoning, Van Buren's draft became the official veto. Jackson inserted notations and several paragraphs into the text.[23] He also added a conclusion. As with the two previous public addresses, the distinct difference between Van Buren's version and the formal veto lies in the presentation of a more formal, decorous address devoid of the draft's more active and determined style.

The final veto was officially registered as "Veto Message Regarding Funding of Infrastructure Development." Jackson informed the House of Representatives that he had "maturely considered the bill to authorize a 'subscription of stock in the Maysville Road Company,'" and that he was returning it to House with his objection. He followed his brief introduction with an eloquent appeal professing his "friendly" support of improvement in roads and canals throughout the country.[24] Jackson regretted "any difference of opinion in the mode of contribution to it [improvement projects]," and he even apologized: "In stating this difference, I go beyond what the occasion may be deemed to call for." The subject, he added, was of "great importance." It came from the House, so he wished "to be correctly understood by [his] constituents in the discharge of his duties." Given our country's foundation on "freedom of opinion," it was only natural for differences to arise on many issues. One principle should remain: "Public good should be the measure of our views, dictating alike their frank expression and honest maintenance."[25]

Exhibiting the decorum of the period, Jackson combined determination and humility, stating at the outset that his veto would carry greater importance than its narrow focus. In other words, a larger strategy was in play. Jackson understood that opposing the House on a majority vote carried its own weight. But in the spirit of free exchange of ideas and within the authority granted to the president, he had to respectfully disagree with the people's representatives. Jackson's task now was to present his case with great clarity.

Jackson informed the House that he had expressed his view on internal improvements in his First Annual Message. He had already noted that the Constitution did not confer the power of funding local projects on the federal government. The bill brought to his attention, he said, "has, therefore, been passed with a knowledge of my views on this question."[26] Jackson admonished congressmen for asking him to sign a bill they knew he would reject. Citing passages from his First Annual Message, he reminded the House that he had already tied it to extinguishing public debt and considering tariffs. These two tasks had to be satisfied with only "a considerable surplus in the Treasury." If the surplus was to fund internal improvements, steps should first be taken for "the adoption of some plan which will reconcile the diversified interests of the States, and strengthen the bonds that unite them." All would benefit from internal improvements, Jackson stated. But such endeavors had to be attained "in a mode which be satisfactory to all."[27]

The issue, then, was not internal improvements per se but the source of their funding. Constitutionally, the federal government could support only interstate or national projects. Money could only come into the states via proportional distributions from the Treasury surplus, and for this venue to open up, the national debt had to be eliminated first. Additionally, any adjustment to tariff rates requested by states had to be understood as further reducing federal government revenues. Those who sought to test the president faced his firm stance on key issues. Noting that financial matters often involved corruption, Jackson further noted that his veto was an attempt to end lingering unethical practices.

Thus far, Jackson elaborated, various improvement projects had been inconsistently implemented. Some were "deprecated as an infraction of the Constitution," while others were viewed "as inexpedient." Yet, he added, "all feel that it [internal employment] has been employed at the expense of harmony in the legislative councils."[28] At issue for Jackson were budgeting concerns, relationships between states, and certain regions' growing strife over government largesse.

Jackson followed with two related justifications for the Maysville Road Veto, both mandated by "the constitutional power of the Federal Government." He pointed to the road project's "bearing on the sovereignty of the States," and he emphasized the appropriation of funds from the "National

Treasury" for work "undertaken by State authority."[29] Jackson supported the first point by stating that no federal government had yet been taken to affect a state's sovereignty. The bill in question sought to do exactly that. Second, Jackson declared his belief that money raised by the federal government could not be used for projects it was not authorized to cover. In this instance, he argued, the Constitution and its "deservedly high authority" ought "to be held in grateful remembrance for its immediate agency in rescuing the country from much existing abuse."[30] Jackson believed the Constitution was the agency of safety and security against abuses. He lamented that such restrictions on federal money were not always practiced, but he was intent on preserving the Constitution and its limitations on the federal government. As in the initial draft, Jackson's final version presents the Constitution as the primary mover of the veto. Constitutional authority was the basis of Jackson's argument for harmony among the states and an improved Treasury balance. The Constitution was also the foundation for Jackson's desire to avoid financial abuses that could corrupt the Union and to maintain the delicately balanced relationship between the federal government and the confederation of states.

Resorting to earlier supportive examples, Jackson referred to the case of Thomas Jefferson, who paid $15 million for the Louisiana Purchase, and to prior appropriations for constructing the Cumberland Road. Under President Madison, money was also allotted for various roads and canals in order to improve "the navigation of water courses, in order to facilitate, promote, and give security to internal commerce among the several States and to render more easy, and less expensive, the means and provisions for the common defence [sic]."[31] James Madison, Jackson averred, objected to financing projects "within limits of the States" and considered it unconstitutional. President Monroe, too, returned to the House with objections a bill regarding the Cumberland Road. Monroe contended that Congress had unlimited power to raise money, and he noted that such funds were restricted to "general, not local, national, not State, benefit."[32] In short, Jackson's objections were not new; previous presidents had ruled similarly.

Jackson opined that he could not be mistaken for his reverence for the Constitution and the need to guard it "with sleepless vigilance against the authority of precedents which have not the sanction of its most plain defined powers." His concern was over the enactment of exceptions to constitutional matters, exceptions that had become precedents further weakening the Constitution. In any event, he added, repeating Monroe's statement, grants by the federal government were only for "general, not local, national, not

State" projects. Jackson affirmed that he could not view the bill as anything but "a measure of purely local character." He acknowledged the possible argument that every local project was also national in character. But he affirmed that a distinction between local and national projects had to be made, for "a disregard of this distinction would of necessity lead to the subversion of the federal system."[33]

Jackson included another testy admonition in the veto: "Considering the magnitude and importance of the power, and the embarrassments to which, from the very nature of the thing, its exercise must necessarily be subjected, the real friends of internal improvement ought not to be willing to confide it to accident and chance."[34] The president made it clear that he would not subvert the Constitution's power if internal improvement's supporters wanted to test him. But Jackson also expressed concern that his veto would embarrass the Maysville Road's promoters. His implication was that these advocates should have known better, especially in light of his stated opinions. Jackson did not wish his views to be considered expedient—he promised erasure of the national debt after four years if no unexpected expenses were incurred. Yet at this point, all bills approved and likely to be approved would exceed revenues by 1830. And since duties (tariffs) on items such as coffee and tea had been reduced, thus indicating flexibility on the issue, Jackson projected decreased revenues and a further delay of paying down the debt. He therefore returned to the financial grounding of his central argument. Fiscal stability had to be restored to the nation before money would be available for various projects, and even then, that money would be used only as the Constitution prescribed.

Jackson lauded the several states independently managing their internal projects and hoped that other states would find ways to do the same in the future. He remarked, "Great as this project [Maysville Road] undoubtedly is, it is not the only one which demands the fostering care of the Government." As was his habit here and elsewhere, Jackson followed a specific argument with a larger philosophical point. He noted "the attachment of our citizens to the Government of their choice, by the comparative lightness of their public burthens [burdens], and by the attraction which the superior success of its operations [would] present to the admiration and respect of the world." In essence, the president argued that America was blessed and its people were happy and prosperous precisely because of the overall exemption "from the pressure of taxation which other less favored portions of the human family [were] obliged to bear." Though some taxes in the past "have, for a considerable period, been onerous," and in some cases "taxes have borne severely upon the laboring and less prosperous classes of the community," they were "necessary to the support of Government, and the payment of the debts unavoidably incurred in the acquisition and maintenance of our national rights and liberties."[35] Jackson maintained that some taxes were a crucial burden, as in times of war. But paying for a road improvement, another form of tax, was not of the same urgent category. He abhorred taxes and considered them a source of corruption.

Jackson had no doubt what the people wanted: "[They will] demand, as they have a right to do, such a prudent system of expenditures as will pay the debts of the Union, and authorize the reduction of every tax to as low a point as the wise observance of the necessity to protect that portion of our manufactures and labor, whose prosperity is essential to our national safety and independence." There were, then, other interests—not just those of the states, but also those of particular segments of the population—hoping for a reduction in taxes. Therefore, increasing taxes, which the Maysville Road Bill would achieve, had to be rejected. Projecting what the people would wish in the form of an efficient economy was a safe argument. Significantly, though, Jackson omitted from the veto his preliminary argument that the election of 1828 gave him a mandate to oppose internal improvements.[36] In fact, many Americans supported road and canal construction and general improvement in transportation and communication, making this argument unconvincing.

Jackson grew quite eloquent about "the effect of presenting to the world the sublime spectacle of a Republic, of more than 12,000,000 happy people, in the fifty-fourth year of her existence—after having passed through two protracted wars—the one for acquisition, and the other for maintenance of liberty—free from debt, and with all her immense resources unfettered!" He called the US experiment in free government the envy of the world, yet he also stated, "A course of policy destined to witness events like these cannot be benefitted by a legislation which tolerates a scramble for appropriations that have no relation to any general system of improvement, and whose good effects must of necessity be very limited." The Maysville project was an expedient appropriation, one seeking to "shift upon the Government the losses of unsuccessful private speculation, and thus, by ministering to personal ambition and self-aggrandizement . . . sap the foundations of public virtue, and taint the administration of the Government with a demoralizing influence."[37] Jackson issued his sharpest criticism thus far, challenging the motives of speculators who wished to profit while burdening the government with any failures.

The final issue, which repeats the idea outlined in the draft, addresses the suitability of the bill in question. As in his previous point, Jackson indicated that the Maysville Road project was an attempt to secure federal support for local projects without the required constitutional amendment, and therefore in violation of that sacred document. Here, too, Jackson admonished those seeking expedient use of federal funds. He described what might happen if the money were to be granted in this case: "The construction of the Constitution may be regarded as unsettled if the right to apply money in the enumerated cases is placed on the ground of usage."[38] In addition to this narrow issue, Jackson was concerned about constant attempts to infringe upon the Constitution and weaken its authority. He took the document as foundational for the political system it created. He would not waver over it—neither with this veto nor with future issues that would come his way.

Jackson acknowledged, "This subject has been one of much, and, I may add, painful, reflection for me. It has bearings that are well calculated, to exert a powerful influence upon our hitherto prosperous system of Government, and which, on some accounts, may even excite despondency in the breast of an American citizen." Repeating sentiments from the veto's introduction, he stated that it pained him to reject the bill in question and face the prospect that some Americans sought to test his resolve and unnecessarily incite their fellow countrymen. Jackson indicated his awareness that the internal improvement project's supporters might have had many friends. Few of them, he declared, "are mindful of the means by which they should be promoted: none certainly are so degenerate as to desire their success at the cost of that sacred instrument, with the preservation of which is indissolubly bound our country's hopes." Jackson now pinpointed his criticism of those pushing for federal government investment in the road project. He lamented some individuals' desire to subvert the Constitution and the Union, but he said more. He even suggested that some had been "reckless of their constitutional obligations" and would "prefer their local interests to the principles of the Union."[39] The veto's increased intensity here is a modest counterpoint to the reality that many Americans supported internal improvements in 1830. Jackson sought a transcendent argument attributing lamentable motives to this wide backing.

Not wanting to end the Maysville Road Bill Veto on a negative note, Jackson declared that he did not "entertain such gloomy apprehensions." If people wanted the federal government to bankroll the construction of canals and roads, a constitutional amendment was needed. The federal government's financing of the Cumberland Road, he said, "should be an instructive admonition of the consequences of acting without this right." The reality, he added, was that one Congress had approved such appropriations and the next one had not. He did not wish to continue this inconsistency. Jackson argued that abiding by the Constitution kept the Union viable. This added argumentative strain emphasizes Jackson's concern over the strength of national authority, necessary for the union of the states.

Ultimately, Jackson pondered whether the nation could not understand simple principles of a free government. In that case, he stated, "then indeed has the world but little to hope from the example of free government." He continued, "When an honest observance of constitutional compacts cannot be anticipated elsewhere; and the cause in which there has been so much martyrdom, and from which so much as expected by the friends of liberty, may be abandoned . . . the degrading truth, [is] that man is unfit for self-government admitted."[40] The United States' failure as a democratic republic, and the international implications thereof, would be the direct result "if expediency be made a rule of construction in interpreting the Constitution."[41] Here and elsewhere, Jackson would resort to the argument that a larger issue was at stake—the American experiment in self-government. He believed that other nations were carefully studying this experiment and hoping it would fail. An American collapse would remove pressure on other countries to adopt the idea that free people could indeed govern themselves. With altruistic reasoning, Jackson believed in America's uniqueness and opposed a constructionist approach to expedient interpretations of the Constitution that weakened the document. He attributed the greatness of the American system to this fact: "In no government are appeals to the source of power, in cases of real doubt, more suitable than in ours."[42] Tampering with the Constitution, which established the country's exceptionalism, put democracy at risk.

Jackson also connected internal improvements with the sticky issue of tariffs. He stated that all knew his opinion on the matter, despite the suggestions of some that he opposed specific individuals and communities. Here he referred to southern states, those most concerned about duties. Jackson offered that he did not deserve such criticism: "There has been nothing in my public life which has exposed me to the suspicion of being thought capable of sacrificing my views of duty to private considerations, however strong they may have been, or deep the regrets which they are capable of exciting." The president felt the need to reassert his integrity and long-standing sense of duty, alluding to his well-known military experience and sacrifices. His approach to any issue would be based on clear principles. Of tariffs he said

"[Those] directed to national ends ... shall receive from me a temperate but steady support."[43] Jackson cautiously supported tariffs, well understanding how other economic concerns could muddy this issue. He emphasized his sole criterion—that projects have a national purpose.

Crucially, stated Jackson, "there is no necessary connection between it [tariffs] and the system of appropriations. On the contrary, it appears to me that the supposition of their dependence upon each other is calculated to excite the prejudices of the public against both." He further criticized the wishes of some for "a forced continuance of the national debt, by means of large appropriations," noting that "such a course would certainly indicate either an unreasonable distrust of the people, or a consciousness for its support, if left to their voluntary choice and its own merits." Those contemplating such a course, he asserted, "have looked upon its history with eyes very different from mine." The president continued, "This policy, like every other, must abide the will of the people, who will not be likely to allow any device, however specious, to conceal its character and tendency."[44] Jackson disapproved of internal improvements and tariffs as a means of unnecessarily exciting the public's passions and continuing the national debt.

COMPARING THE DRAFTS TO THE FINAL DOCUMENT

Jackson came into office determined to change many practices in Washington. The Maysville Road Veto was his initial opportunity to implement and signal his serious approach to political reforms—a theme of his presidential campaign and First Annual Message to Congress. In issuing this first veto of his administration, Jackson highlighted his role as a different president. He was not the tool of political insiders or behind-the-scenes political machinations. Instead, he was a crusader, a political outsider, a man able and determined to do what was needed and expected despite all obstacles. After all, many Americans considered the end of the 1824 presidential election the last straw. Jackson benefitted greatly from the prevailing public opinion that insiders and corrupt politicians had snatched away the presidency.[45]

Jackson's challenge now was framing his administration rhetorically, projecting the large but vague mandate he had received and the reforms he would effect amid growing tension on several fronts. Words would have to be carefully assessed and weighted, and calculated editing would secure the most effective formal statements. Jackson's first veto and first jump into the political fray proved prescient. The Maysville Road Veto is well crafted, eloquent, and moderate relative to his initial points. In its final form, the veto turns a keen eye to political implications, more carefully phrasing the direct arguments and justifications from the first draft. A common practice emerged over Jackson's two terms: The president would often be the first to outline or draft public statements. He would then allow his aides to debate and modify the documents as needed. As with the Inaugural Address and the First Annual Message, Jackson made sharper arguments in the initial Maysville Veto than in the final version. The determined president needed editing for a dose of measured rhetoric. Significantly, one major argument from Jackson's draft—that of his election mandate to reject internal improvement—does not appear in the final veto.

Jackson allowed the Constitution to drive his objection to the Maysville Road Bill, and he projected himself as the agent implementing that long-established, sacred document. Yet the final version of the Maysville Veto modifies Jackson's strong introduction of the Constitution in his initial draft. This document identifies the federal government and the Constitution as co–authorizing agents for the president's rejection. A significant rhetorical move, grounding the veto with federal authority would prove wise. Jackson and his staff assessed the growing tensions between the states and the federal government, and they knew that a lingering tariffs fight from the Adams administration could be the next test case. In positioning the federal government and the Constitution as legitimate sources of power, Jackson signaled that he would use the authority of both to counter future challenges. Nonetheless, the Constitution is foundational to most arguments in the Maysville Veto; it grounds almost every stance and line of reasoning Jackson presented. The president understood and opposed attempts to interpret the Constitution at will. He took a narrow view of the document, and he resisted opening it to precedents in constructive interpretations. If some of Jackson's predecessors had been less careful with the Constitution, he himself would take a strict approach. He regarded the Constitution as the foundation on which the entire Union was established.

The final draft also pays significant tribute to how events in the United States can and do impact the international scene. For a young nation still talking in terms of the War of Independence and the War of 1812, the references to foreign affairs are interesting, even revealing. But Jackson had a point to make: the United States as an experiment, still tested internally and much observed externally, mandated that all political issues be constantly scrutinized. Other world powers wanted to see if a political system of self-governance could succeed. Jackson often implied that other nations welcomed the United States' failure so that they would not be pressured to institute democracy. Therefore, it was incumbent on Americans to make their government succeed. In his other major argument, the president described his task of guarding against any move that could weaken the democratic experiment.

Jackson's describing the nation as an "experiment" after five decades is not a measure of his concern. Rather, this description reflects Jackson's strong belief that the Founders considered their democratic republic an organic institution requiring modifications. Thus they stipulated the mechanism for such changes—the lengthy and purposefully cumbersome process of amending the Constitution. Such a method would assure moderation and contemplation of proposed amendments. Jackson clearly sided with this perspective of gradual development that could secure overall stability and a cautious approach to change. He also looked back for guiding principles that were now forgotten.

The veto thus projects American democracy as unique and worthy of careful treatment to keep it the envy of the world. Jackson asserted that that guarding this unique experiment would continue to make the nation the happiest on Earth. He covered his rejection of a popular bill with a motivational appeal and the hyperbole therein. Jackson exaggerated his reason for opposing the road plans by extending the argument beyond the scope of the issue at hand. If Jackson sought a larger popular appeal, one can find it here. The argument no longer addresses Congress alone but the nation as a whole. Still, the overall point about the world's reaction to US failure is not a serious argument. Jackson worried about the future of the Union, and domestic matters were the primary reasons for his concern. By referencing the international community, a convenient and altruistic commonplace, he informed the nation of its growing importance. He also reminded the country that selfish regional interests could harm a larger democratic project yet to be realized by the world.

Significantly, the initial draft's reference to the Bank of the United States was removed. The veto was not the place to confuse one issue with another. In any event, Jackson said little about the bank thus far, and he and/or his staff felt no need to disrupt his strategic vagueness. Jackson's including the bank in his first version of the veto can be taken as an attempt to address a larger concern over corrupt economic issues, or at least note their overall interdependence. Indeed, the bank would occupy most of Jackson's energy and exhaust much of his two terms in office. Yet, Jackson still focused on economic issues, especially the unethical and improper practices he abhorred.

Only toward the end of the message did Jackson criticize unnamed individuals' reckless pursuit of local advantages over national ones. He purposefully inserted the term "constitutional compact," which carried legal and historical implications for those still debating the nature of the Union's federal compact. Clearly, Jackson calculated a confluence of issues in this first veto. He also criticized attempts to connect internal improvements to the increasingly volatile tariff issue. Jackson saw in these cases deliberate incitement of the populace for personal promotion. Thus the final version of the Maysville Veto also includes admonitions casting doubt on the bill's enthusiasts, questioning their motives and political gamesmanship, especially in light of Jackson's declared stance on internal improvements.

One intact issue, though, remains key to the completed document: the road project in question was a state issue that did not fall under federal jurisdiction. The primary difference between the initial and final vetoes lies in the authority grounding Jackson's distinction between the states and the federal government. Jackson also modified his earlier point that in rejecting the Maysville Road Bill, he was protecting states' independence. He did not side with states' rights; stating otherwise was not his true intent. The Union was Jackson's focus which meant keeping a harmony between the states was only beneficial if the Union remained strong and effective. Yet in rejecting federal expenditures for state projects, Jackson also gave the states a sense of independence from federal interference. This convenient argument gave states' rights advocates something to cling to. Jackson walked a fine line, disputing the federal government's authority but keeping the Union's opponents in check.

The shift from Jackson's initial emphasis on the veto's constitutional grounds to his later emphasis on its basis in federal government authority is a relatively minor point. The federal government draws its power from the Constitution. Consequently, the change involved constructing the most advantageous argument for the moment given other issues lurking in the background. Jackson's close aides understood that the official veto was safer for him than the initial draft. Ultimately, the president did not reject all internal improvement projects. His task in issuing the veto, as he instructed Van Buren, was to frame it such that the people would "fully understand it."[46] Jackson's prohibition was a rhetorical document explaining why he rejected a road project that many supported. Now he had to secure the people's understanding of his views.

Van Buren largely drafted the veto, and Donelson provided final editing. Though Jackson composed a portion and subsequently made extensive insertions, the veto is very much a development of his initial notes.[47] The primary arguments about the supremacy of the Constitution, the harmony between the states, and the states' relationship with the Union and the federal government are all present in both documents. The key argument about the Maysville Road Bill Veto—that the requested appropriation was for a state-based project, not a national one—also remained intact.

✳✳✳✳

A veto, by definition, is a unique rhetorical act. It is a statement rejecting a majority vote in the legislative branch, and as such, it acknowledges that an individual in a position of authority can overrule an agreed-upon policy. The Constitution stipulates that a presidential veto is the prerogative to reject a bill and return it to the House.[48] While this veto's rhetoric justifies the reason for a bill's dismissal, it also seeks to confront the House and the nation at large for moving in a direction that the executive deems unwarranted. Vetoes, write Campbell and Jamieson, have been forwarded on two grounds: constitutionality and expediency. Both rationales were of paramount importance to Jackson. A veto, then, can be considered a formal admonishment of an act taken by the majority in the House, an announcement that this act is unacceptable for one reason or another.

In correcting a course against the wishes of many, a presidential veto does not follow the common rhetorical processes of identifying with the audience, creating a connecting vision, or complimenting the audience's wisdom or actions. Therefore, this course of action can be risky. It is bound to anger Congress and, by implication, constituents whose representatives acted in a manner congruent with their interests. The veto is often based on clear principles whereby Congress, at least initially, is at odds with the executive. Yet this is what Jackson wanted—to assert his authority and that of the executive over the legislative branch. Vetoes are more indicative of presidential character than most other rhetorical acts since they occur at moments of great tension and conflict.[49] Crucially for Jackson, the Maysville Road Bill Veto implied that the executive was responsible for public policy and so ought to have significant input on legislative matters. In consequence, Congress was not the sole legislator of the nation's affairs. Jackson plainly expanded the initial understanding and working of the branches of government, using the veto as a rhetorical imperative to reform the polity. He would veto a total of twelve bills.

Madison and Monroe issued similar objections to federal involvement in state-based projects, but Jackson's veto was more significant by far. This was due primarily to the rise of partisan politics after Monroe's presidency, and to the more competitive if not altogether hostile relationship between the executive and legislative branches following, and likely caused by, the election of 1824. Jackson's candidacy in 1827 ended the one-party preference that had prevailed since the nation's founding. It also ended the practical alignment of congressional and presidential politics. Jackson's Maysville Veto, then, was significant for putting Congress and the nation on notice, that he would be a daring president. The general was strong in conviction and ready to implement that which he promised, even if the majority of the people's representatives thought otherwise. Significantly, Jackson added an ideological argument to the Maysville Veto that separated himself and Van Buren from Clay and John Quincy Adams. This contention promoted a partisan line of thinking and a partisan divide by default.[50] Ultimately, Jackson brought to the White House a clear set of principles grounded in the Constitution, and he was eager to rid politics of corruption. He also extrapolated on the economy to such a degree that, upon assuming office, he signaled a clear focus on domestic issues in general and the economy in particular. If anyone had a preconceived notion about the general-turned-politician and considered Jackson a novice, the Maysville Road Bill Veto proved them wrong.

With the Maysville Road Bill Veto, Jackson strengthened the presidency. The opportunity for the veto came early in his administration, and though it was likely an attempt to test him, those who did so paid dearly. The very act of rejecting a bill made it clear that the executive was powerful and independent of the legislative branch. Jackson would take a serious approach to the nation's financial and economic standing, to preserving the Union and its constitutional foundation, and to strict constitutional interpretation. In so doing, he built a stronger, determined executive. Jackson's veto allowed all to see that the daring general was also a daring politician. He did not hesitate to put principles above expediency. The larger objective of the veto was critical as well: it elevated the Constitution to sacredness and the ultimate guide to matters political. Jackson saw himself as a keeper of the Constitution, and he would define much of his presidency in this way.

The Maysville Veto, though almost two centuries old, remains a timeless statement about the politics of appropriation bills and pork barrels that often endlessly increase the deficit, with one administration after another failing to reverse course. The veto also highlights the tensions between local and national priorities. At the outset of his presidency, Jackson declared he would not only reduce the budget deficit but eliminate it altogether. He also planned to distribute surpluses once they were realized. The Constitution was his weapon, supplying the basis for his arguments against "reckless" spending and narrow interests that ignored the nation's larger needs. Jackson staunchly supported the Union. The Maysville Veto was his first shot fired in its defense. Jackson's veto was sustained when a vote of ninety-six to ninety failed to overrule it.[51]

NULLIFICATION AND RHETORICAL ECONOMY

ANDREW JACKSON'S MANAGEMENT OF A NATIONAL CRISIS

Proceeding from the Nullification Crisis, Jackson's Nullification Proclamation is among his most noted rhetorical acts, one that carried significant impact during his presidency and beyond. While preparing remarks for his first inauguration amid growing strife and threats of southern secession, President Abraham Lincoln referred to Jackson's proclamation of December 10, 1832.[1] That Lincoln's entry into the White House saw him consulting the words of another president who tackled secession threats from the same state is intriguing though not surprising. It was no coincidence that South Carolina was again on the verge of secession as it had been in the 1830s. Few would contend the claim that Lincoln faced the gravest crisis in American history to date, and perhaps ever since. Yet some thirty years earlier, Jackson had faced a similar crisis. Although the nullification debate did not mature into the catastrophic war Lincoln faced, it was prompted by the same threat of secession from South Carolina. Moreover, slavery, the same issue that provoked the Civil War, indirectly incited the Nullification Crisis.

At the most crucial phase of the Nullification Crisis, Jackson issued his Proclamation to the People of South Carolina—a controversial act during a crisis borne of South Carolina's insistence on reducing tariff rates. South Carolina claimed authority to nullify the Tariffs of 1828 and 1832 that Jackson and his predecessor had signed into law. The state declared the duties unenforceable, and even worse, it threatened to leave the Union if it did not get its way. The forceful language of the president's proclamation and the threat of military action by the federal government forced South Carolina nullifiers to retreat to a more moderate, accommodating stance and resolve the crisis. Jackson, in turn, agreed to lower the tariff rates.

The rhetoric in Jackson's proclamation was effective enough to end the Nullification Crisis and provide guidance for Lincoln on the eve of the Civil War. Therefore, the Nullification Proclamation and its preceding rhetorical acts require deeper consideration. Jackson compromised on the tariff issue and the Force Bill against his better judgment. Yet his crisis discourse, specifically that concerning his Unionist stance in the struggle over states' rights, was successful overall. Despite his ambivalence concerning tariffs, Jackson presented a consistent rhetorical stance on the Union's constitutional authority. He took decisive, effective action against South Carolina, and he did so with a distinct sense of strategic timing. The president's rhetoric also sharpened focus on the American constitutional framework. Subsequently, Jackson's Unionism solidified the camps around the issues of states' rights, federal power, and, most profoundly, slavery. However, he was late to realize slavery's pivotal influence on the crisis at hand. Ultimately, Jackson's crisis rhetoric had immediate and long-term effects.

Richard E. Ellis suggests that the constitutional and ideological precepts of the Nullification Crisis are central to understanding Jackson's conduct and the incident's historical impact.[2] Likewise, assessing Jackson's rhetoric helps readers understand the foundational sentiments he set during the crisis. In explicating the Nullification Proclamation's significance and placing it in the context of his other major addresses, I account for Jackson's views on the role of the federal government vis-à-vis states' rights. In so doing, I develop a thematic account of Jackson's Unionism as the principal argument during the crisis. As Jeffrey K. Tulis argues, presidential proclamations were rare during the nineteenth century. Jackson's Nullification Proclamation and Lincoln's Emancipation Proclamation stand out as rather unique rhetorical forms of the presidency.[3]

Admittedly, scholars' accounts of Jackson's handling of the Nullification Crisis and his constitutional perspective have been inconsistent at best. The Nullification Crisis, argues Ellis, was central to Jacksonian democracy, and it would become a major issue that would play itself out up to and beyond the Civil War.[4] Ellis ascribes more failure than success to Jackson's response to nullification. Remini argues that Jackson's adamant approach to crushing the nullifiers and his military preparations in case of secession was an important variable for consideration.[5] Matthew S. Brogdon's take on the proclamation is insightful, illuminating the degree to which Jackson's constitutional understanding was quite unique. A nuanced reading of the Nullification Proclamation reveals the president's original thoughts relative to those of supporters, such as Daniel Webster and even Secretary of State Edward Livingston, the proclamation's coauthor. Brogdon also convincingly argues that Lincoln embraced the proclamation while writing his own First Inaugural Address. Therein, he followed Jackson's line of reasoning quite closely.[6] Jackson's handling of the Nullification Crisis, though, was not independent of the other crises and conflicts he confronted. A certain consistent rhetorical approach can be detected throughout seemingly disparate issues. It is also worth noting that Jackson portended the first major crisis of his presidency in his First Inaugural Address. The speech's principal arguments prescribed the approach he would take with this and most other pivotal issues of the day.

THE CONSTITUTIONAL QUESTION

The tariff issue became a crisis once the anonymous document titled *South Carolina Exposition and Protest* was issued on December 19, 1828, arguing the right of a state to oppose the federal government. According to Ellis, Jackson encountered three positions regarding the federal Union when he became president: nullification, nationalism, and traditional states' rights. All of them impacted the crisis at hand, and all of them had supporters who reacted to the *Exposition and Protest*. Nullifiers gave the federal government no authority over the states. They opposed the concept of majority rule and considered a "Constitutional government, and the government of a majority . . . utterly incompatible."[7] Nationalists believed the federal compact was based on the Constitution as created by people and not by states. The federal Union, then, held the authority over the states, and the Supreme Court adjudicated all constitutional questions. Traditional states' rights supporters opposed the nullifiers' extreme position that each state had the right to decide what was good for it. Their principal belief was that any power not under federal jurisdiction belonged to the states.[8]

Jackson supported a clear demarcation between the authority of the federal government and states' rights. This view was especially evident in his Maysville Veto. Yet until he issued the Maysville Veto, Jackson's support of states' rights was the stance most politicians assigned to him. Calhoun concealed his authorship of the 1828 *South Carolina Exposition and Protest* because, as John Quincy Adams's vice president, he had strongly opposed the tariff bill passed in May of that year.[9] Keeping his authorship hidden was even more crucial to Calhoun once he became Jackson's vice president. Calhoun hoped that Jackson, a southerner, would be more sympathetic to southern states over tariffs and calm their growing concern over states' rights and their way of life (a euphemism for slavery). Ultimately, Calhoun wanted the *Exposition and Protest* to force Jackson to repeal or lower the 1828 tariff rates.[10]

However, Jackson took the balanced view of a divided authority between the federal government and the states. At least initially, he did not see the slavery issue as the real issue at hand; the Nullification Crisis focused on tariffs. Georgia's plan to remove its Indian tribes further complicated the issue, as did tension over states' rights vis-à-vis the federal government. Jackson supported Georgia over the Indian removal plan and opposed South Carolina over nullification. In so doing, he strategized that he would not subsequently be viewed as a strict Unionist. Jackson in turn got the support of the National Republican Party and its pro-Unionist position, and he was also not taken as opposing states' rights. Thus Jackson formed a large "moral force" that stood behind the preservation of the Union and critically included several southern states.[11]

Yet on one key issue Jackson would not compromise. The nullifiers' contention that constitutional government was incompatible with majority government and that South Carolina would secede if it did not get its way on tariffs incensed him. Indeed, Jackson's overall sentiments regarding the narrow issue of tariffs were not identical to his view of the constitutional question at hand and the threat of secession. This perspective would define his crisis rhetoric, but his opponents in South Carolina would also misunderstand it. It is fair to say that Old Hickory entered the White House with tremendous popular support despite his unclear position on some issues. He outlined few specifics in his First Inaugural Address. Additionally,

Jackson's remained vague on the issue of tariffs in his First Annual Message to Congress, instead promoting a general objective of fighting corruption and advocating reforms.[12] He called for transcending regional interests with national interests but that, too, was not specific enough to be taken as a warning. If he meant in his early addresses to frame major issues without specific commitments, he kept many guessing with his strategic vagueness. As Arthur Schlesinger opines, "Jackson had an impressive mandate, but it was unclear what the mandate was for."[13] In any event, the 1828 act that South Carolina named the Tariff of Abominations was passed during the Adams administration. Crucially, and as Jackson also pointed out, protective tariffs did not decrease the price of cotton, though southerners conveniently believed that they did.[14]

Jackson's primary concerns were the integrity of the Union and the power of the Constitution to mandate it. As the proceeding account illustrates, he remained rhetorically firm and consistent on these key issues. Jackson's words were aimed at diffusing the crisis, and he developed a two-track approach to accomplishing this objective. He took a moderate position on states' rights and tariffs, but he kept a firm stance regarding the integrity and preservation of the Union. Jackson made several attempts to accommodate and calm the parties involved. He sought a reasonable path that would allow the crisis to dissipate and the antagonists to retreat from extreme positions. Yet, when all else failed, Jackson resorted to the third option: decisive rhetoric in a proclamation spelling out actions he would take to preserve the Union.

JACKSON'S UNIONIST RHETORIC

Though tariffs were an economic concern for quite a while, Jackson had managed to walk a fine line regarding his views since his second senatorial stint some six years earlier. He deemed the national picture more complex than the merits of a single regional issue, and he proposed a moderate approach to tariff rates. But the issue would simmer, and South Carolina in particular wanted to force the incoming president to state his position. The opportunity came during the celebration of Thomas Jefferson's birthday on April 13, 1830, an event that included toasts by various prominent politicians. Jackson saw the list of the event's participants in advance. He also realized that growing tension over tariffs and nullification threats would make the much-anticipated event a crucial one. So would the Webster-Hayne debate preceding it. Jackson noted his dismay "that the celebration was to be a nullification affair altogether."[15]

A toast called for unique rhetorical skills. Jackson would have to make a succinct statement in a highly charged atmosphere of competing toasts and general anticipation of his remarks. He had no choice but to prepare a statement he did not wish to make, at least not at this point. As was his practice with other rhetorical acts, he drafted three different toasts and opted for one after consulting with close aides.[16] With one short and succinct sentence, Jackson commenced his Unionist position. His silence, now broken with the toast "Our Union—It must be preserved" would be a game changer.[17] The Nullification Crisis intensified tenfold once the nation's chief magistrate defined it in terms of the United States' constitutionality as a union. With Jackson's statement in the open, "the veil was rent," stated Van Buren.[18]

Jackson's toast came after one by Senator Robert Hayne of South Carolina, a key proponent of states' rights. Hayne's toast specified "the Union of the States, and the Sovereignty of the States." The impact of Jackson's one-line salute was most significant if not altogether shocking. All attendees gasped as they learned that Jackson favored the Union over states' rights. Senator Thomas Hart Benton commented immediately thereafter that the president's words "electrified the nation."[19] To add fuel to the fire, Vice President Calhoun followed with his toast: "The Union, next to our liberty, the most dear. May we all remember that it can only be persevered by respecting the rights of the States, and distributing equally the benefit and burden of the Union."[20] For Jackson, Calhoun's toast ruined any cordial relationship left between them. Though relations between the two had improved in recent years, especially during the formation of a successful Democratic coalition, their connect was now severely strained.

A few days later, Jackson, finding another opportunity to state his position unequivocally, was asked by a visiting South Carolina congressman what message he had for his friends back home. Jackson replied tersely, "Please give my compliments to my friends in your State, and say to them that if a single drop of blood shall be shed there in opposition to the laws of the United States, I will hang the first man I can lay my hands on engaged in such treasonable conduct, upon the first tree I can reach." Jackson's response must have had its desired effect. He knew full well that this private statement would soon be made public. When Senator Hayne asked Jackson's friend Senator Thomas Hart Benton if Jackson really meant to hang people,

Benton answered, "I tell you, Hayne, when Jackson begins to talk about hanging, they can begin to look out for ropes."[21] Jackson's toast defined the crisis, as it explicated positions clearly. In hindsight, speechwriters were wise to remove from Jackson's First Inaugural Address his statement about not accusing anyone of treason for interpreting the Constitution differently.

Jackson's toast and "message" to friends in South Carolina effectively conveyed his views on the growing national tension over states' rights. He was adamant that any attempt to undermine the authority of the federal government would be opposed militarily, and that those supporting secession would face the ultimate punishment. The president meant to be harsh. He hoped that such succinct rhetoric would end the dangerous crisis, and he referenced measures he had used successfully as a military leader—issuing clear statements about where things stood and executing those engaged in treasonable or illegal behavior. Indeed, the nation's capital "buzzed with discussions about 'the meanness uttered by the President against South Carolina,' his 'threatening the gallows,' and his frequent assertion 'that he considers himself authorized by the *existing* laws, to use military force against South Carolina.'"[22] If Jackson thought that his few words would magically bring the crisis to some accommodation, he was wrong. The crisis would only intensify.

On the narrow issue of tariffs, Jackson had no strong opinion. He sympathized with southern states' concern over high rates, but he also weighed this issue against his previously stated plan to balance the federal budget. Tariffs had been a continuous thorn since President John Quincy Adams raised them from 33 percent to 50 percent.[23] Yet once the tariff issue was transformed into opposing the federal government's right to decide the matter, the crisis took on a new form. At the heart of the Nullification Crisis stood the principle that guided the United States as united states with a central government overseeing the federation. Such was the controversy from 1776, through the confederation and the Great Compromise of 1787, and beyond.

The differing views of Founding Fathers and state-based constitutional conventions further complicated the matter. For the most part, the Federalists had the upper hand early on, and by 1800, even with the agrarian president Jefferson, the national government strengthened more by default than due to any ideological argument. By sheer practice, territorial expansion, and the growing need for consistent foreign and domestic policy, the central government acquired increased authority. Yet the nation was young, and contrary sentiments were in vogue and would be reiterated at different intervals in the South and the North. The words used to describe the central government—*federal, central, general,* or *national*—proved the American experiment's tenuousness during the nation's first five decades.

Jackson's military experience, his bravery and courage, and his notorious military acts were known to all. But so was his immense popularity. Thus the president's toast and "message to friends" at the height of the Nullification Crisis must be understood within the larger context of his decisive acts during serious controversies. Given most politicians' (including Jackson's) penchant for expounding opinions in lengthy speeches and with a measurable sense of decorum, eloquence, and politeness, Jackson's short, terse statements on nullification were significant anomalies.

Jackson's toast to the Union would likely not have been made had the Senate not debated the issue to great effect. There, the issue was dissected, and its rhetorical framing was very much as Jackson wished—a debate over the nature of the Union itself. Daniel Webster's six-hour retort to Robert Hayne was a piece of grand oratory. The Webster-Hayne debate in Congress began over the issue of tariffs, letting others than Jackson set the context and outline the primary arguments. However, it quickly turned to the issue of states' rights and the nature of the Union, subordinating tariffs to a greater cause. Webster, who opposed many of Jackson's policies, ended his famous speech by stating, "Liberty and Union, now and forever, one and inseparable!" This line was clearly consistent with Jackson's thinking, and it prompted his toast.[24]

An equally impressive oration of the day (March 9, 1830), though often discounted, was that of Edward Livingston. The Louisiana senator and old friend of Jackson's depicted the president as securing the nation by advocating a Unionist position and subduing the people's passions. Jackson was calling for a more sober assessment of opinions and a reasoned way out of the conflict. For Livingston, the pride and emotions of the moment were not conducive to managing the emergency. He, too, hoped for a measured solution and a constructive approach to the Nullification Crisis. Though from a southern state, Livingston called for the "continuance of the Union" and voiced his "fears, on the madness of party that [might] destroy it."[25]

It was left to South Carolina to make the next move, and the move would indeed be most significant. In the Fort Hill Address, published on July 26, 1831, Calhoun openly repeated the sentiments he expressed anonymously in the *Exposition and Protest*, adding an insightful caveat. The tariff act was a pretext. Calhoun identified the real issue as follows: "The peculiar domestick [sic] institution of the Southern States and the consequent direction which that and her soil have given to her industry, has placed them in regard to taxation and appropriations in opposite relation to the majority of the Union."[26] In short, the real issue was slavery. South Carolinians experienced growing fear that the central government might oppose its "domestic institution."

After Jackson signed the duties into law, South Carolina declared in November 1832 that the Tariffs of 1828 and 1832 were unconstitutional and unenforceable, citing the right of the state to decide so. Additionally, the state issued the South Carolina Ordinance of Nullification. This edict drew on Calhoun's primary argument in the *Exposition and Protest*: "It would seem impossible to deny to the States the right of deciding on the infractions of their powers, and the proper remedy to be applied for their correction. The right of judging, in such cases, is an essential attribute of sovereignty, of which the States cannot be divested without losing their sovereignty itself, and being reduced to a subordinate corporate condition."[27] In short, Calhoun believed that states' sovereignty allowed them to challenge the federal government. Though not all South Carolinians supported this great test of federal authority, momentum shifted in the radicals' direction.[28]

THE NULLIFICATION CRISIS IN JACKSON'S MAJOR ADDRESSES

Since the tariffs issue simmered for a while, even before he took office, Jackson's public rhetoric leading to the Nullification Proclamation was a model of decorum and reserved eloquence. The president did his best to walk a fine line between states' rights and the authority of the federal government. More specifically, as the crisis intensified, Jackson retreated to a moderate stance, hoping he could prevent an eruption.

Jackson stated in his First Inaugural Address on March 4, 1829, "As the instrument of the Federal Constitution it will devolve on me for a stated period to execute the laws of the United States, to superintend their foreign and their confederate relations, to manage their revenue, to command their forces, and, by communications to the Legislature, to watch over and to promote their interests generally." As he entered office, the president subtly outlined the federal government's role and constitutional foundation as management of several issues including "confederate relations," a careful phrase that did not push too hard against states' rights. To balance his stated duty as the chief magistrate of the nation, and to indicate his cognizance of states' rights sentiments, Jackson added a tempered note: "In such measures as I may be called on to pursue in regard to the rights of the separate States I hope to be animated by a proper respect for those sovereign members of our Union, taking care not to confound the powers they have reserved to themselves with those they have granted to the Confederacy."[29] The authority of the national government was carefully balanced with the sovereignty of states on issues not entrusted to the federal government.

In his First Annual Message to Congress on December 8, 1829, Jackson briefly addressed the issue of tariffs in most transcendent language, calling on patriotism and the avoidance of partisanship, which often turns injurious.[30] Clearly attempting to appease states' rights advocates, Jackson later opined, "I cannot . . . too strongly or too earnestly, for my own sense of its importance, warn you against all encroachments upon the legitimate sphere of State sovereignty. Sustained by its healthful and invigorating influence the federal system can never fall." Without sounding Unionist, the president carefully suggested equalizing regional and local sentiments with the greater good of the nation. And in a masterful rhetorical line, he praised the "legitimate sphere of State sovereignty" as essential for the strength and vitality of the federal government. This is a complementary twist whereby the states gave strength to the Union and not the other way around, a point Jackson had already made in his First Inaugural Address.

In his Second Annual Message to Congress on December 6, 1830, Jackson took a longer view of the crisis at hand. In an early paragraph that on the face of it is innocuous and even generous, Jackson stated, "The apparent exceptions to the harmony of the prospect are to be referred rather to inevitable diversities in the various interests which enter into the composition of so extensive a whole than any want of attachment to the Union—interests whose collisions serve only in the end to foster the spirit of conciliation and patriotism so essential to the preservation of that union which I most devoutly hope is destined to prove imperishable."[31]

This paragraph reveals only a hint of undercurrent difficulties. Its phrasing, couched in the president's mildest language and demonstrating his generous forbearance. That this calm message followed a shocking toast few months earlier suggests Jackson's style of forwarding most moderate and tempered public and official statements. Here, he considered the "exceptions to the harmony" as natural growing pains of the Union. A note of irony is also imbedded therein. Jackson suggested that the current "collisions" would not work, and that in the end they would bring "conciliation" and "patriotism" necessary to preserve the Union. Ultimately, the Union's destiny would prove, in Lincoln's similar phrasing thirty-three years later, "imperishable." Importantly, Jackson's mild, even charitable tone did not diminish his ultimate stance on protecting the Union.

Jackson devoted a larger portion of his Second Annual Message to the intensifying crisis, hoping to counter his rather terse and angry private tone. He repeated his desire to see personal ambition and local prejudices put aside for the "public good." He called again for a balance between states' rights and federal government authority, advocating "the importance of sustaining the State sovereignties as far as is consistent with the rightful action of the Federal Government, and of preserving the greatest attainable harmony between them."[32] He also added a bit of his political philosophy: "Diversities in the interests of the different States which compose this extensive Confederacy must be admitted. Those diversities arising from situation, climate, population, and pursuits are doubtless, as it is natural they should be, greatly exaggerated by jealousies and that spirit of rivalry so inseparable from neighboring communities. These circumstances make it the duty of those who are intrusted [sic] with the management of its affairs to neutralize their effects as far as practicable by making the beneficial operation of the federal government as equal and equitable among the several states as can be done consistently with the great ends of its institution."[33]

Jackson acknowledged that different states and regions had developed along differing circumstances and objectives that would naturally create tensions among them. The role of the federal government was to manage this diversity in an "equitable" way.[34] Jackson preferred to acknowledge these hostilities rather than criticize them; he asked states and regions to rise above conflict for the greater good of the Union. Yet he added, "Our course is a safe one if it be but faithfully adhered to. Acquiescence in the constitutionally expressed will of the majority, and the exercise of that will in a spirit of moderation, justice, and brotherly kindness, will constitute a cement which would forever preserve our Union."[35] The mild and accommodating tone did not weaken Jackson's principal stance—that the constitutionality of the federal government, a government of the majority, was the central principle of the Union.

At the conclusion of the Second Annual Message, Jackson returned to the crisis at hand. He called upon constitutional history, acknowledging that while the states initially had power to impose duties on imports, "the states [had] delegated their whole authority over imports to the General Government without limitation or restriction."[36] Against this principal notion, Jackson asserted, "To make this great question, which unhappily so much divides and excites the public mind, subservient to the short-sighted views of faction, must destroy all hope of settling it satisfactorily to the great body of the people and for the general interest. I cannot, therefore, in taking leave of the subject, too earnestly for my own feelings or the common good warn you against the blighting consequences of such a course."[37]

As the Nullification Crisis intensified, so did Jackson's rhetoric. He maintained a moderate and respectful tone but issued more admonitions and warnings once positions were stated and antagonists identified. Nevertheless, he avoided overusing words he knew would anger the nullifiers. Instead of "Union," Jackson preferred the ever-innocuous phrases "the great body of the people" and "the general interest," hoping South Carolina would realize it had positioned itself against a patriotic mass. The president also wished to counter those clinging to a constitutional interpretation favoring the states' right to withdraw from the national confederation.

Jackson included no reference to the growing crisis in his Third Annual Message of December 6, 1831. Even so, his mention of the nation's budgetary balance was of great importance to the Nullification Crisis. Jackson presented the balance sheet on which payments on the national debt had improved as revenues increased. In particular, expanding sales of public lands increased the government coffers, and revenues entered the Treasury as a result. Subsequently, Jackson could talk about his "confidence" in "the extinguishment of the public debt." He could also allude to "[a] modification of the tariff which [should] produce a reduction of our revenue to the wants of the Government and an adjustment to the duties on imports with a view to equal justice in relation to all our national interests." Jackson observed that this circumstance would add "Justice to the interest of the merchant as well as the manufacturer," and he hoped that the "spirit of concession and conciliation which ha[d] distinguished the friends of our Union in all great emergencies, it is believed that this object may be effected without injury to any national interest."[38] Ever so subtly, Jackson compromised on his important issue of balancing the budget. He was willing to reduce tariff rates by absorbing a deficit to accommodate the nullifiers.

Even after he reduced the tariff rates, none of Jackson's rhetorical efforts yielded the course he hoped South Carolina would pursue. To the contrary, South Carolina declared during a special convention in November 1832 that the tariffs were "unconstitutional" and "unenforceable." With his compromise rejected, Jackson waited until delivering his Fourth Annual Message to Congress on December 4, 1832, to respond to the most serious challenge. He devoted only one paragraph of his lengthy address to the recent development in the Nullification Crisis. But that paragraph issues a stern warning:

> It is my painful duty to state that in one quarter of the United States opposition to the revenue laws has arisen to a height which threatens to thwart their execution, if not to endanger the integrity of the Union. Whatever obstructions may be thrown in the way of the judicial authorities of the General Government, it is hoped they will be able peaceably to overcome them by the prudence of their own officers and the patriotism of the people. But should this reasonable reliance on the moderation and good sense of all portions of our fellow citizens be disappointed, it is believed that the laws themselves are fully adequate to the suppression of such attempts as may be immediately made. Should the exigency arise rendering the execution of the existing laws impracticable from any cause whatever, prompt notice of it will be given to Congress, with a suggestion of such views and measures as may be deemed necessary to meet it.[39]

Jackson issued a serious warning though his phrasing was still vague. Key words in the conflict such as "nullification," "secession," "tariffs," or even "South Carolina," were not to be found in the address. Jackson preferred instead the more innocuous "one quarter," "opposition," and "revenues." Yet only a few important words and phrases such as "the integrity of the Union," "obstruction," "exigency," and "suppression" were sufficient to send a clear message of Jackson's determination to assert the authority of the federal government if prudence did not prevail.

In planning this address, Jackson informed Van Buren that he intended soft peddle the issue of nullification, at least until South Carolina's intentions were clear. He stated, "I mean to pass it barely in review, as mere buble, [sic], view, [sic] the existing laws as competant [sic] to check and put it down, and ask merely a general provision to be enacted, to authorize [sic] the Collector . . . to demand of all vessels entering our harbours, where a state by law has authorized her citizens to oppose & resist the collection of the revenue."[40] And so he did, saying little of what he really had planned, limiting his words to the collection of duties under the tariff law. Yet Jackson's hint about a state resisting revenue collection would be appreciated only a few days later—as would his plan of notifying Congress of necessary measures to be taken if the crisis was not resolved.

To balance his insistence, Jackson followed with what is by now a familiar note of constitutional history. He pointed to the wisdom of the Founding Fathers in authorizing the general government "to regulate the great mass of the business and concerns of the people." He continued, "[The Founders' plan] have been fully justified by experience, and . . . it cannot now be doubted that the genius of all our institutions prescribes simplicity and economy as the characteristics of the reform which is yet to be effected in the present and future execution of the functions bestowed upon us by the Constitution."[41] Jackson hailed the Union as a successful and brilliant experiment that had yet to be fully realized. To reinforce this view of the limited yet clear function of federal authority, the president provided this view of the general government: "[It ought to possess] superintending power to maintain peace at home and abroad, and to prescribe laws on a few subjects of general interest not calculated to restrict human liberty, but to enforce human rights, this Government will find its strength and its glory in the faithful discharge of these plain and simple duties. Relieved by its protecting shield from the fear of war and the apprehension of oppression, the free enterprise of our citizens, aided by the state sovereignties, will work out improvements and ameliorations which cannot fail to demonstrate that the great truth that the people can govern themselves is not only realized in our example, but that it is done by a machinery in government so simple and economical as scarcely to be felt."[42]

In short, the role of the federal government was rather clear; its authority was quite limited, and it worked best when its presence was scarcely noticeable. By implication, Jackson questioned those keen on nullifying the authority of the Union. He asked them to explain their unjustified criticism of a central government that was barely felt, had never been oppressive, and was often keen to ameliorate difficulties. Jackson also took a broader view of the crisis at hand, a perspective he resorted to in previous addresses. The president called on the nullifiers to realize what a successful experiment the United States had been. He urged them to understand that in their hands lay the potential to disprove the simple truism that there could ever be a political system of self-government. Jackson appealed to their patriotism and loyalty to the Union, not to any faction therein. His argument about transcending local sentiments by securing a historical experiment of great significance was an appeal to altruism and to political ideals. Jackson almost begged South Carolina not to destroy that which thus far had been a successful limited government.[43]

Since issuing the Nullification Ordinance, South Carolina clearly would not retreat from its position, even after Jackson offered a major concession on tariffs. The timing was ripe for a dramatic change in the president's crisis rhetoric. He issued a hint in his Fourth Annual Message to Congress designed not to get antagonists to retreat, but to implement a rhetorical process that formally sequenced and addressed appeal, warning, and action. Four days later, Jackson issued the Proclamation to the People of South Carolina containing shocking statements and threatening language.

THE PROCLAMATION

Jackson drafted the initial version of the Nullification Proclamation himself, furiously writing some fifteen to twenty pages, according to one witness.[44] Edward Livingston edited this work, but Jackson complained that the changes did not convey his intended point or the necessary passion. The president then worked into the night to complete the proclamation to his satisfaction, even documenting the time he completed his task: "11 ocloke [sic] P.M. on Decb 4th, 1832."[45] The draft was dated the same day Jackson delivered his Fourth Annual Message. Jackson, then, was ready, and he knew the crisis would not dissipate. As he affixed the time and date to the proclamation, he was likely aware of its rhetorical and historical significance in the present and for posterity.

The final version of the Proclamation drew from Livingston's 1830 Senate speech, Livingston's amendments to Jackson's initial draft, and Jackson's extensive reworking of the proclamation for three more days until finalizing it on December 7. Major Lewis suggested modifying the document in order to assuage those who advocated states' rights but objected to nullification. Jackson rebuffed him, stating, "Those are my views," and "I will not change them nor strike them out."[46] In no mood for middle-of-the-road compromise, the president opted for clear statements on the key principle of the safeguarding the Union.

In his lengthy proclamation, Jackson stated his position succinctly, refuting South Carolina's arguments, questioning its motives, and calling on its people to realize their actions and retreat from secession plans. Jackson defined the Nullification Act as insurrection and treason, and he made it clear that he would take necessary action to preserve the Union.[47] The Nullification Proclamation rationalized the Union's operative principles and historical underpinnings. Moreover, it laid out the illogical implications of South Carolina's actions, and Jackson's own determination to save the

Union. Principally, the president argued that the Union had authority over the states, and that the Union was of the people, not of its states. Hence, its sovereignty was of the people of the Union. The South Carolina Ordinance, Jackson stated,

> prescribes to the people of South Carolina a course of conduct in direct violation of their duty as citizens of the United States, contrary to the laws of their country, subversive of its Constitution, and having for its object the instruction of the Union—that Union, which, coeval with our political existence, led our fathers, without any other ties to unite them than those of patriotism and common cause, through the sanguinary struggle to a glorious independence—that sacred Union, hitherto inviolate, which, perfected by our happy Constitution, has brought us, by the favor of Heaven, to a state of prosperity at home, and high consideration abroad, rarely, if ever, equaled in the history of nations; to preserve this bond of our political existence from destruction, to maintain inviolate this state of national honor and prosperity, and to justify the confidence my fellow-citizens have reposed in me, I, Andrew Jackson, President of the United States, have thought proper to issue this my proclamation.[48]

In its pursuit of selfish interests, South Carolina forgot the basic principles on which the nation was founded—patriotism, common cause, and independence—principles "our" Constitution made perfect. Instead, argued Jackson, the "ordinance is founded . . . on the strange position that any one State may not only declare an act of Congress void, but prohibit its execution; that they may do this consistently with the Constitution; that the true construction of that instrument permits a State to retain its place in the Union, and yet be bound by no other of its laws than those it may choose to consider as constitutional."[49]

In surveying several case studies, including the Nullification Crisis, David Zarefsky and Victoria Gallagher contend that the Constitution functions as a sacred document and a symbol whose values are held in great esteem. They also opine that the Constitution's very ambiguity allows opposing sides in a conflict to use it to support their views. At the same time, such ambiguities in the Constitution cannot solve serious conflicts. Specifically, Zarefsky and Gallagher contend that Jackson used the Constitution to argue the authority of the federal government, and that nullifiers likewise argued that their actions preserved the Constitution. Nullifiers also argued that federal tariffs were meant to collect revenues to "be used to subsidize the

American Colonization Society, which promoted the return of freed slaves to Africa."[50] In other words, on the strict legal matter, the issue for South Carolina was not the federal government's right to impose tariffs but the *motive* behind this action—supporting an antislavery association.[51] Yet, if slavery was the central issue, other southern states would have supported South Carolina, which they did not. In any event, per this interpretation, the new issue of slavery was inserted to oppose the federal government.

For Jackson, however, the principal issue was the authority of the Union. In his view, South Carolina made a mockery of the Constitution, and those promoting the conflict ignored the prosperity and peace it had brought the people. Most explicitly, Jackson added, "I consider, then, the power to annul a law of the United States, assumed by one State, *incompatible with the existence of the Union, contradicted expressly by the letter of the Constitution, unauthorized by its spirit, inconsistent with every principle on which it was founded, and destructive of the great object for which it was formed.*"[52]

Jackson engaged South Carolina's reasoning in order to refute it. He argued the following about South Carolinians: "[They consider their right to secede as] deduced from the nature of the Constitution, which they say is a compact between sovereign States who have preserved their whole sovereignty, and therefore are subject to no superior; that because they made the compact, they can break it when in their opinion it has been departed from by the other States. Fallacious as this course of reasoning is, it enlists State pride, and finds advocates in the honest prejudices of those who have not studied the nature of our Government sufficiently to see the radical error on which it rests."[53]

Jackson sought to tackle the pivotal point of the nullifiers who argued that "because the Union was formed by compact . . . the parties to that compact [might], when they [felt] themselves aggrieved, depart from it." However, he maintained, "it is precisely because it is a compact that they cannot. A compact is an agreement or binding obligation."[54] He then explained how nullifiers' reasoning was in error: "[The] Constitution of the United States . . . forms a *government*, not a league; and whether it be formed by compact between the States, or in any other manner, its character is the same. It is a Government in which all the people are represented, which operates directly on the people individually, not upon the States."[55] Here, Jackson argued the key point that the Union was of people and not of states. Crucially, for Jackson, the foundation of the Union was not in its compact, but in its perpetuation: "We were the *United States* under the Confederation, and the name was perpetuated and the Union rendered more perfect by the Federal Constitution."[56] This is an innovative and significant argument, as Jackson was the first to define "the doctrine of the Union as a perpetual entity." Unlike Daniel Webster, who, in his reply to Hayne, described the Union as "a blessing to mankind," Jackson offered "a dynamic new reading of constitutional law."[57]

Having outlined the Nullification Proclamation's legal aspects and pointed to South Carolina's unconstitutional actions, Jackson then employed the tradition of classical rhetoric to narrate the crisis's evolution and his own plans to respond. He characterized the emergency as borne of "[a] small majority of the citizens of one State in the Union" who "ordained that all the revenue laws of the United States . . . be repealed, or that they [would] no longer [be] a member of the Union." The president continued, "The governor of that State has recommended to the legislature the raising of an army to carry the secession into effect, and that he may be empowered to give clearances to vessels in the name of the State." Jackson ultimately acknowledged, "No act of violent opposition to the laws has yet been committed, but such a state of things is hourly apprehended, and it is the intent of this instrument to *proclaim* . . . the duty imposed on me by the Constitution, 'to take care that the laws be faithfully executed,' shall be performed to the extent of the powers already vested in me by law."[58]

The Constitution, then, gave the president authority to ensure the Union's survival and resort to all necessary actions to this end. The key word *already* clearly signals that no special approval for such action is required. Jackson did not need to go to Congress with additional authorization, which would confuse and delay the situation; the president had all the authority needed. The president minced no words in his severest statement of the proclamation. He wrote: "[I warn]the citizens of South Carolina, who have been deluded into an opposition to the laws, of the danger they will incur by obedience to the illegal and disorganizing ordinance of the convention— [I want] to exhort those who have refused to support it to persevere in their determination to uphold the Constitution and laws of their country, and to point out to all the perilous situation into which the good people of that State have been led, and [I maintain] that the course they are urged to pursue is one of ruin and disgrace to the very State whose rights they affect to support."

Jackson, who often avoided emotional and sentimental language on principle, concluded the Nullification Proclamation with an anguished yet determined appeal:

Fellow-citizens of my native State! let me not only admonish you, as the first magistrate of our common country, not to incur the penalty of its laws, but use the influence that a father would over his children whom he saw rushing to a certain ruin. In that paternal language, with that paternal feeling, let me tell you, my countrymen, that you are deluded by men who are either deceived themselves or wish to deceive you. Mark under what pretenses you have been led on to the brink of insurrection and treason on which you stand! First a diminution of the value of our staple commodity, lowered by over-production in other quarters and the consequent diminution in the value of your lands, were the sole effect of the tariff laws. The effect of those laws was confessedly injurious, but the evil was greatly exaggerated by the unfounded theory you were taught to believe, that its burdens were in proportion to your exports, not to your consumption of imported articles. Your pride was aroused by the assertions that a submission to these laws was a state of vassalage, and that resistance to them was equal, in patriotic merit, to the opposition our fathers offered to the oppressive laws of Great Britain.[59]

The crisis, argued Jackson, bore no relation to the situation at hand, and the people were deceived in supporting a greater cause not related to the issue—namely, tariffs. The true causes of the local economic difficulty, he iterated, were not truthfully addressed. Instead, those wanting to mislead others were promoting a constitutional crisis bordering on treason and insurrection. Jackson challenged, elevating a local conflict to a constitutional crisis on par with the fight for independence against an oppressive Great Britain.

If Jackson thus far avoided pinning the crisis on specific nameless individuals—particularly Calhoun—he made a point of doing so here, assigning the crisis to the deceitful actions of a few. He exhorted the majority of South Carolinians to influence those few to retreat from their position. In repeated paternal metaphors that he had employed in previous addresses, Jackson sought to empower the citizens of South Carolina to take their state back from the brink of disaster. He reserved the venom of the proclamation for the few deceiving individuals, not the majority they had deluded and exaggerated to. Anger and even fury creep out of the Nullification Proclamation resembling nothing in Jackson's previous public statements. If the proclamation can be likened to any prior address it is to the president's short "message to friends" in South Carolina, in which he mentioned hanging the first person shedding blood over the Nullification Crisis. It is also noteworthy that Jackson formally addressed the Nullification Proclamation to the people of South Carolina and not the State of South Carolina. Consistent with his argument that the Union was not of states but of the people, the president retained this reference in the proclamation. He stood by his conviction that the people had the power and authority to undo the damage done thus far. Jackson also avoided using the word Union, opting for the more neutral reference to "our common country."

The support for Jackson's Nullification Proclamation was quite overwhelming. Joseph Story thought it "excellent," and Daniel Webster stated his unquestionable backing. Webster and other supporters of Jackson also held a meeting at Faneuil Hall in Boston to champion the proclamation. Similar meetings were held in Baltimore and Philadelphia. Even southern states hailed the president's proclamation and handling of the crisis. Appalled by its intensity and threatening language, the decree's opponents considered Jackson a despot keen on setting himself above the law. One senator from North Carolina was "deeply mortified," and another opined that Jackson's principles "[were] at war with all our opinions of state power." Even close allies such as Senator Benton did not agree with all aspects of the Proclamation. A New York City supporter saw in it "the broad errors of doctrine on some of the fundamental principles of the Constitution."[60]

Jackson was very pleased with the effects of the Nullification Proclamation's rhetoric, and he encouraged pro-Union meetings throughout the country. He used his newspaper "to speak up for the principles he had so eloquently conveyed in his proclamation," writes biographer Remini.[61] And though historians and constitutional experts have quibbled about the proclamation's legal aspects, especially Jackson's rejection of the "compact theory of the origin of the Union,"[62] from a rhetorical perspective, the statement was unique, forceful, and even lethal.

But most crucially, the Nullification Proclamation ended the crisis effectively and rather quickly. For Jackson, as Zarefsky and Gallagher point out, the Constitution was indeed a sacred document. In my view, the president's crisis rhetoric cannot be appreciated without understanding his esteem for the Constitution as a sine qua non authoritative document grounding the Union—hence its sacredness. To give credence to this point, I note that the word "constitutional" appears 16 times in Jackson's Proclamation, the word "unconstitutional" 23 times, and the word "Constitution" 47 times, for a total of 86 references to the Constitution as a concept. By comparison, the word "Union" appears 46 times, often qualified as "happy" or "sacred." The most visible verbs associated with the "Union" are "to retain," "forming" or "to form," "to preserve," and "to secede." When taking these references as condensation symbols or God terms, they help us understand that Jackson's approach to and resolution of the Nullification Crisis was borne of clear principles embodied in the Constitution and the Union.

In Jackson's view, argues Brogdon, "the Constitution formed a government, not merely a league." On this particular point, Lincoln adopted Jackson's view, rejecting Webster's argument for the Union's nationhood and emphasizing instead its legal and contractual foundation. In essence, Lincoln accepted Jackson's perpetuity view of the Union, the seventh president's argument that "the terms of the Constitution itself would bind the federal government to disallow nullification by a state."[63] Finally, the Nullification Proclamation emphasizes Jackson's confidence as president. After the election of 1832, he was no longer hesitant about the Union but convinced that the people and their votes were sufficient to sustain it via the ballot box.[64] Realizing how well the "moral force" of his rhetoric was received nationwide, Jackson used his press to continue this line of argument, especially his points about the "perpetual union" and the Constitution as the ultimate authority of the Union.[65]

THE AFTERMATH

The federal government took specific measures in January 1833. Jackson explicated appropriate military actions if South Carolina obstructed tariff collections or, worse, ended the crisis. Congress approved a Force Bill that authorized military intervention (but more as a face-saving measure for the administration when the crisis had clearly passed its peak). A compromise was quickly under way: the federal government agreed to reduced tariff rates, and South Carolina agreed to repeal its Nullification Ordinance. Jackson prevailed, at least for now, yet secession sentiments did not subside. And though he compromised on tariffs, Jackson did not modify his principal stance, continuing to consider "the right of secession . . . a virtual dissolution of the Union."[66]

At least initially, Jackson and the Unionists did not fully understand that the Nullification Crisis and its advocacy of states' rights were indirectly tied to slavery. Ellis argues that Jackson belatedly realized that embedded in the tariff and Nullification Crisis was South Carolina's fear that Unionism would ultimately bring the federal government to force slave owners to free their slaves.[67] Remini altogether rejects slavery as a cause of the crisis. He maintains that slavery was instead no more than a pretext for secession, just as tariffs were a pretext for secessionist sentiments manipulated by specific ambitious individuals, especially Calhoun. Remini claims that had other southern states understood the crisis to evolve around slavery, they would not have supported Jackson. In April 1833, once the crisis was over, Jackson was prescient enough to state as much. He said in a letter to John Coffee, "Nullification is dead . . . the coalition between Calhoun, Clay, Poindexter & the Nullifiers in the South intend[s] to blow up a storm on the subject of the slave question." Tellingly, the president also opined, "The next pretext will be the negro, or slavery question."[68] Yet in both statements, Jackson considered slavery a pretext for secession and not a cause.

There was no doubt that after the infamous toast, John C. Calhoun would either resign or be dumped as Jackson's vice president. Calhoun resigned in late 1832 in order to run for the Senate. If he used the Nullification Crisis for personal promotion, its resounding defeat ended his presidential aspirations. In contrast, Jackson's stand on nullification would be enshrined in a memorial and a statue in front of the White House.

In some historians' assessment, the Nullification Proclamation hurt Jackson more than it helped him. Yet South Carolina's cautious behavior after its issuance—carefully avoiding any pretext for federal intervention and fairly quickly withdrawing its Nullification Ordinance—can hardly be construed as Jackson's failure to manage the crisis. If anything, the proclamation carried a clear threat, and its effect in quickly ending the constitutional crisis was significant. Key South Carolina politicians, Calhoun being the most prominent, cautioned against any state action that could provoke a federal response. This circumstance proves that Jackson's Unionist stand and threats of military action were effective.

The Nullification Proclamation did suffer some setbacks, emanating primarily from the perception of its harsh intent and Jackson's embarkation on a dangerous path.[69] More significantly, Jackson's proclamation opened the door to a growing debate in most southern states over the constitutional issues therein. Discourse on this subject would affect political alignments for decades to come. Yet several states such as Alabama, Mississippi, and North Carolina, which opposed Jackson's military threat, criticized South Carolina's reckless behavior, rejected nullification as "contrary to the letter and spirit of the Constitution," and asserted that the ordinance was "essentially revolutionary."[70] And the fact that Calhoun hurried to Charleston to persuade "the reassembled state convention that the compromise tariff represented a victory for nullification" proves that it was not much of a victory for South Carolina.[71]

✳✳✳✳

The president followed two rhetorical tracts corresponding to the two parts of the Nullification Crisis: the tariffs dispute and federal government authority over the states of the Union. Until he issued the proclamation, Jackson expressed his Unionism and adamant opposition to states' rights via several warnings in the clearest moderate tone. On the tariff issue he released more moderate, sympathetic statements. Throughout the crisis, he sought to temper local sentiments and transcend them with the needs of the nation and its growing interdependence on commerce, agriculture, and manufacturing. The Nullification Proclamation was Jackson's ultimate rhetorical act following South Carolina's Nullification Ordinance declaring the Tariffs of 1828 and 1832 "utterly null and void."[72] With consistent efforts at diffusing the crisis, Jackson attempted to mitigate the most serious challenge to the Union yet. He sought to end it with a brief toast and a "private" message to friends in South Carolina, as well as by including appeasing statements in several of his official addresses.

Once his moderate tone failed and the Nullification Ordinance was issued, Jackson quickly went for the jugular. He issued clear statements about the authority of the Union and outlined the actions he was willing to take in enforcing federal authority. And though Tulis contends that "it is striking that Jackson seems prevented by the requirements of the form from attempting the blatant appeal to passion for which his oratorical abilities were reputedly well suited," I argue that the seventh president was not as constrained as suggested. His Nullification Proclamation was rather forceful if not altogether threatening, including paternal appeals to the people of South Carolina. Additionally, it was rather pointed despite the decorum and constraints of the period.[73]

In the end though, Jackson also compromised, perhaps to balance his tough stand. In the words of Major Wilson, "He [Jackson] agreed with Daniel Webster that liberty and Union were one and inseparable, but he shared no less with John C. Calhoun the view that the Union, as a means for free men to pursue happiness, was one of limited powers."[74] Jackson compromised on the question of tariffs because he considered it the initial cause of the crisis, but also because it came after he issued the Bank Veto and won a second term.

The issue for Jackson was embracing "a new synthesis view of the Union" in which the people wanted to preserve the Union but also wanted to enjoy its fruits by "being left alone." Jackson stated as much in the proclamation, referring to securing Americans "complete enjoyment of civil liberty."[75]

The issue of states' rights versus federal authority would surface again.[76] South Carolina would do more than threaten to secede when the issue became slavery rather than tariffs. President Lincoln's challenge amid South Carolina's secession and opening military assault on Fort Sumter in 1861 was the most daunting act yet. It would tear the nation apart. The issue of states' rights and the challenge to the federal government would rear its ugly head yet again in the form of opposition to civil rights, voting rights, equal education, and related racial ordinances across the South. This conflict endured all the way through the 1950s and the 1960s, testing different administrations into the mid-twentieth century. Other presidents faced challenges to such sentiments with varying degrees of success, but also with delays and inaction. Yet Jackson stands alone in being the first to encounter such a dangerous rift in the young nation. With relatively few determined words over a four-year period, he met the challenge and stabilized the Union for some thirty years. John Quincy Adams lamented that Jackson was not "'Federalist' enough," while Calhoun condemned Jackson "for not being 'Republican' enough," thus testifying to the president's astute management of the Nullification Crisis.[77]

It is difficult to prove the degree to which other presidents have learned from Jackson's experience, especially those removed from the Nullification Crisis of the 1830s by the passage of a century and more. But Lincoln carefully examined Jackson's nullification rhetoric. Though initially of the Whig Party and quite critical of the former president on other matters, it is safe to assume Lincoln actively studied Jackson's approach to South Carolina's challenge to the Union when he himself faced the threat of secession from the same state. As early as 1856, Lincoln stated in one speech that "during Gen. Jackson's administration, the Calhoun nullifying doctrine sprang up, but Gen. Jackson, with that decision of character that ever characterized him, put an end to it."[78] Jackson sought to diffuse the crisis by arguing that while the Union was above the states, the central government had a limited and well-defined role vis-à-vis the states. With patience and a good sense of kairos, Jackson took time asserting his position and issued repeated accommodating statements while hoping South Carolina would find the way to retreat without losing face. But when all attempts failed, he enacted a principled crisis rhetoric decisively and effectively asserting the authority of the federal government and the Union over states' rights.

6

ANDREW JACKSON AND THE INDIAN TRIBES

AN UNCOMPROMISING APPROACH

I know your humanity would feel for them.
—Andrew Jackson to his wife, Rachel

Upon becoming president, Jackson had to confront the growing tension between the federal government, states, and the Indian nations. Local governments and private white citizens pressured various tribes, seeking to take over their land and end their sovereignty over specific territories. The tension was most acute in several southern states where the Creek, Cherokee, Choctaw, and Chickasaw Nations resided in territories legally secured by earlier treaties. In 1802, the federal government also promised the State of Georgia to terminate the "Indian title within the state 'as early as the same [could] be peaceably obtained on reasonable terms.'"[1] Just prior to Jackson's presidency, Georgia, Alabama, and Mississippi spelled out their jurisdiction over their Indian territories, and Jackson opted not challenge the states, thus signaling his intention to remove the tribes westward.[2]

No other issue Jackson dealt with would linger and become a historical mark of shame like his uncompromising approach to the question of the Indian tribes. Jackson's dealings and experience with American Indians was long, arduous, and intricate. He had faced them in numerous battles, he respected their fighting skills, and he had good reasons to fear their terror on the frontier. And when he settled on a course of action, he took the one that was most practical—the Indians' removal from the land they lived on, which white people now quite coveted for expansion and settlement. Jackson would send several tribes packing. He moved them across the Mississippi River, far enough away for an early nineteenth-century president to deem both sides of the conflict safe. Indeed, Jackson rationalized that such a course of action would benefit both the tribes and the growing white population. He also considered his policy benevolent given the dire alternative: American Indians' annihilation if they stayed. Yet the tribes' physical removal and uprooting from their land would later be described as a "Trail of Tears." Thousands of Indians perished along the long and slow march.

Though Jackson did not prepare a single message addressing the nation on the Indian question, he said plenty in several public addresses. He often expressed his sentiments without rhetorical flourishes in private letters. On October 12, 1829, he wrote the following to his friend Capt. James Gadsden: "You may rest assured that I shall adhere to the just and humane policy towards the Indians which I have commenced. In this spirit I have recommended them to quit their possessions on this side of the Mississippi, and go to a country in the west where there is every probability that they will always be free from the mercenary influence of White men, and undisturbed by the local authority of the states: Under such circumstances the General Government can exercise a parental control over their interests and possibly perpetuate their race."[3] In this statement, the president summarized his attitude and policy toward tribes. Moving Indians facing growing dangers from local whites was the best approach to saving them.

In ordering tribal removal, Jackson took a decisive step that would even run against the Supreme Court's decision. Due to his experience and knowledge of the tension between whites and Indians, he strongly believed that physical separation was the only way to guarantee the tribes' survival. Jackson noted previous administrations' failure to handle the growing conflict, observing that it was left for him to resolve a miserable situation.

Talks of removal date to the first presidency. George Washington's secretary of war, Henry Knox, sought in 1789 to advance a humane policy toward American Indian tribes. According to Knox, the principle of justice would reject "any neighboring community, however compatible and weak it might be."[4] In 1803, President Jefferson sought the removal of the Cherokees following the Louisiana Purchase. Jefferson considered the Cherokees allies of Great Britain and thus suggested their removal west. He also purposefully sought Indians' accrual of debt through trading with whites so that tribal land could be confiscated when payments were not made.[5] As early as 1809, Governor Blount of Tennessee proposed the transfer of the Cherokees and the Chickasaws west of the Mississippi as the only solution to the growing tension between whites and local Indian tribes.[6] President James Monroe stated in his Sixth Annual Message to Congress, "It is essential to the growth and prosperity of the Territory [Pensacola], as well as to the interests of the Union, that those Indians should be removed."[7] John Quincy Adams tackled the same issue, though more humanely and with reservations.

Where John Quincy Adams vacillated over the tribes' predicament, especially in Georgia, Jackson determined to remove them from their land but also provide compensation for the loss of land transfer. Jackson expressed the principle in play in this statement: "Our national security requires it, and their security requires it . . . It must be done."[8] Even the tribes that were friendly to the popular general and the US government were forced to transfer their land as punishment for not stopping other Creeks from committing raids and killing Americans, and for heeding Tecumseh's order to fight the United States.[9] Despite protestations, Jackson forced peace on the Creeks, who had lost land and crops and were no longer in a position to resist him. Jackson also insisted on feeding and clothing tribal members. He conveyed his ambivalence in a letter to his wife, Rachel, writing, "I know your humanity would feel for them," and identifying the still-unfinished war with Great Britain as the real culprit.[10]

The Indian tribes suffered also for their unintended role in the larger nineteenth-century regional geopolitical battle over North America. This clash engulfed the United States, Great Britain, and Spain. American Indians would also be involved in presidential politics not of their making. In 1818, under orders from General Gains, Jackson was instructed to protect the southern border from the Seminoles. The command from President Monroe carried a specific limitation "not to pass the line" into Florida, which was Spanish territory. The order also instructed Jackson to "exercise a sound discretion as to the necessity of crossing the line," which he read as tacit permission to invade Florida.[11]

Spain and England protested Jackson's expedition into Florida, and the Monroe administration found itself on the defensive. Jackson quickly became the central figure in a high-stakes political controversy. Many in the nation considered him a national hero, but the Washington elite began worrying that his growing popularity—three years after the Battle of New Orleans—would allow for political ascendancy over his military acumen. If Jackson's presidential prospects were to be stopped, some rationalized, now was the time. That Monroe's cabinet included all primary presidential contenders for a post-Monroe era, including John C. Calhoun, Henry Clay, John Quincy Adams, and William Crawford, did not help. These aspirants tried everything to stop Jackson from gaining too much popularity.[12] Calhoun, then the secretary of war, claimed that Jackson violated his instruction not to enter Florida.[13] Calhoun worried that if the United States did not return Pensacola to Spain, another war was upon the nation. Others called for Jackson's censure.[14] Monroe, however, refused, lending some credence to Jackson's later contention that they had an informal understanding.

This entire episode would surface during the 1828 campaign and the early years of Jackson's presidency. Calhoun, the prime instigator of the nullification debate, made it a particular focus. In his view, Jackson's strong advocacy of the federal government superseding the states during nullification did not look good because he had earlier sided with the State of Georgia over its Cherokees and the dispute over their land.[15] Jackson, however, benefitted from siding with Georgia over its treatment of the Indians since this action afforded him "proof" that he was not completely opposed to states' rights.

The tension between the tribes and the State of Georgia was precipitated when President John Quincy Adams and Georgia governor George M. Troup clashed over the Cherokees, who declared themselves an independent nation in 1827. The governor, fearing that federal troops' arrival entering his state would provoke a civil war, threatened to use Georgia troops to defend the state's "sovereignty." As the state took over the Cherokees' lands, the tribe appealed to the Supreme Court for an injunction but lost on a technicality. Importantly, though, the court maintained that the Cherokees had a right to their land but not to file a lawsuit against the federal government. A year later the Supreme Court affirmed the Cherokee Nation as a political entity, and it declared that Georgia laws had no effect inside its borders. Both Jackson, now president, and the State of Georgia had no intention of following the court's ruling. Within this context Jackson supposedly uttered, "John Marshall has made his decision, now let him enforce it."[16] The president likely did not make this statement, but it has been attributed to him nonetheless.

As noted earlier, Jackson included no statement regarding the tribes when drafting his Inaugural Address. This omission ought to mean that for strategic reasons, a clause regarding the tribes was inserted later, most likely constrained by his predecessors' statements in their Inaugural Addresses.[17] Jackson provided strong hints of the direction he would pursue in key phrases such as "humane," "our people," "dependent situation," and "our national character."

In his March 23, 1829, letter to the Creek Indians, Jackson took a markedly different approach from the oblique statement in his inaugural speech. Addressing his "Friends & Brothers," he told them, "I . . . now speak to you as your father and friend, and request you to listen." He expressed love for his "white and red children," and promised to "always speak straight" to them, "and not with a forked tongue." "I have always told you the truth," he reminded the Creeks. The president also voiced displeasure with some of the tribes' "bad men" who had murdered a white man in Georgia, stating, "Where you now are, you and my white children are too near to each other to live in harmony and peace. Your game is destroyed and many of your people will not work and till the land." Jackson asked the Creeks to move beyond the Mississippi, where other tribes had gone. There, he asserted, "your white brothers will not trouble you; they will have no claim to the land, and you can live upon it."

Jackson then added a biographical account, reminding the tribe that he had told them "many years ago . . . of this new country, where [they] might be preserved as a great nation, and where [their] white brothers would not disturb [them]." "Where you live now," he declared, "your white brothers have always claimed the land. The land beyond the Mississippi belongs to the President and to none else; and he will give it to you forever."[18] Patronizing the tribes or just following the whites' customary style of addressing them, Jackson sought to cash in on his credibility. He had spent many years clashing with Indians, fighting them and negotiating with them on behalf of the federal government. The president was now ready to make a drastic move, telling the tribes they had no other choice given whites' encroachment.

Jackson's initial draft of his First Annual Message to Congress sheds much light on his plan and overall attitude toward the Indian tribes. He offered a sympathetic view of their plight and summarized past efforts to civilize them. But he objected to American Indians' attempts at self-government, which he considered impractical. "No people were ever free, or capable of forming & carrying into execution a social compact for themselves until education & intelligence was first introduced," he stated.[19] For Jackson, education and intelligence were necessary for progress and potential self-government, and were foundational to American democracy. The tribes lacked these qualities and thus could not ask for self-governance while residing among those who were more civilized. In any event, stated Jackson, since many preferred to maintain their own ways, "it [could not] be conceded to them to continue their efforts at independence within the limits of any of the States."[20] They had to pass "beyond the Mississippi," despite the reality that they "were once the uncontroled [sic] & indisputable owners of this immense region of country." American Indians had been "yielding from time to time to the solicitations of their white brethren, until they [were] only to be found far in the interior." Now, opined Jackson, "it is but Justice that a proper degree of sympathy should be awakened in [sic] their behalf."[21]

Either Jackson was truly benevolent, or he added a dose of humanity to his remarks at the urging of many. Yet his term "uncontrolled" appears to be a legalistic reference and a subtle suggestion that the tribes could not claim legal rights to lands they presumably owned outright. Jackson ended the lengthy portion of his remarks devoted to the tribes by referencing a balancing act: "Generous feeling is entertained towards this race, it should not be at the sacrifice of principles, and of the interests of others concerned." Put differently, they believed the sovereignty of the states could not accommodate a separate sovereignty within, and that "power [could not] be concurrent." With this principle stated, Jackson asked and began to answer a rhetorical question: "What then is to be done? Let the plan of removal beyond the Mississippi."[22] The sentence ends abruptly and Jackson's thoughts are incomplete.

Secretary of War Eaton also forwarded the president a draft centering exclusively on Indian removal. Eaton continued the passage that Jackson abandoned, pointing to the primary dilemma facing the federal government: not implementing removal would "require the Executive to enforce it [separate sovereignty within the states] by the employment of a military force," that "would trample upon the rights of the states and the liberty of the Country." The Secretary of War further wrote, "It is a power that should be placed in the hands of no individual; the consequences & dangers to which it might lead, are so obvious that no reason on it, seems to be uncalled for & unnecessary."[23]

In his draft, Eaton acknowledged previous governments' many errors in addressing the tribes: "[Since 1814] they have been called upon the assist in our wars without any exercise of opinions & discretion on their part." The government, he added, sought to restrain "intrusion upon Indian lands" dating back to the Indian Intercourse Act of 1802. But different states had developed inconsistent policies regarding the tribal property within their borders. Eaton also noted the difference in the federal government's treatment of American Indians in southern states and those in northern ones. Northern tribes' experience was more positive while southern states pressed their jurisdiction over Indian lands. The federal government, Eaton stated, could not prevent the states from exerting their jurisdiction. He described the solution to the tribes as follows: "[Either] they give obedience to the laws as others residing in the states must do; or if dissatisfied . . . remove to the west, where they can be maintained under their own customs." The government would help the tribes "with the spirit of kindness" and "agree to defray their expenses, supply the means of transportation, & grant supplies to their families for a year." Removal would be a better solution, Eaton reiterated, "while the contest between the general & state governments, [could] give assurance of nothing that [was] agreeable or cheering."[24] The legal entanglement between the states and the federal governments, then, complicated matters to the point of threatening the tribes' safety.[25]

In his First Annual Message, Jackson assumed the rhetorical perspective that he had no choice but to recommend removal given the facts on the ground. The alternative would be devastating and dangerous. He was left, he stated, with a tough decision that previous administrations had hesitated to take, and the situation had gotten much worse. Yet this was not Jackson's best argument. As had been his practice, the president preferred a constitutional cover. Clearly, he presented an inconsistent picture. Jackson at once claimed that tribes' lack of civilization precluded them from residing among white people, and that the Constitution principally prohibited such a construction. He ignored the fact that the Supreme Court had actually ruled in favor of the tribes as an entity within a state.

Explaining the matter further, Jackson asked what would have happened if the constitutional principle were not operative. In such a case, "Would the people of Maine permit the Penobscot tribe to erect an independent government within their state?" Or would the people of New York allow the

Six Nations to do the same? Would other states act similarly, thus establishing separate republics within different states? These rhetorical questions would yield the obvious answer—that the tribes of Georgia and Alabama could not establish a separate independent government, and that the US government had advised these Indians "to emigrate beyond the Mississippi or submit to the laws of those states."[26] Jackson employed a generally weak and inconsistent rhetorical approach to his case for tribal removal, mixing practical and constitutional arguments. In the end, his syllogistic reasoning pointed to removal as the only viable option.

Jackson modified his overall tone relative to the drafts but remained direct nonetheless. He assumed the role of a benevolent leader surveying the tribes' history and providing conclusions. "Their present condition," he narrated (leaving portions of his draft intact), "contrasted with what they once were, makes a most powerful appeal to our sympathies." Early settlers found American Indians "the uncontrolled possessors of these vast regions." The president continued, "By persuasion and force they have been made to retire from river to river and from mountain to mountain, until some tribes have become extinct and others have left but remnants to preserve for a while their once terrible names." Jackson advanced a historical portrayal of the tribes' gradual fall from great heights. He did not minimize whites' responsibility for the demise of tribal cultures, yet he noted that long-gone tribes' fate awaited those still remaining "within the limits of the states."[27] The benevolent tribute to the tribes' past did not diminish the impact of Jackson's careful description of Indians as "uncontrolled possessors" of "vast regions" but not, significantly, as owners of specific land. Hence, their removal from land already questioned any legal claim they had made to its ownership.

Jackson acknowledged, "[The nation's] conduct toward these people is deeply interesting to our national character," and "humanity and national honor demand that every effort should be made to avert so great a calamity." Indeed, as the tribes' treatment would reflect on the nation's character, the current attitude of benevolence was the correct one. With this observation, Jackson ever so subtly acknowledged the influence of many who sympathized with the tribes. Yet Indian removal was conditioned by historical forces and by implication; it was not the fault of anyone in particular. Now, the government had to develop a practicable solution to avoid calamity. The agent—Jackson—was thus absolved of ill will, and the tribes' removal was the agency of the lesser of all evils, benefitting both the tribes and white people. Jackson added that it was "too late to inquire whether it was just in the United States to include them and their territory within the bounds of new states, whose limits they could control." And since it was too late for that, he said, "that step can not be retracted."[28]

Now, Jackson stated, "actuated by feelings of justice and a regard for our national honor, "[I] submit to you the interesting question whether something can not be done, consistently with the rights of the states, to preserve this much-injured race." Jackson publicly activated the principles of humanity, honor, and justice in suggesting "the propriety of setting apart an ample district west of the Mississippi for their [American Indians'] future residence." He foresaw several tribes living across the Mississippi and "subject to no other control from the United States than such as [might] be necessary to preserve peace on the frontier and between several tribes." The president even conceived a union of tribes, a commonwealth of sorts, "destined to perpetuate the race and to attest the humanity and justice of this government." Jackson hoped for a voluntary removal since it would be "cruel and unjust to compel the aborigines to abandon the graves of their fathers and seek a home in a distant land." Alternatively, he declared, "they should be distinctly informed that if they remain within the limits of the states they must be subject to their laws."[29]

Jackson had one more significant point to make. Tribes could not claim tracts of land "on which they [had] neither dwelt nor made improvements, merely because they [had] seen them from the mountain or passed them in the chase."[30] American Indians' claims to vast lands, forests, and lakes made no sense to early nineteenth-century settlers.[31] Now Jackson further explicated his previous reference to "uncontrolled possessors," taking a rather direct tone. Those wishing to stay, he iterated, had to submit to and be protected by the laws of the state like all other citizens. These individuals also had to hope that in the long run they could be "merged in the mass of our population."[32] Despite the Supreme Court's ruling, Jackson thus rejected the argument against an independent state within a state.

Though Jackson would say more in other addresses, he stated everything he wanted to in this one. He wished this issue to be settled soon, and he would see the legislation he advocated pass in his first year in office. The Senate voted 28 to 19 for removal, with the chief argument that this measure was the only way to save the tribes. The vote in the House, however, was extremely close—102 for and 98 against. Approved and signed on May 28, 1830, the Indian Removal Act garnered support from the majority of southern states and opposition from the majority of northern states.[33] Jackson savvily pushed for the removal vote before coming out with his Maysville

Veto. He correctly calculated that the Removal Act might have been defeated had he presented the two measures in reverse. The close vote did not bode well for a controversial policy, yet the strong opposition to an overall harsh measure did not dissuade Jackson from forcing tribes to accept removal.

On August 23, 1830, Jackson sent a message to the Chickasaw Indians. Secretary of War John Eaton and Gen. John Coffee, the commissioners designated to meet with the tribe's delegates, read the president's remarks. In this lengthy address, Jackson assured the twenty Chickasaw representatives of his "continued friendship." Though he had agreed to the meeting per their request, the delegates had refused to meet with him. Now, "by an act [of Congress it was placed] in his power to extend justice to the Indians, to pay the expences [*sic*] of their removal, to support them for twelve months, and to give them a grant for lands which should endure 'as long as the grass grows or water run.'" Justifying their removal, Jackson narrated the tribes' past glory before whites settled near them. At present, Jackson said, "states have been created within your limits which claim a right to govern and control your people as their own citizens; and to make them answerable to their civil and criminal laws. Your great Father has not the authority to prevent this state of things." He added, "[These laws are not oppressive,] for they are those to which your white brothers conform and are happy." Such laws ought to mean that the tribes cannot "be permitted to seek private revenge." This way, they could enjoy the same benefits as white people. Thus the choice was adjusting to states' laws or, if tribal happiness could only be preserved through keeping "ancient habits," facing removal.

Jackson was quick to tell the Chickasaws, "There is no unkindness in the offers made to you," and "No intention or wish is had to force you [from] your lands; but rather to advice [*sic*] you to your own interest." The president acknowledged the tribes' attachment to "the [bones] of [their] ancestors." But he also stated, "Our forefathers had the same feeling, when a long time ago, to obtain happiness they left their lands beyond the Great waters and sought a new and quiet home in those distant and unexplored regions." Finally, Jackson asked that the delegates attend to this "serious consideration" and indicate the terms of their removal if they agreed to it. But, Jackson added, if you "determine to remain where you are candidly say so, & let us be done with this subject no more to be talked of again."[34] Though his sentiments resembled those in his First Annual Message, Jackson addressed the Chickasaws straightforwardly, hoping to impress them with a fait accompli. He sought to ease the pain of removal by suggesting analogically (an argumentative strain he would use time and again), a deterministic view of the world and its history. Removal could be justified as just another chapter in people's lives. Nonetheless, the president offered a naïve appeal comparing Indians' and whites' different circumstances and motivations and rejecting the cultural significance of each.

Yet legal and political challenges remained, and several tribes' refusal to move across the Mississippi continuously frustrated Jackson. He blamed corrupt white advisors for complicating matters. Writing to Maj. William B. Lewis on August 25, 1830, Jackson described the difficulties of negotiating with the tribes and referenced the Creeks' refusal to meet government officials. He repeated a point in his address to the Chickasaw tribal delegates: "We leave them to themselves, and to the protection of their friend Mr. Wirt . . . to whom they have given a large fee to protect them in their rights as an independent Nation; and when they find that they cannot live under the laws of Alabama, they must find, at their own expence [sic], and by their own means, a country, and a home."[35] Jackson considered William Wirt in particular a "truly wicked" person. In persuading the Creeks to refuse to move across the Mississippi, Wirt ignored the reality that such a denial would "lead to the destruction of the poor ignorant Indians."[36] In a spirit of frustration and resignation, Jackson added, "I have used all the persuasive means in my power. I have exonerated the national character from all imputation, and now leave the poor deluded Creeks and Cherokees to their fate, and their annihilation, which their wicked advisers has [sic] induced."[37]

The federal government, in Jackson's mind, had done all it could. Any refusal to abide by the safe course it carved for the tribes could not be pinned on the United States, and neither could its national character be impugned thereof. The president ended the letter on a more hopeful note, wishing that "the Indians [would] now think for themselves, and send to the City [Washington] a delegation prepared to cede their country and move X [across] the M [Mississippi]."[38] A much frustrated Jackson put in letter what he had to say more cautiously in public. Though his tone differed, his overall sentiments were the same. As a corrective, the letter is nevertheless instructive for its consistency with Jackson's public pronouncements.

In another letter to William B. Lewis on August 31, 1830, Jackson reported that the Chickasaws had signed the treaty and agreed to cross the Mississippi in 1832. The president added, "Thus far we have succeeded, against the most corrupt & secrete [sic] combination that ever did exist, and we have preserved my Chickasaw friends and red brethren."[39] On September 29, 1830, Brig. Gen. John Coffee informed Jackson that all five to six thousand Choctaws had also signed the treaty and agreed to move. The general wrote, "The terms allowed them are liberal, as you instructed us to make for their comfort, yet I think it is a good treaty for the U. States."[40]

In early December 1830, Jackson outlined the topics he wished to include in his Second Annual Message to Congress. He listed eleven items, and under item six, titled "War Department," he included the following matters: "Military academy—Indians—The course pursued since last cession [sic] under The Act of Congress—The result."[41] Jackson was eager to report some successes of the Indian Removal Act of May 26, 1830; he hoped that positive news would entice other tribes to follow suit. The portions of the Second Annual Message devoted to Indian tribes required extensive drafting, thus making the address rather important. Jackson was the first to draft this passage. Donelson and Kendall then worked off his draft. The objective now was to show the Removal Act's achievements precisely because it remained controversial. As a result, the president again explicated the act's legal grounding. Moreover, he and his aides included an extensive narrative appealing to the sentiments of many, especially those with strong feelings about the unjust removal.

In his Second Annual Message of December 6, 1830,[42] Jackson made his most elaborate case for Indian removal. Though he addressed the case of the tribes in Georgia, he covered the general circumstances of Indian tribes. In his reflective message, Jackson sought to persuade Congress and the nation that the removal policy was necessary. The close vote in the House and its nationwide implications likely convinced the president to forward a kinder justification for the Removal Act. The removal policy was described as "benevolent," and it accounted for more than thirty years of various governments' treatment of the tribes. Two tribes, announced Jackson, had already agreed to move. The removal of others, he said, "will be important to the United States, to individual States, and to the Indians themselves."

Jackson quickly refuted the notion that the policy presented "pecuniary advantages" to the government (in the materiality of land) and, therefore, the chief reason for advocating removal. No doubt, sending the tribes far away would open vast lands to whites. Jackson justified the Removal Act by stating, "It will incalculably strengthen the southwestern frontier and render the adjacent States strong enough to repel future invasions without remote aid." Frontier security, then, more than land acquisition was Jackson's primary objective. Though consistent with his long-standing concern with the porous frontier and its risks to settlers, Jackson did not use this inventive argument in advancing Indian removal. Nor did he mention this reasoning in his First Annual Message—hence its likely expediency.[43]

Jackson did acknowledge that tribal removal would enable several states "to advance rapidly in population, wealth, and power." He further noted, "It will separate the Indians from immediate contact with settlements of whites; free them from the power of the States; enable them to pursue happiness in their own way and under their own rude institutions; will retard the progress of decay, which is lessening their numbers, and perhaps cause them gradually, under the protection of the Government . . . to cast off their savage habits and become an interesting, civilized and Christian community."[44] Jackson repeated the conventional wisdom of the time—whites' vocation to civilize the "uncivilized" and show them the light of the Christian faith. As whites pursued this calling, Indian tribes would cease their savage ways and improve on their "rude institutions."[45]

Jackson was convinced of his good intentions concerning Indian tribes: "Toward the aborigines of the country no one can indulge a more friendly feeling than myself, or would go further in attempting to reclaim them from their wandering habits and make them a happy, prosperous people." He also opined that, though people may have their own opinion about how to treat the tribes, "as a Government we [had] as little right to control them as we [had] to prescribe laws for other nations." Jackson sought to distance himself from people's opinion about the act of removal—which was quite negative in some quarters—to argue the government's limitation in controlling other nations. His pseudo legalistic perspective essentially considered the tribes a separate nation whose residence could only be sustained outside states' jurisdiction. The rhetorical distance Jackson inserted into the equation allowed many to consider the tribes not as indigenous people but as a foreign nation. This very reality mandated treating them like any other foreign entity. Accordingly, the president asserted, the government offered a liberal policy toward the tribes. Since they "[had] preferred maintaining their independence in the Western forests to submitting to the laws of the States in which they now reside," he argued, their removal was the only option left. Jackson also added a threat, calling the proffered treaty "probably the last which [would] ever be made with them."[46] Jackson saw himself as the president who would find a solution to the Indian issue. None of his predecessors was willing or able to pursue this feat.

Jackson did not discuss the weakest points of his policy—that the tribes preferred staying to being removed, and that the issue at hand was not the laws of the states but the hostility and prejudice of white people. Jackson came closest to seeing the issue from the tribes' perspective with this statement: "If it be their real interest to maintain a separate existence, they will there [west of the Mississippi] be at liberty to do so without the inconveniences and vexations to which they would unavoidably have been subject in Alabama and Mississippi." The president was fully aware of the prejudicial attitudes toward the tribes. Yet for his public statements he preferred to highlight the benevolent treaty, enumerating the "liberal sum in consideration of their removal, and comfortable subsistence on their arrival at their new homes."[47]

Jackson also presented a historical perspective on the matter of the tribes' removal. Though he believed in benevolence and empathy whereby "humanity ha[d] often wept over the fate of the aborigines of this country," he nevertheless asserted, "Progress has never for a moment been arrested, and one by one have many powerful tribes disappeared from the earth." With a dose of historical determinism, Jackson put the current situation in the context of natural progression whereby "the extinction of one generation" was necessary in order "to make room for another." He subsequently stated, "[There is nothing which] upon a comprehensive view of the general interests of the human race, is to be regretted." The fate of the tribes had now to be accepted in the larger context of human evolution and progress; the trajectory of human nature moved forward. In any event, Jackson asked, "What good man would prefer a country covered with forests and ranged by a few thousand savages to our extensive Republic, studded with cities, towns, and prosperous farms, embellished with all the improvements which art can devise or industry execute, occupied by more than 12,000,000 happy people, and filled with all the blessings of liberty, civilization, and religion"?[48]

True to the progressive ideals of his time, Jackson believed in expanding the nation's territory and encouraging many to move westward in search of new opportunities. Whites stood for the values of improvements, liberty, progress, civilization, and religion, and it was their time to determine the country's future. The tribes stood in the way of this manifestation of historical and material reality. They had to move, in Jackson's words, just as earlier "tribes which occupied the countries now constituting the Eastern States were annihilated or [had] melted away to make room for the whites." Believing his policy continued those of previous governments, Jackson stated bluntly, "We now propose to acquire the countries occupied by the red men of the South and West by a fair exchange, and, at the expense of the United States to send them to a land where their existence may be prolonged."[49] The president then added a fatalistic note to his address. He suggested that, while westward removal could prolong tribes' existence, earlier American

Indians' disappearance meant that the same fate could await those now seeking to save their way of life by refusing to move.

Jackson acknowledged that Indians would find it "painful to leave the graves of their fathers." Yet, their experience would be no different from that of white Americans' forebears and children. People always moved "to better their condition in an unknown land." Now, Jackson asserted, "Our children by thousands yearly leave the land of their birth to seek new homes in distant regions." He took the defensive, seeking the best argument to assuage the strong opposition to Indian removal and finding it in comparative experiences whites could relate to. The president asked rhetorically, "Does humanity weep at these painful separations from everything, animate and inanimate, with which the young heart has become entwined? Far from it." Many move, stated Jackson, "hundreds and almost thousands of miles at their expense, purchase the lands they occupy, and support themselves at their new homes from the moment of their arrival." By comparison, Jackson suggested, the tribes should be grateful for the financial assistance the government had offered. "Can it be cruel," he asked, "when, by events which it can not control, the Indian is made discontented in his ancient home to purchase his lands, to give him a new and extensive territory, to pay the expense of the removal, and support him a year in his new abode?"[50]

Jackson's comparison ignored the obvious—that the tribes' culture, and ways of life were detrimental to their connection to the land and ancestors. But he intended his address more for whites than for tribal members. He sought to put the removal of people under the heading of progress, yet he overlooked the disparate reasons for it: progress as a choice and progress as an imposition. Whites' migration to the western territory and tribes' forced relocation were hardly the same, except for the fact that both groups traveled in the same direction.

Jackson wanted to present an inevitable situation in the best light, and he suggested as much when stating that events could not be controlled. The alternative would be "utter annihilation," a point he raised in an earlier letter. Thus Jackson strategized that the benevolent offer would convince many that the help the government offered "toward the red man" "[was] not only liberal, but generous." Jackson hoped that even zealous objectors to tribal removal "[would] unite in attempting to open the eyes of those children of the forest to their true condition, and by a speedy removal to relieve them from all the evils, real or imaginary, present or prospective, with which they [might] be supposed to be threatened."[51] In summarizing his policy and its appeal, Jackson subtly questioned those opposing the removal, asking whether they were exaggerating the evil they described, and whether they were being unrealistic about the tribes' plight. In the president's opinion, removal was the best option, and other alternatives could be worse.

The Second Message is quite straightforward. Jackson designed it as a comprehensive argumentative tract justifying a controversial policy anchored on securing the frontier and ensuring expansion to new lands. The president delivered a manifest for white progress. At the same time, he portrayed the tribes as belonging to an old civilization that refused to move with the times. Jackson revealed his overall attitude toward American Indians when he described them as "savage hunters," "children of the forest," "red m[e]n," and "wandering savage." He could not have emphasized a clearer dichotomy between the races, especially within the context of his progressive era and its westward orientation.

The delay in the actual removal of the tribes concerned Jackson; he was anxious to put the issue behind him. On September 7, 1831, he wrote to General Coffee, "I am anxious to hear from you whether you are likely to make with the Choctaws, the necessary arrangements for the accommodations of the Chickasaws, within the boundary of the Choctaws west of the Mississippi. This is a subject of great importance to us, and if made, will induce the Creeks and Cherokees to remove."[52] When the Senate opted to "inquire into the moral character of the Agent employed by [Andrew Jackson] to negotiate treaties with the several bands of Indians residing within that state [presumably Ohio]," Jackson made it clear that he understood the inquiry as a form of opposition to the treaty. He added that, even if the agent in question "conclusively proved that he is a bad man, that fact would in no manner affect the validity of the Treaties or enlighten the Senate in relation to their duties."[53] In private, Jackson made it clear that the removal treaty would be implemented no matter what.

Indeed, Jackson's usual nemeses tried to use the treaty to hurt him, just as they would use the Bank of the United States. When the Supreme Court was asked to adjudicate the matter of two missionaries residing among the Cherokees against the State of Georgia's prohibition, it ruled in *Worcester v. Georgia* in favor of the missionaries. In its March 3, 1832, decision, the Supreme Court declared the State of Georgia's laws unconstitutional.[54]

Some historians believe that at this juncture Jackson retorted, "Well, John Marshall has made his decision, now let him enforce it." Horace Greeley, rather than Jackson, likely made this statement. The context for this declaration lay in the reality that once the Supreme Court ruled on the issue, the decision would be sent back to the Superior Court of Georgia. Once the Georgia court failed to act accordingly, the Supreme Court was in recess. Nothing would come out of the Supreme Court's decision until it reconvened. In the meantime, Jackson could do nothing legally, and events on the ground could be detrimental to the tribes.[55] The Indians' fate was now an open question, and the president feared local whites would subject tribes to a potentially devastating attack.

Whether for the situation on the ground, or the larger fait accompli, a treaty was reached with the Creeks, "who had ceded all their lands East of the Mississippi River to the United States with certain reservations to chiefs & heads of families."[56] The Senate ratified the treaty, and the vote was unanimous after Clay and Calhoun failed to generate an effective opposition. The removal plan called for surveyors to complete their work so that lands could be sold. However, the Chickasaws still hoped to get the Supreme Court to issue an injunction against Georgia. Jackson was particularly concerned with this tribe that fought to stay. He worried that if the court did not issue the injunction, "one regiment of militia could not be got to march to save [the Chickasaws] from destruction." He asserted, "This the opposition know, and if a collision was to take place between them & the Georgians, the arm of the Government is not sufficiently strong to preserve them from destruction."[57]

This, for Jackson, was the crux of the matter and probably a correct one—the tribes faced real danger unless they moved far away from whites. Jackson was aware of those who protested the treaty and the removal of the tribes, commenting, "Surely the religious enthusiasts, or those who have been weeping over the oppression of the Indians will not find fault with it [the treaty] for want of liberality or justice to the Indians." He added, "We want them in a state of safety removed from the states & free from collision with the whites, & if the land does this it is well disposed of and freed from being a corruption source to our Legislation."[58]

In his Fourth Annual Message, Jackson devoted one paragraph to the tribes' situation, informing Congress that despite "the strongest disposition on the part of the Government to deal justly and liberally with [them]," the Cherokees of Georgia had rejected their removal. He mentioned how anxious he was "to remove all the grounds of complaint and to bring to a termination the difficulties in which they [were] involved."[59] Opposition to Jackson's treatment of the tribes constituted a serious setback to his rhetorical efforts.

Overall, Jackson exhibited practicality with regard to the Indian tribes.

He understood the one particular force that stood in the way of all those opposing Indian removal—the State of Georgia would expel the Cherokees no matter what. Jackson was under no illusion that events would scuttle the Supreme Court decision. Realizing that federal troops could not be on hand in time to protect the tribes, he saw no other choice but their removal. He thus pressed the Cherokees to sign the treaty, assuming all along that he was their savior.

THE SECOND TERM

On March 3, 1833, the day before assuming the presidency for his second term, Jackson wrote Robert J. Chester to inform him that the Senate had ratified the treaty with the Chickasaws. The president appointed Chester surveyor for the purpose of settling the tribes across the Mississippi.[60] Yet when drafting the Second Inaugural Address (the text is in his own handwriting, and it was presumably written before the letter to Robert J. Chester), Jackson made no mention of the tribes' situation, just as he had avoided the issue while drafting the First Inaugural Address. In contrast to his first inaugural speech, Jackson included no reference to Indian removal in his second inaugural speech. He would henceforth say very little in public concerning tribes. Once the Removal Act had been passed and ratified, and several tribes had reluctantly accepted it, Jackson felt no need to address the issue. The Bank of the United States was front and center during his second term, and it would occupy most of his time. Even so, tribal removal remained a sore point involving local and legal challenges. Jackson would be slightly more forthcoming in private, enough to gauge his views on the matter during his second term.

Jackson addressed the Indians' situation at the end of his Fifth Annual Message to Congress, stating as a matter of fact the passing of several treaties with local tribes to relinquish territories and move westward. Now, the president hoped the remaining southern tribes would finalize their plans to move as well:

> The only remaining difficulties, will realize the necessity of emigration, and will speedily resort to it. My original convictions upon this subject have been confirmed by the course of events for several years, and experience is every day adding to their strength. That those tribes can not exist surrounded by our settlements and in continual contact with

our citizens is certain. They have neither the intelligence, the industry, the moral habits, nor the desire of improvement which are essential to any favorable change in their condition. Established in the midst of another and a superior race, and without appreciating the causes of their inferiority or seeking to control them, they must necessarily yield to the force of circumstances and ere long disappear."[61]

Biographer Remini notes that "Jackson's hideous, not to mention racist, judgment was stated flatly without the slightest realization that it was hideous or racist. Quite simply, it was typical of American thought in 1833."[62] Since Jackson kept repeating this line of thinking about the tribes' inferiority relative to whites, one is hard-pressed to disagree with this observation.

Difficulties with southern tribes continued as several of them refused removal. Jackson, however, was determined: "[Since] the Government of the U.S. has promised them [the tribes] protection, it will perform its obligations to the tittle."[63] He issued this instruction after violence erupted and one John Walker Jr. was shot. In a September 15, 1834, letter to Jackson, John Ross, head of the Coosa tribe, refuted the president's assertion that the tribes were responsible for the murder. Ross demanded protection from Jackson and profusely denied American Indians' involvement in the crime.[64] Writing Jackson again on January 23, 1835, he explicated the "continued unavailing struggle against the Cruel policy of Georgia." Ross stated, "On the part of that State, it [the policy] has been One, of unparalleled aggravated Acts of Oppression upon the Nation. Actuated by an inextinguishable love of Country, Confiding implicitly in the good faith of the American Govt." Ross continued to complain about how Georgia had defied the US Congress and the Supreme Court. He observed that "armed bands of her Citizens [were] now parading thro' their Country," terrorizing tribes who were hoping for the Supreme Court's reversal of their removal to Arkansas. Now Ross asked Jackson, "Upon what terms will the President negotiate for a final termination of those sufferings, that their people may repose in peace and comfort on the land of their nativity under the enjoyment of such rights and privileges as belonging to freemen."[65]

In his Sixth Annual Message, Jackson stated, "No important change has during this season taken place in the condition of the Indians." Creeks and Seminoles were arranging their removal, and some Cherokee tribes had yet to decide on the move. The president opined, "The experience of every year adds to the conviction that emigration, and that alone, can preserve from the destruction the remnant of the tribes yet living among us."[66]

On May 25, 1835, Jackson received a letter from William A. Underwood indicating that Ross was doing everything in his power to prevent the Cherokees from agreeing to their removal (and that he would likely fail). But in the meantime, Underwood said, the Cherokee Nation "shall be so far mislead by him as they reject the very liberal offer now made them it will be long before the difficulty Can be settled and in the meantime the Common Indians will be ruined."[67] This is precisely what Jackson feared. In hindsight, he was prescient to suggest that removal from Georgia was the only way to save the tribes from whites' wrath.

On May 20, 1835, Gov. Wilson Lumpkin of Georgia wrote Jackson that all attempts to reverse removal would fail since the "Indians [could not] live in the midst of a White population and be governed by the same laws." Lumpkin was also appalled and "truly disgusted" to "reflect upon the enormous frauds . . . committed upon the Indians by a small, but abandoned and selfish portion of our white population." Under current conditions, he wrote, "we are unable to retrain and punish these enormities." At the same time, the governor enumerated menace, injury, and murder committed by tribal members. Therefore, he added, many whites "are living in a state of constant apprehension." Lumpkin summed his account with rhetorical questions: "Have not these Indians lost all just claims to national character? Ought not these Indians to be considered and treated as the helpless wards of the Federal Government?"[68] The tribes' plight in Georgia had worsened due to unscrupulous white advisors and a hostile population bent on pushing them out. Jackson ended the presidency with the issue not fully resolved. The worst was yet to come.

Jackson said nothing about the tribes in his Seventh Annual Message to Congress. But he could not avoid briefly referencing the situation in his last Annual Message, delivered on December 5, 1836. Skirmishes on the Florida frontier likely prompted these remarks. Yet the president stated that "the protection of our frontier settlements from the incursions of the enemy" called for military action, especially due to the "savage inroads" of the Indians. He also declared, "Difficulties apprehended in the Cherokee country have been prevented, and the peace and safety of that region and its vicinity effectually secured."[69] The irony of Jackson ending his presidency with a reference to fighting Indians on the frontier brought his lifelong battles with the tribes full circle.

THE AFTERMATH

On August 27, 1837, after his presidency, Jackson wrote Secretary of War Joel R. Poinsett about the lessons his long experience with the Indians had taught him: "They are only to be well governed by their fears. If we feed their avarice we accelerate the causes of their destruction. By a prudent exertion of our military power we may yet do something to alleviate their condition at the same time that we certainly take from them the means of injury to our frontier." Ever concerned with the growing nation's safety, Jackson followed with his suggestion to build a "cordon of forts on our western frontier" to protect it from potential American Indian attacks.[70] From the beginning of his military career to the end of his political career, one primary objective—defending the frontier—conditioned Jackson's negative view of American Indian tribes. He was a man of the frontier who believed in westward expansion and the justness of this cause. His words and actions were consistent throughout his life.

Jackson's overall policy and its rhetorical manifestations stemmed from his keen understanding of frontier life, his close familiarity with the tribes, and his acute reading of the growing tension between whites and Indians. Though he did not establish the removal policy, he believed in it as the situation on the ground worsened. Jackson understood both parties to the conflict. If anything, he attempted to portray a strife that would become worse unless a separation between the warring parties soon took place. Jackson also understood his audiences. He recognized the plight of the tribes and their growing desperation while living among whites. He comprehended the uncompromising local feelings and local and state officials' corrupt handling of the Indians' affairs. And at the same time, Jackson witnessed a youthful nation eager to expand territorially. Moreover, the president scoffed at the federal government he headed, especially the judicial branch and its unrealistic assessment of the situation. Ultimately, the solution—removing tribes west of the Mississippi—was consistent with Jackson's long-standing plan formulated over his many years of fighting them before becoming president. After assuming the presidency, he saw nothing that would change his mind. The tribes had to go, and Jackson considered his plan a benevolent one.

No other president knew the tribes as intimately as Jackson did. Though twenty-first century judgment would render the seventh president insensitive and cruel, many of his contemporaries shared his sentiments. Jackson's views were borne of his several decades' experience with savagery on both sides of the Indian-white conflict. Multiple attacks and retaliations meant that it was no longer clear what cruel act preceded other ones. Like most whites, Jackson considered American Indian tribes un-Christian, uncivilized, unruly, and different. He saw their situation through simplistic dichotomous lenses—civilization versus barbarism, culture versus savagery, Christianity versus heathenism, and modernity versus backwardness. This perspective translated rhetorically to a list of principles guiding Jackson's public and private statements. Often resorting to familial and paternalistic metaphors, the president applied authoritarian rhetoric to tribal matters. He was prone to lecturing American Indians.[71] As early as 1815 and through 1821, when serving as the primary negotiator with the tribes, Jackson spoke to their members in patronizing, harsh language. Jason Black describes Jackson's words as "the rhetoric of dominance in the vein of pretentious grandiosity."[72]

Jackson also prided himself that when he addressed the tribes he was benevolent but more importantly truthful. Consider this statement to Creek chiefs: "Have I not by the orders of your father the President sent goods into the Nation, to cloath [sic] you and your naked woman [sic] and children . . . Listen I send you true talk. You know I have never deceived or told you lies, and I now tell you if you listen to the talk of wicked men . . . you will bring immediate destruction on your selves."[73] Historian Walter Russell Mead argues "that Jackson was fixated on viewing the American polity as a family," and that this view undergirded American nationalism as well as allowed "white control over the entire continent in the name of Manifest Destiny."[74] Calling the tribes "red children," argues Black, was a silencing device that helped Jackson's authoritarian and fatherhood rhetoric. The by-product of this language allowed Jackson to argue whites' moral superiority over American Indians.[75]

Just as civilized whites had uprooted themselves from their land to build new homes, the tribes had now to do the same in the name of progress. Jackson could not see the matter in any other way. Neither did he believe in American Indians' ability to "learn" the civilized ways of the whites. His guiding principles were few but detrimental to the tribes: the country was expanding, foreign powers continued to challenge the United States and constantly disrupt the tribes, and attacks on the frontier caused much fear. Thus, securing the frontier was essential for the young nation. Jackson's overall approach to tribal policy was rhetorical and not legal. He calculated how to convince many of the need to remove the tribes despite legal challenges and protestations against his inhumane policy. As a result, Jackson developed a rhetorical stance that was strategically reserved. Yet his actions were harsh. The president knew that removal was painful and had generated much criticism. For this very reason, he dwelt in his public addresses on the government's compassionate, generous attendance to the tribes' situation. Jackson sought in his public statements a moderate tone replete with a sense of understanding historical forces. He presented Indian removal as scenic rhetoric—not a measure of his doing, but rather the consequence of larger forces and constraints he had to tackle.

Andrew Jackson by Ralph E. W. Earl, c. 1817. National Portrait Gallery, Washington, DC.

Caucus curs by James Akin, 1824, presenting a critical commentary on the press's treatment of Andrew Jackson and on the practice of nominating candidates by caucus during the presidential race of 1824. Library of Congress.

Inaugural reception of President Andrew Jackson, 1829. Illustration by Robert Cruickshank for The Playfair papers, 1841. Library of Congress.

Lithograph by Edward W. Clay, c. 1832, praising Jackson for destroying the Second Bank of the United States. Library of Congress.

The Modern Balaam and His Ass, 1837. Jackson portrayed as a caricature of Old Hickory followed by Martin Van Buren. Library of Congress.

1896 portrait of Andrew Jackson that would be used as the basis for the engraving appearing on the twenty-dollar bill. Library of Congress.

Engraved portrait from the United States Currency. Bureau of Engraving and Printing and Smithsonian Institute.

Andrew Jackson by D. M. Carter, 1860. Library of Congress.

Tomb of Andrew Jackson in Nashville, Tennessee, 1908. Library of Congress.

THE BANK VETO AND
RHETORICAL LEADERSHIP

Andrew Jackson held a long-standing aversion to the Bank of the United States, perhaps partially out of personal experience, but also out of strong convictions about fairness and ethics. As early as 1820, Jackson stated his view that the Constitution "prohibited the Establishment of Banks in any state."[1] Though the source of Jackson's animosity toward the bank is unclear, it is likely related to earlier financial dealings in Tennessee. However, one incident at the outset of his presidency may have solidified his viewpoint. The attitude of bank president Nicholas Biddle irked Jackson. Biddle sent a letter to Secretary of the Treasury Samuel Ingham regarding the conduct of the president of the bank's branch in New Hampshire. Biddle wrote Ingham, "[The directors of the bank and its branches] acknowledge not the slightest responsibility of any description whatsoever to the secretary of the Treasury touching the political opinions and conduct of their officers—that being a subject on which they never consult and never desire to know the views of any administration."[2] Such an attitude infuriated Jackson; he found it beyond the pale and completely unacceptable.

When drafting the First Inaugural Address, Jackson made no mention of the Philadelphia-based Bank of the United States as a consideration. He came closest to discussing banking in his passage on public revenue, but there was a hint of a guiding perspective in key words such as "trust" as essential for government operation and the need for "a strict and faithful economy." The absence of any specific remark regarding the bank, though, would attract notice much later. With preparation for the First Annual Message under way, the Bank of the United States would be a major issue of concern. On November 20, 1829, Amos Kendall sent Jackson a memorandum in which he suggested, "[The banks'] "constitutionality . . . has been maintained only on the ground that it is necessary to furnish a safe depository for the moneys of the United States and facilitate their transmission from one section of the Union to another." Kendall doubted "whether the people of several states intended to delegate to the general government the power to create any corporation . . . except within the District of Columbia." He further contended that the people "did not intend to grant to this government the power to withdraw from the jurisdiction and taxing power of the states, persons, or property located within their borders."[3]

Kendall expanded his views on the Bank of the United States, detailing that the government owned only one-fifth of the institution's stock and could appoint only one-fifth of its directors. The fact that four-fifths of the bank's stock was in private hands made for an unacceptable reality. He opined that the bank violated the Constitution on several grounds: It enjoyed "exclusive privilege" and disallowed, by the terms of its charter, the creation of any other national bank. It allowed its stockholders to use money in ways from which "the rest of the community [was] excluded." Moreover, while the Bank of the United States permitted stockholders to use public revenues for private business without paying state taxes, the transactions of all other banks were taxed. Here, Jackson added a notation that the Supreme Court in *McCulloch v. Maryland* (1819) upheld the bank's constitutionality and denied states the power to tax it.[4] Kendall's memorandum recommended the establishment of a "purely national" bank that would be "attached to the Treasury" and would function primarily to generate revenues. The president and the Senate would appoint the institution's directors. Then the bank would "receive, safely keep, and when required, faithfully transmit the moneys of the United States from one section of the Union to another and to foreign parts."[5]

Kendall's memo would guide much of Jackson's rhetoric during the Bank War. The president well understood the constitutional issue and Kendall's emphasis on the Bank of the United States' unchecked powers and abuses. Jackson also received a draft concerning the bank from Secretary of War John Easton. Pointing to the government's limited management of the bank, Easton posited that the bank's unconstitutionality lay in its "exclusive privileges," as well as in its permission of public revenues "to augment individual gain."[6] For the most part, the secretary of war repeated Kendall's earlier arguments. Eaton acknowledged that the Supreme Court had affirmed the constitutionality of a previous charter for the Bank of the United States. Yet he added a significant caveat: "The ground on which it was granted by congress and has been sustained by the Supreme Court, is, that a Bank is a necessary agent of this government in executing its delegated powers." The remaining question, added Eaton, was whether "it was the intention of the people to delegate to this government directly or indirectly, the power to create any corporation whatever, except within the District of Columbia for District purpose."[7] Jackson took note of this particular argument.

Jackson forwarded Kendall's and Easton's drafts, including his own views on the matter, to James Hamilton. In turn, Hamilton wrote his own memorandum for insertion in the First Annual Message.[8] The bank's charter was due for renewal in 1836. Hamilton alluded to this fact in his draft paragraph, having Jackson state in 1829, "Its [the bank's] Stockholders will most probably apply for a renewal of their privileges," and "In order to avoid the evils resulting from precipitancy in a measure involving such important principles and such deep pecuniary interests, I feel that I cannot in justice to our constituents and to the parties interested too soon present it to the deliberative consideration of the Legislature and the people." Hamilton also questioned the constitutionality of the law because it infringed on states' rights, asserting, "it grants to those who hold the Stock exclusive privileges of a dangerous tendency." He included a final statement justifying Jackson's challenge to the bank: "Its expediency is denied by a large portion of our Citisens [sic] while others insist that its operation is extensively injurious to various parts of our Country and it is believed none will deny that it has failed in the great end of establishing a uniform and sound currency throughout the United States." With his initial rhetoric about the bank, Jackson invoked the Constitution as well as public sentiments. This language was consistent with his conception of his presidency as a corrective to a corrupt and unrepresentative polity.

Hamilton's draft was further modified for the final version of the December 8, 1829, First Annual Message. Removing references to "constituents" and "states' rights" shortened the statement overall. The charter of the bank, Jackson stated in matter-of-fact language near the end of the message, "expires in 1836, and its stock holders will most probably apply for renewal 'of their privileges.'" He left the rest of the draft sentence intact.[9] The president also retained the reference to the "evils" of "pecuniary interest," as well as questions about the current charter and its implication regarding "sound currency." Jackson added one short paragraph suggesting that the legislature should contemplate a national bank "founded upon the credit of the government and its revenues," such that it "would avoid all constitutional difficulties and at the same time secure all the advantages to the government and country that were expected to result from the present bank."[10] Though mild and noncommittal, Jackson treaded lightly on a significant issue. He left his audience with the initial impression that the bank rechartering was not necessarily in question. It could be read as a task Jackson left Congress to address. If Jackson had more serious intentions, he did not yet state them, but he nonetheless provided strong hints in the topoi of "trust," "evil," and "pecuniary interest." Removing references to states' rights was strategic, as Jackson saw no advantage to connecting this issue to other important ones, namely tariffs. The president had no intention of rechartering the Bank of the United States.

Hamilton followed on January 4, 1830, with his "Outline of a Substitute for the United States Bank."[11] In his outline, he raised two central objections to rechartering the bank: "It is unconstitutional," and "it is dangerous to Liberty." Hamilton acknowledged the bank's important functions, writing, "It cheapens and facilitates all the fiscal operations of the government," and "it tends to equalize domestic exchange and produce a sound and uniform currency." However, a substitute to the bank was warranted, one "which [should] yield off its benefits, and be obnoxious to none of its objections."[12] Primarily understanding banks' two central functions as discount and exchange, Hamilton sought a simplified bank under the authority of the secretary of the Treasury. He then made several points concerning the constitutionality question. Hamilton opined that "Congress ha[d] no constitutional power to establish," the current bank; that it has mixed private business with that of the states including the "purchases of lands and other real estates within the States and without their consent," and that in all these transactions, the bank had claimed to be authorized by Congress.

On the issue of the Bank of the United States endangering liberty,

Hamilton outlined five concerns: First, that the bank's officers were powerful, wealthy stockholders who could grant or refuse loans at will. Moreover, he stated, the bank "embodies a fearful influence which may be wielded for the aggrandizement of a favorite individual, a particular interest, or a separate party," and it concentrates power in a few individuals "which may be perverted to the oppression of the people, and in times of calamity, to the embarrassment of the government." Added to this was the fact that foreigners held much of the bank's stock, thus allowing foreign influence "in the most vital concerns of the Republic." In addition, as the bank would "ever support *him* who support[ed] *it*," it was an institution prone to undue influence. Finally, Hamilton argued, "it weakens the States and strengthen[s] the General Government."[13] In short, Hamilton contended that an independent Bank of the United States was an anathema to a nation conceived as a republic. Such an institution allowed the concentrated power and selfish motives of a few to dictate America's finances. This outline would become the shorthand template for Jackson in his long battle with the bank.

Hamilton proposed replacing the Bank of the United States with another bank involving few officers, no stockholders, no ability to make loans, and no financial interests in commercial projects. This new, government-controlled outfit would allow no foreign influence, and it could oppress no one. Rather, it would aid the American government's financial functions. The new bank's operation would be cheaper to run, it would sustain cash equal to its outstanding bills, and it would not favor one region over another. In this most compact document, Hamilton laid out a succinct list of reasons to reject rechartering the bank and revamping the nation's banking system.

As in his First Annual Message, Jackson addressed "the Bank of the U.S." at the end of his draft of the Second Annual Message to Congress (dated December 6, 1830, the same day as the formal address, though likely written earlier). [14] The president stressed the critical point of the bank's unconstitutionality, noting that states were sovereign prior to the formation of the federal constitution and stating, "No state is deprived by the Constitution of any power it once possessed, unless in the exercise of its own sovereign powers it has made an express surrender to the Federal Government." Jackson asked rhetorically, "Who can point his finger to the paragraph in the constitution which this power is conferred?" He immediately declared, "I answer no person. . . . Now all ought to admit, if such power exists, it is doubtful from what paragraph it is to be inferred."[15] With some legal jingoism. He announced that no constitutional ruling disallowed the establishment of the bank, and that no ruling conferred such an authority outside the jurisdiction of a legislative body. In short, stated Jackson, "The very circumstance of this disagreement, is a strong argument that it cannot be legitimately, deduced from any of the grants of power which have been made."[16] The Bank of the United States was unconstitutional because no specific statement in the Constitution supported its formation.

In the final version of the Second Annual Message, Jackson stated, "[The] importance of the principles involved in the inquiry whether it will be proper to recharter [sic] the Bank of the United States requires that I should again call the attention of Congress to the subject."[17] He further lamented, "Nothing has occurred to lessen in any degree the dangers which many of our citizens apprehend from that institution as at present organized." In addition, Jackson observed, "In the spirit of improvement and compromise . . . it becomes us to inquire whether it be not possible to secure the advantages afforded by the present bank through the agency of a Bank of the United States so modified in its principles and structure as to obviate constitutional and other objections." The president specifically called for making the bank part of the Treasury Department. He wanted the bank to be "without power to make loans or purchase property." He did not want it to function as a corporation. Thus Jackson suggested the bank operate without "stock holders, debtors, or property," and with a reduced staff.[18] The official message contains nothing of Jackson's rather severe attack on the bank and its corrupt practices. Nor does it push the constitutional question, which Jackson left rather inconclusive in the draft. In delivering his Second Annual Message to Congress, Jackson knew that it was not the right time to up the ante. But it was the time to seek compromise, and he hoped that a mild approach would carry the day. Equally plausible was the hope that Congress would not act. In this event, Jackson would have a stronger justification for refusing the bank's recharter.

Importantly, Jackson was willing to go only as far as modifying some of the Bank of the United States' activities. Equally important, he envisioned a structure for the bank that would avoid "the constitutional objections . . . urged against the present bank." He stated, "Having no means to operate on the hopes, fears, or interests of large masses of the community, it would be shorn of the influence which makes the bank formidable." In return, added Jackson, states would operate more efficiently by having the means "of furnishing the local paper currency through their own banks." The national bank would regulate local banks by redeeming state paper currency for specie. Jackson clarified that he did not offer these suggestions as recommendations. Rather, he characterized them as attempts to call "the attention of Congress to the possible modifications of a system which [could] not continue to exist in its present form without occasional collisions with the local authorities and perpetual apprehensions and discontent on the part of the states and the people."[19] Jackson employed a moderate tone in this limited passage, but he outlined significant change and pinpointed reforms as necessary. The pro-state policy in his approach is not to be discounted; it can be construed as a strategic balancing act in the midst of the Nullification Crisis.

Jackson said little regarding the Bank of the United States in his Third Annual Message to Congress. He addressed the Bank in the last paragraph of his lengthy remarks, stating in the most innocuous way the need for Congress to attend to this "important subject . . . that it might be considered and finally disposed of in a manner best calculated to promote the ends of the Constitution and subserve [sic] the public interests."[20] If some thought Jackson had abandoned his refusal to recharter the bank, they had good reason. This mild paragraph is almost an afterthought. However, Jackson privately discussed the subject with friends, allies, and confidants. Preparations for the Third Annual Message allowed for rhetorical insights of significance. In his lengthy draft, Amos Kendall devoted only a very short paragraph to the bank. He specifically focused on its discount rate and profit margin, questioning why "an institution, which, without the power to discount, should perform the domestic exchange business of the United States."[21] In short, Kendall asked why the Bank of the United States' profits should be granted to stockholders and not the nation at large.

In a letter to Van Buren, Jackson indicated that Louis McLane, the new secretary of the Treasury, had "an honest difference of opinion" with him concerning the bank. He further said of McLane, "in his report he acts fairly, by leaving me free & uncommitted, this I will be, on that subject, still I like his frankness."[22] McLane, who was instructed to provide the paragraph about the bank for Jackson's Annual Message, opted to say very little. He suggested a short passage about leaving investigation of the institution's practices to "an enlightened people and their representatives"—in other words, Congress. When Jackson read the draft of the Annual Message to his cabinet, Atty. Gen. Roger Taney was annoyed by what he perceived to be a withdrawal from previous attempts to challenge the bank. He worried that Jackson might have given up the fight. Jackson, however, operated differently. He did not wish to contradict McLane in front of other cabinet members during the reading of the draft message, leaving the Treasury secretary to assume that the Bank of the United States was safe.

In another letter to Van Buren, Jackson argued that he did not change his mind about refusing to recharter the bank. McLane and, in turn, Biddle and Clay thought that the president's seeming retreat provided an opportunity to bring the bank's recharter to a vote in Congress. The men assumed they would trap Jackson into either agreeing to the plan or vetoing it, and they also thought that in both cases they would win. Ellis and Kirk suggest that in all likelihood, Jackson began to waver on the Bank of the United States' recharter. They also assert that, after his presidential nomination at the National Republic Convention, Clay knew the election would be difficult and sought a controversial issue to help his cause. He asked Biddle to apply for the bank's recharter four years early for this very reason, thinking a bank war "a win win situation." His campaign assumed that a veto after Congress's passage of the recharter by a comfortable majority would turn the nation against Jackson. Clay's win in the next presidential contest would then be ensured.[23] The rechartering of the bank was now a trap calculated to be used against Jackson. This rhetorical gamesmanship is intriguing, especially when observing how Jackson operated and accurately forecasted how each player in the drama would act. The president would have had the upper hand not only for planning rhetorical acts but also for keeping strategic silence and hitting hard when necessary.

Behind the public scene, and over several months, Jackson solicited as well as received input from various individuals across the nation. Not all of them supported his plan to dismantle the Bank of the United States. On June 19, 1831, for example, Jackson received a confidential letter from Worden Pope of Louisville reacting to an article in the *Globe*, the administration's newspaper. Pope advocated the president's plan, but not on all points. He suggested that replacing the Bank of the United States with state banks would depreciate banknotes. Pope also thought that metallic currency would not suffice for the nation's needs. In any event, he stated, "The safety of the national revenue requires a Bank of the United States." If strong opposition to the national bank emerged, Pope recommended that a new bank be chartered with added restrictions as well as congressional control. In assessing public opinion, Pope offered a view contrary to Jackson's. Unlike the president, he believed that the vast majority of people would likely support the Bank of the United States unless a substitute bank was offered.[24]

Jackson's silence over the bank brought others to assume that he might have retreated from his initial plan not to recharter it. Jackson wrote James Hamilton exactly that, stating, "I thought it useless to make an unnecessary repetition of the objections which were stated in my former messages, as some of my friends are persuaded that something more explicit than has been stated would have had a good effect in preventing an error into which some have fallen, to wit, that I have changed my ground on that subject." Jackson added, "A superficial reading of Mr. McLane's report [the formal paragraph in the Third Annual Message] was also calculated to lead to the same false conclusion."[25]

In his December 22, 1831, response to the same charge by John Randolph, Jackson maintained that he had not retreated from his initial plan. The president argued that he had "uniformly on all proper occasions held the same language in regard to that institution [the bank]." He insisted, "[The Bank] has failed to answer the ends for which it was created, and besides being unconstitutional, in which point of view, no measure of utility could ever procure for it my official sanction, it is on the score of mere expediency dangerous to liberty, and therefore, worthy of the denunciation which it has received form the desciples [sic] of the old republican school."[26] Jackson also elaborated on McLane's differing opinion, saying, "it would have been unbecoming in me to control" it. The president further stated and the Secretary of Treasury merely sought "arrangements that might be favorably accommodated with the aid of a Bank."[27]

The question remains, though, about Jackson's muted language in his Third Annual Message. Given his careful strategizing of all previous rhetorical acts, it stands to reason that he preferred to leave the bank issue with another reminder of what he had asked Congress to look into since 1829. In a letter to Van Buren on December 17, Jackson provided another possibility. Though he did not mention the bank directly, Jackson reflected on the recent rumors that Clay and Calhoun, whom he called "these two antipodes in politics, [had] come together on the tariff." Jackson also mentioned the recent Baltimore convention nominating Clay to the presidency. The nomination was not necessarily due to his chances of success in the next election. Rather, it was an effort to save Clay from oblivion.[28] At this juncture, it is possible that Jackson calculated his muted language about the bank to make debate less intense. The president might have sensed that Clay would make the Bank of the United States his campaign issue. A master of timing, Jackson could then have saved his objection to rechartering the bank for later in 1832, the election year.

On January 12, 1832, James Hamilton sent Jackson a letter reiterating his opposition "to the renewal of the Present Bank." Hamilton provided a reason for his disapproval that he had not specified earlier. He now believed that in the very application of renewing the bank's charter, the bank and its supporters were "determined to brave the General."[29] In short, the Bank of the United States had refused to look into its practices and correct perceived infractions. Especially given Jackson's mild statements thus far, the bank's preferring to fight him was in itself a warranted reason for refusing its recharter. Hamilton added that the bank would continue to oppose Jackson if it succeeded in renewing its charter. If given another twenty-year charter, it would be too strong an institution for the government to challenge.[30] Hamilton was right on this point. His argument gives credence to the political aspect of the Bank War, which Jackson understood rather well. Hamilton developed a full-fledged plan for the president to dismantle the bank by revealing its manipulative actions, including subsidizing the press, mismanaging its affairs, and behaving "most injuriously as . . . respect[ed] the Country."[31] Bribes and temptations for enriching directors and stockholders at the public's expense numbered among the bank's other egregious offenses.

Hamilton followed the outline with a plan of action Jackson could use. The first step would be calling for the removal of Nicholas Biddle, the Bank of the United States' president, and demanding a full investigation. Hamilton urged Jackson to make his disapproval known during this investigation: "Throw the weight of your opinion & character into the scale . . . and thus justly put a mark of opprobrium upon the Bank, more effectual and more lasting than anything that could be done and I think that by doing so you would gratify in a very high degree the Public feeling without the slightest risk of injustice."[32] In short, a thorough investigation of the bank's president and public accusations of improper and corrupt practices would suffice for this campaign's success. For Hamilton, Americans' perception of Jackson's popularity and integrity was key to a successful rhetorical campaign against the Bank of the United States. The president's fight with the bank ought to take place in public for all to witness. Popular sentiments would then carry the day. The timing of this dramatic change was calculated to be an important feature in the upcoming presidential campaign.

Despite repeated calls, Jackson's request that Congress examine the bank and its recharter was ignored. On June 11, 1832, the Senate passed a bank bill by a vote of 28 to 20, and on July 3, the House passed the bill by a vote of 107 to 85. Both houses voted along partisan lines.[33] As a result, Jackson was determined to "kill this 'hydra.'"[34]

The president began work on his "Memorandum on the Bank in View of Veto" early, recording arguments and drafts in his memorandum book in

1830 and again in 1831. This would serve as the initial draft of the final veto. A forwarding note in Jackson's papers credits early versions of the document to Jackson himself, Andrew Jackson Jr., and Jackson's secretary George Breathitt. Amos Kendall wrote a later major draft, and Andrew Donelson edited and finalized Kendall's version.[35] Nonetheless, the memorandum's initial plan, key arguments, and overall rhetorical strategy are instructive.

Jackson began the document by stating, "The U.S. Bank is unconstitutional and impolitic." He explained that the word "impolitic" related to the bank's monopoly: "It puts the community at large and their property at the mercy of a corporation which will in the end pursue its own interest."[36] In a later draft, the president wrote, "It has been often inquired, would I approve no Bank charter. I have always answered, that I would approve no Bank charter that violated the constitution, but I would approve any Bank charter that was presented where none of its provisions violated the principles of the organic law."[37] The Constitution, whether in principle or as a matter of expediency, was the pivotal reasoning behind the bank controversy. If Jackson drafted this memorandum himself, as he might have, the primacy of this argument is significant given his long-standing view of how to navigate political issues relative to the Constitution. The document's next point strengthens the possibility that Jackson indeed wrote the memorandum: "I have always viewed that the powers granted by the constitution to our Federal Government were for general purposes, for national not local objects." The Bank of the United States, Jackson added, "must be national, not for a few stockholders, and the charter securing to this few exclusive privileges, from which all the rest of the community are excluded," cannot continue.[38]

Jackson also included the following instruction and warning to Congress: "Before it usurps any power not expressly granted & before creating a Bank with stockholders and the united states [sic] becomes a member of that corporation, which grants exclusive privileges to a few stockholders—let them submit to the people by way of amendment of the constitution, and ask them (in the true spirit of the Sages who formed it) whether you will grant this power. If they say nay, then I say to congress [sic], now and then, 'touch not, handle not, this accursed thing.'"[39] These are tough words. In hoping Congress would heed the people's wishes, Jackson offered a not-so-subtle hint about the 1824 presidential election.

Jackson argued that citizens had to be involved in any change to the Bank of the United States' charter. Otherwise, he declared, "three millions of people, under the present census are unrepresented in the present Congress who ought to be heard, and that the people might deliberate, and at the next election for representatives might select those who would truly represent their wishes on this important subject." In any event, the president concluded, "No inconvenience can result from my veto." The charter was in effect for four more years, providing ample time for a constitutional amendment.[40] Jackson was convinced that the majority of voters would reject the bank once an investigation revealed it to be the tool of the wealthy. He also believed that any move via the mechanization of Congress that ignored public sentiments would be consequential to the people's representatives in the next election. The stakes over the Bank War were high, with both sides of the conflict anticipating gains from the upcoming presidential race.

THE BANK VETO

On July 10, 1832, Jackson issued the official Bank Veto, which would follow most of the arguments spelled out in the earlier memorandum.[41] Historians consider this veto one of the most effective presidential documents in American political history and perhaps the most important presidential veto ever issued. Therein, Jackson presented a list of arguments against the Bank of the United States and the reason for returning the bill to Congress.[42] His primary reason for the veto centered on "the principles of the Constitution," and he listed numerous practices that were "unauthorized by the Constitution, subversive of the rights of the States, and dangerous to the liberties of the people." Jackson reminded Congress that he had made numerous requests for it to examine the bank's organization. He had also recommended that Congress modify the bank's charter as needed. But since Congress had failed to honor either request, and it had also voted to recharter the Bank despite his urgings, Jackson now enacted his veto.

Jackson's primary argument against the Bank of the United States appears in the veto's first paragraph, where he stated, "Some of the powers and privileges possessed by the existing bank are unauthorized by the Constitution."[43] Importantly, he did not label the bank unconstitutional. He labeled its practices unconstitutional. Jackson then detailed the bank's abusive practices, which included its president and directors enjoying "an exclusive privilege" and "a monopoly" over domestic and foreign exchange, as well as an increase in the value of bank stock "far above its par value, operated as a gratuity of many millions to the stockholders." The rechartering of the bank would allow current directors—seven of whom had maintained their position since the last rechartering twenty years earlier—an extensive annuity of some $200,000 a year. Noting that eight million stocks were held by foreigners who would also gain much from the bank's rechartering, Jackson stated, "For these gratuities to foreigners and to some of our own opulent citizens the act secures no equivalent whatever."[44] These privileges and financial rewards, noted Jackson, came at the expense of the public that enjoyed none of these benefits.

The president employed a classic rhetorical strategy, pitting the few rich who abused public money against the majority of hardworking people who lacked such privileges and advantages. For Jackson this was not just a tactical move but a fundamental one. He believed in the principles he advocated, and he abhorred unfair advantages in the hands of a minority. The Bank Veto afforded Jackson one of the best popular appeals. Thus he took full advantage of displaying his long-standing principle that he was the people's president.

Jackson argued that the call to recharter the bank was essentially a fear tactic based on the false assumption that "calling in its loans [would] produce great embarrassment and distress." To claims that denying the recharter could cause economic harm, Jackson replied that there was enough time to recall loans without problem (the bank was chartered until 1836). Any distress caused would be the bank's fault. The institution's arguments, stated Jackson, though of the "most odious features . . . retained without alleviation." Furthermore, the bank had made itself difficult to deal with. Individuals in different states faced an unfair situation in which they could only sell notes to the Bank of the United States. As Jackson noted, these people had to sell at a loss such that "it [did] not measure our equal justice to the high and low, the rich and poor."[45] The seventh president had been critical of the bank and practices before. He was now appalled that the organization could use its ability to cause economic harm to keep the government from denying its recharter. The Bank of the United States would do exactly that.

Jackson focused a large portion of the veto message on foreign holders of the bank's stocks. He also emphasized the reluctance to tax these owners, which further increased the value of their stock. That the majority of foreign stockholders were from Great Britain further irked Jackson. Recent withdrawals of funds from the Bank of the United States to pay dividends to stockholders (including foreigners) had depleted the nation's reserves and caused financial distress, especially in western and southern states. While some states had no citizens owning bank stocks, non-Americans did own such stocks. Jackson summarized the situation in this manner: "American people [are] debtors to aliens in nearly the whole amount due to this bank, and send across the Atlantic from two to five millions of specie every year to pay the bank dividends." Subsequently, a large number of stockholders had no responsibility to the government or to the management of the Bank of the United States. This fact brought Jackson to wonder, "Will there not be a cause to tremble for the purity of our elections in peace and for the independence of our country in war?" For all of these concerns, the Bank "should be *purely American*," he stated, and its stockholders should also be "composed exclusively of our own citizens."[46]

Jackson disagreed with those who claimed that precedent and the Supreme Court had established the conditions of the bank. He countered this argument by stating, "Mere precedent is [a] dangerous source of authority, and should not be regarded as deciding questions of constitutional power except where the acquiescence of the people and the States can be considered as well settled." Jackson also refuted constitutional reasoning. He observed that Congress had decided to support the bank in 1791, then had decided against it in 1811 and 1815, and then had supported it once more in 1816. So much for the argument about a precedent that "ought to weigh in favor of the act before me," stated Jackson.[47]

A progressive thinker, Jackson was not impressed by appeals to tradition and habit. The inconsistencies therein were sufficient to discount the constitutional argument in favor of the bank. But Jackson's thinking encompassed a more significant point. As for the Supreme Court's adjudication on the matter, he countered, "The opinion of the judges has no more authority over Congress than the opinion of Congress has over the judges, and on this point the President is independent of both."[48] This assertion was an altogether significant and radical development. Jackson argued that the president could have an opinion regarding decisions by the judicial branch. If presidential power was an evolving matter, Jackson asserted a new position consistent with his view of a powerful executive. In one short rhetorical stroke, the balance of power between the three branches shifted its weight to the executive, with Jackson arguing its independence from, not its coequality with, the other branches. This major political shift in favor of the presidency allowed Jackson once more to strengthen the office of the executive, just as he did while facing previous challenges.

Jackson talked at length about the Supreme Court's emphasizing specific functions of the Bank of the United States as "necessary and proper." He declared, "[it is] the exclusive province of Congress and the President to decide whether the particular features of this act [of incorporating a bank] are *necessary and proper* in order to enable the bank to perform conveniently and efficiently the public duties assigned to it as a fiscal agent, and therefore constitutional, or *unnecessary and improper*, and therefore unconstitutional." In short, Jackson rejected the Supreme Court's and Congress's exclusive privilege to decide the future of the bank, mocking time and again the use of the terms "necessary" and "proper" as warrants to an argument he found absurd.[49]

Jackson declared that Congress's right to establish a bank, as granted by the Constitution, meant that it could establish more than one bank. But in 1816 Congress had decided to have only one Bank of the United States. In 1832 it decided to extend this decision by fifteen years. Of this decision Jackson opined "[it] can not be considered 'necessary' or 'proper' for Congress to barter away or divest themselves of any of the powers-vested in them by the Constitution to be exercised for the public good," because in so doing they have decided a future in which others may have a different view.[50] In short, the president argued that the bank recharter was unconstitutional because what was "necessary" and "proper" at one time might not be so at a later time.

Jackson pushed the constitutional question further. He stated, "On two subjects only does the Constitution recognize in Congress the power to grant exclusive privileges or monopolies." Citing the Constitution, he noted that document's power "to promote the progress of science and useful arts by securing for limited times to authors and inventors the exclusive right to their respective writings and discoveries." Given this limitation, Jackson continued as follows: "On every other subject which comes within the scope of Congressional power there is an ever living discretion in the use of proper means, which can not be restricted or abolished without an amendment of the Constitution." In short, he contended that Congress had no constitutional right to grant monopolies or exclusive privileges either for "a limited time, or a time without limit." He continued, "to restrict or extinguish its own discretion in the choice of means to execute its delegated powers is equivalent to a legislative amendment of the Constitution, and palpably unconstitutional."[51]

As for granting Bank of the United States stocks to foreigners and exempting them "from all State and national taxation," Jackson asserted that such an act "[was] calculated to convert the Bank of the United States into a foreign bank." The subsequent effect of such an authority would be "to impoverish our people in times of peace, to disseminate a foreign influence through every section of the Republic, and in war to endanger our independence." Clearly, the president considered these privileges neither necessary nor proper; he called them "vitally subversive of the rights of the States."[52] Jackson emphasized just how unconstitutional such a practice was when the federal government could only purchase state land for defense purposes. Even those purchases were subject to state legislatures' consent, while the bank's foreign stockholders could buy state lands at will.

Focusing on the institution's balance sheets, Jackson noted that the old Bank of the United States had a total of $11 million, a sufficient sum for all governmental functions. Now, the bank had $35 million, $24 million more than necessary for covering all its responsibilities. Since the public debt had been nearly paid off, the only possible conclusion one could draw was that "this increase of capital [was] therefore not for public but for private purposes." With such straightforward, easily understood facts and figures, Jackson returned to the bank's argument about "necessary" and "proper" duties. He deemed the government the best judge of these two key questions. Only Congress had the right to coin and regulate money, and Jackson thus contended, "It is neither necessary nor proper to transfer its legislative power to such a bank, and therefore unconstitutional."[53] The president came close to ridiculing the bank's justification of its rechartering, as the bank had not only increased its holdings unnecessarily, but also exempted itself from paying state taxes. As a corporation, he posited, the bank was no different from any other business paying state taxes. Jackson thus hammered at another privilege the bank assigned itself—unfairly enriching its directors and stockholders. This privilege had no constitutional basis and was clearly neither "necessary" nor "proper."

Jackson critically remarked, "Had the Executive been called upon to furnish the project of such an institution, the duty would have been cheerfully performed."[54] Since the bank had ignored his administration's request for it to correct its practices and end abuses, what was left for the president to do? Jackson answered as follows: "In the absence of such a call it was obviously proper that he should confine himself to pointing out those prominent features in the act presented which in his opinion make it incompatible with the Constitution and sound policy." Pointing out the bank's tactic of fighting him instead of suggesting a restructuring plan, Jackson said that he was thus forced to consider its entire operation unconstitutional and worse. For him, the Bank War was the bank's fault. He framed the issues as falling under a disturbing situation that the people's agent had to correct. With the veto now issued, Jackson anticipated "[a] general discussion . . . eliciting new light . . . settling important principles," and allowing the new

Congress to get the people's view on the matter. The "verdict of public opinion," he averred, would "bring this important question to a satisfactory result."[55] Jackson knew that the looming presidential election in the midst of the Bank War would bring Clay to use the bank crisis against him. The president was also sure he would win the battle for public opinion. Clay felt the same about his own prospects.[56]

Near the end of the Bank Veto, Jackson amplified his charges: "Under such circumstances, the bank comes forward and asks a renewal of its charter for a term of fifteen years upon the conditions which not only operate as a gratuity to the stockholders of many millions of dollars, but will sanction any abuses and legalize any encroachments." Jackson charged that the bank had incurred suspicions and committed "gross abuse and violation of its charter." He further indicated that an investigation into the bank's practices had been circumvented. The hurried, incomplete inquiry was "enough to excite suspicion and alarm." What Jackson found most surprising was the fact that the Bank of the United States, "conscious of its purity and proud of its character, would have withdrawn its application for the present and demanded the severest scrutiny into all its transactions."[57] But the bank did not do that. In the veto, Jackson waxed philosophically but with a purpose: "Every man is equally entitled to protection by law; but when the laws undertake to add to these natural and just advantages artificial distinctions, to grant titles, gratuities, and exclusive privileges, to make the rich richer and the potent more powerful, the humble members of society—the farmers, mechanics, and laborers—who have neither the time nor the means of securing like favor to themselves, have a right to complain of the injustice of their Government."[58] He kept repeating the primary charge against the bank's abusive practices, syllogistically listing one improper practice after another to irrefutably show just how far the bank had strayed from principles of fairness and equitability. Jackson knew what conclusion the people would draw.

Jackson tapped directly into his own experience and that of his large constituency to make the case against the bank. He spoke for the hardworking people who he knew would side with him against the Bank's privileges and corrupt ways, asserting, "There are no necessary evils in government. Its evils exist only in its abuses." Now, he suggested, the nation needed to pause and review its principles, "and if possible revive that devoted patriotism and spirit of compromise which distinguished the sages of the Revolution and the fathers of our Union." In Jackson's opinion, the country needed "a stand against all new grants of monopolies and exclusive privileges, against any prostitution of our Government to the advancement of the few at the expense of the many, and in favor of compromise and gradual reform in our code of laws and system of political economy."[59] In the same breath, Jackson lambasted the bank and called for renewed patriotism like that of the Founding Fathers, who were individuals of many Americans' own generation.

The veto's conclusion is clearly in line with the genre of campaign speeches as the president declared, "I have now done my duty to my country." He hoped that his veto would be sustained. In that case, he said, "I shall be grateful and happy; if not, I shall find in the motives which impel me ample grounds for contentment and peace." This peroration is more than the concluding paragraph of a veto—it is a summary campaign appeal. Whether he succeeded or failed in the next election, Jackson had made his points about the bank. The people would judge him accordingly.[60]

A lengthy document, Jackson's veto message details and structures arguments justifying his rejection of the Bank of the United States' charter, a rejection that would destroy the bank by default. The message reads as an extended syllogism. Each argument further strengthens Jackson's only possible conclusion—that the bank, its president, and its directors were corrupt; that its practices were contrary to the Constitution; and that its mechanisms were those of the rich, who made their profits on the backs of the majority of hardworking people. It is also important, though, to situate the Bank Veto's rhetorical strategy within the larger context of Jackson's focus on the nation's finance and economy, and the reform of both. Bothered by corruption in general, Jackson sought major governmental reforms upon becoming president. He paid close attention to the working of the Treasury, opposed budget deficits, and thought it proper to distribute federal surpluses to the states. He worked toward more efficient tax collection and overall management of public money. Jackson particularly abhorred private interests' use of public money for their own selfish rewards. His strong words against the bank reflect his unmistakable hatred of the institution.

With its significant focus on the bank's constitutionality and corruption, the veto remains short on economic reasoning. Jackson did not make a strong argument on purely financial grounds. Rather, he appealed to Americans' sentiments and sense of justice, seeking to convince them that he was attuned to the majority who rejected the moneyed, privileged elite. Jackson clearly spoke to the masses in his veto. The popular appeals therein use classic campaign rhetoric to address one of the most acute issues of his day. The veto message often reads as though Jackson asked the bank, "Are you kidding me?" and then countered its argument in favor of a recharter by stating, "I will show you how corrupt you are." He understood that many Americans would support these sentiments. Such going-public appeals reflect Jackson's and his staff's approach to governing and campaigning—which his opponents often misunderstood.

Though many in Congress were shocked by the veto and its rejection of their votes, no majority could be assembled to override it.

THE RHETORIC INTENSIFIES

If the timing of the veto message was strategized as an opening salvo for the 1832 presidential campaign—as Clay likely planned—Jackson again showed his political acumen. Significantly, Jackson, whom Clay and the Republicans accused of ignoring the people's will, argued the opposite position. He declared the election of 1832 "a referendum on the Bank."[61] On July 15, 1832, John Randolph told Jackson, "[rejecting the Bank Bill] diffuses universal joy among your friends & dismay among your enemies."[62] Likely crediting the veto's chief architect, Jackson wrote confidant Amos Kendall on July 23, 1832, "I am off this morning; *the veto works well.*"[63] But the fight over the bank had just begun. The next step was to articulate a different mechanism to replace the Bank of the United States. For Jackson, the solution was to develop several state banks that would function under the authority of the Treasury. Funds from the federal bank would be gradually withdrawn and transferred to selected state institutions. Vice President Van Buren supported this plan in a March 1833 letter to Jackson, writing, "A National Bank can be dispensed with without serious injury or embarrassment to the public service or to the substantial interests of the Country."[64] However, the bank was not ready to acquiesce, and since the current charter would last four more years, Biddle opted to intensify the fight with Jackson.

As Jackson predicted, the bank's best tool for fighting him was limiting the money supply. The bank also sought to prevent the withdrawal of its funds to be transferred to state banks. In his Fourth Annual Message on December 4, 1832, following his reelection, Jackson informed Congress that due to Bank actions, "the Government [would] be deprived of the use of the public funds longer than was anticipated," and "a surrender of the certificates of this stock [might] be postponed until 1833 October."[65] Jackson argued that the bank had continued to fail in performing its duties, incurring a loss for the federal government as a result. He called on Congress to investigate it: "[An] inquiry into the transactions of the institution, embracing the branches as well as the principal bank, seems called for by the credit which is given throughout the country to many serious charges impeaching its character, and which if true may justly excite the apprehension that it is no longer a safe depository of the money of the people." By causing financial hardships, the bank hoped to blame Jackson for mishandling its recharter. This was a foolish move, and once Jackson was reelected, the thorough investigation would begin.

On March 19, 1833, Jackson issued a memorandum to his cabinet about the plan for a new national bank, outlining several points of discussion for his cabinet. He began with overarching questions: He wondered whether "anything ha[d] occurred to lessen the expression . . . as to the safety of the Bank of the united states [*sic*], so far as regards the pubic deposits." He asked whether the government could rely on the bank's current management "in carrying into effect the fiscal arrangement of the Treasury, as well as whether it ha[d] been heretofore a faithful agent in that respect?" Jackson then inquired "[What is] the propriety of acquiescing in the renewal of the charter of the present bank, under any circumstances or with any modifications? And if with modifications, what ought they to be?" He considered "the propriety of assenting to the establishment of a new Bank," and the best way to introduce his opinion about it. Finally, he asked "What system ought to be established for the future disposition of the public moneys; so far as [it] relates to the places for their deposit, and the manner of their distribution?"

The aforementioned questions are reasonable, but Jackson did not stop here. He also offered his cabinet a short list of his preferences: that the charter of the bank "ought under no circumstances and upon no conditions whatever to be renewed"; "that the ground gained by the veto ought to be firmly maintained"; that no support should be given to establishing a bank outside the District of Columbia; that a new bank in the nation's capital ought to have branches in other states; that "Congress should retain the right to repeal or modify the charter from time to time as it may deem proper, as security against the corruptions and evils which are now experienced from the uncontrollable authority of the current Bank"; and that a new system of deposit and distribution of the public funds be devised.[66] Public opinion lined up behind Jackson, as indicated in his reference to "the grounds gained by the veto." The president was now ready to finish the bank.

Replying to the memorandum, Attorney General Roger Taney reminded Jackson that the House Ways and Means Committee had voted to recharter the Bank of the United States (with Rep. James Polk writing for the minority). He thus cautioned the president to let an investigation into the bank's conduct take place before he acted. Taney provided facts and numbers proving the bank's loss of public trust. For example, the bank could not pay $6 million in national debt even though it had $9 million on hand. This was the case, Taney noted, because the bank "had traded so extensively and profusely upon it [the $9 million] for its own benefit . . . that the government was compelled to postpone the payment for three months longer than it originally contemplated." Additionally, Taney emphasized that the bank's charter did not include trading public funds. Yet in 1831, the bank had significantly increased the number of loans it issued, and its stockholders sought to hide the transactions from the government. Taney charged the bank with using these loans "to influence the press and to enlist newspapers in their service." He advised the government to stop depositing its funds in the Bank of the United States, and to identify state banks as agents of the Treasury.[67]

Jackson solicited input from Amos Kendall, at this time an auditor of the Treasury, and he outlined a policy for the president to follow: designating proper state banks and depositing government funds in them; transferring all books regarding public debt to the Treasury, which would now handle this function; withdrawing public money now in the federal bank; and instructing public officers to transfer funds to the designated state banks. Kendall maintained that these actions would "cripple the Bank of the United States and deprive the conspirators of the aid which they expect[ed] from its money and power." Like Taney, Kendall thought that the government would respond to the bank's strong resistance to the veto by gradually depriving the institution of funds and causing its demise.[68]

Kendall urged Jackson to pursue specific measures. After crippling the bank, Jackson should expose Clay's corrupt land bill and Clay's and Calhoun's attempt to circumvent Jackson's fight with the bank. Kendall assured the president that these revelations would rally the nation behind him.[69] The bank issue was now intertwined with the Nullification Crisis—while Clay sought a compromise on the tariff issue whereby budget surpluses would enable the bank to increase its deposits, Jackson was planning to deplete its funds.[70] The same day that he noted his and Clay's opposing policies, Jackson repeated Kendall's contention that Clay's tariff idea "[would] enable the Bank to survive its present depressed state, and wield by this large surplus its corruption influence over the legislation and destinies of this union."[71]

In Jackson's estimation, Clay and Calhoun had become "printers to Congress" seeking to promise various states funds—which were now lacking due to the bank's credit crunch. The two men hoped to influence a large number of House members to generate the two-thirds majority needed to undo the Bank Veto. Furious, Jackson wrote, "Here is the picture then as to the remedy. I see and will meet the crisis fearlessly, but in meeting it, care must be taken, that we weaken, not strengthen its power or its friends."[72] Jackson labeled the actions of Clay, Calhoun, and others a "hydra of corruption" in which the bank loaned money to congressmen in the hopes of surviving the veto.[73] The president turned his questioning of the bank's constitutional grounding into anticorruption rhetoric that was easier to prove, especially during the depression the bank crisis caused. Jackson's language also resonated well with popular sentiments. The president proved his rhetorical skills again, correctly reading the growing distress over the economic downturn and adjusting his public appeals to generate support in the administration.

※·※·※

Though Jackson often engaged in polemics against the moneyed aristocracy, he also revealed a moral strain in his rhetoric during the Bank War. Jackson advocated economic reform in line with the laissez-faire perspective, aligning the working class against the common enemy of the wealthy upper classes. The juxtaposition between the two groups can be seen in the tension between the moneyed aristocracy that favored paper currency and the common laborers who preferred gold and silver, as well as between those given to speculation and those who were not.[74] The Bank War fleshed out the growing resentment many held against the eastern elite and struck "a blow to an older set of capitalists by the newer, more numerous set." Constructing a new banking system was a necessary step in the "democratization of business, the diffusion of enterprise among the mass of people, and the transfer of economic primacy from an old and conservative merchant class to a newer, more aggressive, and more numerous body of businessmen and speculators of all sorts." Subsequently, Jackson joined his "simple agrarian principles of political economy" with the "doctrine of laissez faire."[75]

The most significant development of the Bank War was the degree to which Jackson asserted the president's power to speak for the people, the president's coequal right with Congress to interpret the Constitution, and his own belief that "Congress needed to consider the president's views as it constructed a legislative agenda."[76] Jackson set forth a new, changing view of the executive, and in so doing he opened the door to charges of dictatorial intent.

THE SECOND INAUGURAL ADDRESS

A WATERSHED IN PRESIDENTIAL
POWER AND POPULAR EFFECT

If the election of 1828 saw the formation of a new two-party system that coalesced around Jackson and Adams, the election of 1832 further solidified this system. The Jackson coalition merged with the Democratic Party and the Adams-Clay coalition with the National Republicans. Jackson was the head of the Democrats, and when he announced that he would run for a second term, there was no doubt that the party would nominate him. He ran the administration and implemented his own agenda, including the Indian Removal Act and the Maysville Veto. The Jackson administration and the Democratic Party were practically indistinguishable; the same person headed both, and the party convention followed his lead.[1] The Bank War in particular gave Jackson the perfect cause, proving his savvy political sense as well as his willingness to engage in "indirect electioneering." These qualities proved his rhetorical sense, ensuring that though his messages were "formally addressed to Congress . . . their language was more suited to the hustings." While Clay and Biddle were sure that such public appeals would help defeat Jackson, the popular appeal was most suited to the new "democratic environment."[2]

Jackson won his second term decisively, receiving 219 electorate votes to Clay's 49 and about 700,000 popular votes to Clay's 485,000. Unlike his 1828 campaign, his 1832 campaign also made significant inroads into New England. Jackson was as popular as ever, and his handling of the Nullification Crisis and especially the Bank War did much to aid his victory. The election of 1832 was partially a referendum on Jackson's Bank Veto,[3] but it was also a vote for Jackson as a person and the trust, devotion, and confidence many had in him, independent of any policy issue.[4] Those who promoted the rechartering of the Bank of the United States to a nationwide discussion, especially the National Republicans in Congress, did so in order to win the election. The ensuing Bank War made the Bank Veto a major campaign issue. It also changed American politics to the extent that future presidential campaign rhetoric would promote candidates' specific policies.[5]

Arthur Schlesinger opines that Jackson was resolute in his "offensive against the American 'nobility system'"—in other words, his attack on the Bank of the United States. Jackson's efforts to squash the bank and his successful presidential campaign convinced him that he had a mandate to fight and end the bank shortly after his reelection. This belief would make for a focused agenda for his second term.[6] It would also change presidential politics forever, prompting victorious candidates to consider election results mandates for the actions they stipulated during the campaign.[7] Yet Jackson did not include a clear agenda in his Second Inaugural Address. Instead, he would offer a sobering reflection on the future of the Union with the Nullification Crisis taking center stage.

As he did while writing his First Inaugural Address, Jackson drafted his Second Inaugural Address and showed it to Van Buren before it was revised and finalized for delivery on March 1, 1833. Though the final address contains large portions of the first version, it still went through major revisions.[8] As in the draft of his first inauguration speech, Jackson employed eloquent, expressive phrasing and language while composing his second address. But unlike the draft of his first address, the draft of Jackson's second address proved so forceful and replete with fury at the nullifiers in particular that it had to be revised and toned down. The Nullification Crisis directly influenced Jackson's writing, turning his speech into invective targeting its promoters.

THE INITIAL DRAFT

Jackson addressed the initial draft to his "Fellow Citizens," acknowledging the "will of the American people, expressed through their unsolicited suffrages," that had called on him to be president for another term. He then characterized his victory as an affirmation of his actions during the first term. This was a significant statement for Jackson's time; presidents of that period hesitated to claim such a mandate. Jackson also described his first term as not "without its difficulties," but given the country's vote of confidence, he humbly promised "to administer their [Americans'] government [so] as to preserve their liberty, and promote their happiness." With these words, the president began an address consistent with his long-held belief in the Constitution's primacy in the nation's affairs.

Already in the second paragraph, Jackson offered general commentary on his previous term, addressing "incidents . . . necessarily called forth, sometimes under circumstances . . . most delicate and painful." He provided no specifics, assuming many could fill in the blank. However, one can surmise that Jackson alluded to serious issues such as the Nullification Crisis, the Indian Removal Act, and the Bank War, but also petty but troubling cases such as the Eaton affair and acrimonious relations with key congressional leaders. Jackson stated that his method of handling these unnamed circumstances was to abide by the "principles and policy which ought to be pursued by the general government." He did not elaborate on this vague reference, as if he preferred to let the implied strength of the Constitution and the role of the federal government stand on its own. Jackson's phrasing can also be read as a summary statement of where things stood at the time. Questions regarding the authority of the "general government" were settled, and the authority of the federal government was now confirmed, a subtle reference to the strengthening of the executive.

On matters of policy, Jackson devoted one paragraph to foreign affairs, which he considered an "almost compleat [sic] success," iterating, "We are not only at peace with all the world, but few causes of controversy, and those of minor importance, are left to be adjudicated." On the domestic front, Jackson identified two related issues of concern: "The preservation of the reserved rights of the several states and the integrity of the union." Given his "observation of a life somewhat advanced," he pointed to the potential "destruction of our state governments, or the annihilation of their control over the local concerns of the people, [that] would lead directly to revolution and anarchy, and finally to despotism and military domination." These strong references to the Nullification Crisis, its subsequent threat of secession, and its danger to the Union are more than a reflection on the conflict with South Carolina. They indicate Jackson's wider view of the crisis's implications, of what the crisis could foretell. In hindsight, the seventh president rather accurately predicted events that would unfold some thirty years hence.

The president considered states' rights essential for the stability of the nation. But in the face of anarchy, he said he would "repress any measures which [might] directly or indirectly, encroach on the reserved rights of the states or tend to consolidate all political power in the general government." Jackson was willing to allow the states' rights stance only up to a point. He left no doubt that he would crush any attempt to disrupt the Union's stability. This strong message about the growing importance of the federal government includes a warning in case the Nullification Crisis continued. Though all knew he believed in a strong central government, Jackson astutely and strategically expressed himself in the name of states' rights, not the federal government's interests. With the Nullification Crisis nearing its final phase, Jackson preferred a balanced expression that incorporated a pro–states' rights stance and deprived the nullifiers of their very argument. He could state that he had now won the crisis. The statement can also be read as a preemption of any reemerging secession sentiments. Jackson knew that though the Nullification Crisis was almost over, its supporters' feelings would linger.

Lest his intentions be misunderstood, Jackson presented this succinct principle in the style of a toast: "Without union our independence and liberty would never have been achieved, without union they can never be maintained." He espoused this principal idea here and throughout his presidency. Dissolution of the Union, Jackson expounded, would result in twenty-four states competing with each other, complicating trade, obstructing communication, and turning farmers into soldiers who would spill blood in the "fields they now till in peace." Such dissolution would result in the "loss of liberty," he stated, while "in supporting the union . . . we support all that is dear to the freeman and philanthropist."

The Union and the freedom it guaranteed trumped all other considerations for Jackson. He argued the case for the Union by touting its strength, and by going further than ever before and describing what the nation could look like without it. In so doing, he projected an effective and quite prescient rhetorical image. For a young nation in which many citizens retained firsthand memories of the War of Independence (Jackson among them), the president's account was probing, and such an ominous prospect was credible. Jackson had fought in that war, and he had fought the same enemy again thirty-six years later. He could thus reliably state how quickly the nation could lose its independence over local sentiments. The president clearly feared for the future of the Union, and he described possibilities that proved similar to events before the Civil War. In all, Jackson's reading of the political map is astonishingly acute.

Hoping that a balanced view would ease states' concerns, Jackson presented the advantages of a strong but limited federal government, especially in the midst of the Nullification Crisis (though by Inauguration Day, the crisis was practically over). Jackson himself defined the situation as a crisis, telling the nation, "The time at which I stand before you is one of portentous importance," and "The eyes of the world are fixed on our Republic. The event of the existing crisis will be decisive in the opinion of mankind of the practicability, or impartibility of the federal system of government." Jackson sought to impart the nation's crucial situation to the public. As in previous addresses, he noted how the world would view the American experiment. The Nullification Crisis, then, was the primary test of the United States' viability as the sole democracy, and it impacted more than an internal conflict. Jackson added, "Great is the stake which mankind have in our hands; great is the responsibility which must rest upon [us]." The future of the United States was at stake. The first modern experiment in democratic federal government was in danger of faltering. Concerned by this state of affairs, Jackson took an internationalist perspective, finding therein a possible means of influencing the domestic crisis. He had used this argumentative strain before, but on balance, it was not a strong one. Opinions of foreigners rarely impacted domestic issues.

In a series of sentences more characteristic of twentieth-century presidential rhetoric—including John F. Kennedy's Inaugural Address, with its anaphora of "Let us begin"—Jackson appealed to the nation's better reason: "Let us realize the interesting attitude in which we stand before the world. Let us exercise forbearance and firmness. Let us extricate our country from the dangers which surround it and learn wisdom from the lessons they inculcate." The crisis at hand, then, ought to be instructive to the nation. Clinging to his paternal image, Jackson saw himself as the nation's father, a figure who wished all to realize important lessons from difficult times.

With the "Let us" anaphora, Jackson projected identification with the American people and a joining of forces to overcome current dangers. He summarized his appeal with a key value: "That people is [*sic*] not best governed who have the most laws." This is a profound statement phrased with great eloquence and economy. Jackson elaborated on his principle: "[Partial legislation, the kind] which depresses one man or interest at the expence [*sic*] of another, or is supposed to do so, will ever lead to discontents, murmurings, dissention and revolution." This vague statement probably references the end of the elitist Bank of the United States. Instead, Jackson offered the following idea: "Government should treat all alike; and the surest means of attaining that end, is to let all alone as far as is compatible with publick [*sic*] justice, peace and safety." He stated his objective to convince the nation of what a wise government ought to look like.

These insightful statements concern a government of few laws and key principles of proper conduct, a government that oppresses no one and treats all alike. Jackson sought this ideal government. He used neutral and even philosophical terms, but he likely aimed his extended point at the national bank and the corruption he had previously encountered. Importantly, Jackson outlined here the essence of a progressive government founded on laissez-faire philosophy, limited in its reach, economic in its outlook, trusting of its people, and abiding by few essential principles. This would become the essence of Jacksonian democracy.

As in his previous paragraph, Jackson alluded to the "world" watching the United States, wondering whether its unique government would sustain itself, and whether democracy had a chance to be implemented elsewhere. This line of thinking is intriguing, as it reveals a more elaborate international viewpoint that Jackson did not discuss during his first term. Jackson's remarks coincided with Alexis de Tocqueville's visit to the United States, during which he, too, asked whether the country's unique form of government, a federal republic, was sustainable, here and elsewhere. Jackson's contemplating how other nations regarded his own was also a sign of the times. He was considering expanding territories, increasing trade, and growing foreign relations, all of them crucial to the young nation. If Jackson deemed the United States a special country, he came close to stating this very idea.

The Union, then, was important to the future of the nation both domestically and internationally. Yet "in the meantime," Jackson adamantly announced, "misguided men must not be permitted, in effect to correct existing abuses or in pursuance of less worthy designs, to impair or overthrow a system of government which is the pride of our fathers." His key adversaries among the nullifiers had gotten the best of him. Jackson therefore used his

Second Inaugural Address as the platform to attack them and their ruinous principles. He disagreed with the nullifiers' tactics, even if they intended for their advocacy to correct some abuses.

Jackson followed with a threat, in which he included a likely reference to John Calhoun and phrasing almost identical to the Nullification Proclamation. "If, in madness or delusion," he declared "any one shall lift his paracidal [*sic*] hand against this blessed union, which, like Heavens Canopy, spreads over us all, and if it does not make us all happy, protect us from unnumbered ills, the arms of tens of thousands will be raised to save it, and the curse of millions will fall upon the head which may have plotted its destruction." These harsh words do not truly befit an Inaugural Address. But on the heels of the serious Nullification Crisis, Jackson sought to warn the nation of the larger risks stemming from a seemingly local dispute over tariffs, and from the disastrous actions of several of that dispute's leaders. Using biblical allusions and the divine metaphor of "Heavens Canopy," Jackson portrayed the Union as a sacred entity not to be trifled with. Like a prophet of yore, the president warned his audience that lifting a hand in defiance, often an act against God, was the ultimate form of betrayal. In Jackson's charge, only a single hand and one head "[might] have" sought to destroy the Union. Thus the president qualified the accusation but hinted again who the culprit might be—his nemesis Calhoun. The Union was a sacred entity, protected by the Almighty and his servant, Jackson. No one had the right to destroy it.

Jackson strengthened the religious metaphors describing the Nullification Crisis with his next statement. "For myself," he said, "when I approach the sacred volume and take a solemn Oath to support and defend this constitution, I feel in the depth of my soul, that it is the highest, most sacred and most irreversible part of my obligation, to *preserve the union of these states, although it may cost me my life*" (italics in the original). In the transition between his first and second term, Jackson determined to fight secessionists and do his best to preserve the Union, even if his efforts cost him his life. In a dramatic way, he declared the stakes and asserted his courage. Jackson purposefully heightened the stakes in order to impart the severity of the situation. As a result, the severe crisis turned personal.

Jackson concluded this draft with an appeal to the Almighty. In his words, God "protected our country in war, and so signally blessed it in peace, that He will teach us justice and moderation, allay excited passions, lead back the misguided to the path of reason, and spare me the painful necessity of resorting to these terrible powers which are vested in me by the constitution and acts of congress [sic], to execute the lays, suppress insurrection, and repel invasion." Jackson issued a clear threat to crush insurrection with military power unless reason and moderation prevailed, repeating the same warning from the Nullification Proclamation. He left no doubt that any talk about secession was insurrection, and that he considered himself authorized by the Constitution to act accordingly. This is not an Inaugural Address befitting the celebration of values and tradition while ushering in a new president. This is a deliberative address with a clear statement of intention in the face of a threat to the Union. Jackson hoped strong words would eliminate the need for action.

The Nullification Crisis consumed Jackson, and he selected his Second Inaugural Address as the most auspicious, highly publicized opportunity to make his stand on the matter. The speech contains some obligatory references to reelection and foreign affairs, but the serious threat facing the young nation otherwise dominates it. Jackson's rhetoric regarding the crisis in this speech is no different from his other forceful utterances. Yet no other issue (though the Bank War came close) roused the president's ire as vehemently as nullification. A constitutional crisis, a threat to the Union, and the unfavorable actions of key politicians, including his former vice president, combined to produce his most extreme rhetorical act.

Jackson's Second Inaugural Address provided him an opportunity to spell out constitutional principles and threaten military action against the nullifiers. These elements set the speech apart from traditional Inaugural Addresses. And in 1833, Jackson could no longer deliver such a speech. He needed to vent his frustrations on paper, and given the limited rhetorical opportunities available to him, Jackson used the Inaugural Address to do so. In the end though, these remarks were confined to a draft. His close aides reworked most of the address, deleting material conveying anger, personal attacks, and threats. Jackson and his staff did, after all, have a semblance of a genre to consult, and they did have a sense of what such presidential speeches ought to concern.

THE FINAL VERSION

The final version of the Second Inaugural Address differs markedly from Jackson's initial draft. Jackson acknowledged his election "expressed through" the people's "unsolicited suffrages," and as in the draft, he briefly mentioned his "public conduct through a period which [had] not been without its difficulties." Humbly accepting the people's "renewed expression of their confidence in [his] good intentions," he also stated that he would continue to emphasize the people's liberty and "promote their happiness."[9] Yet Jackson retreated from a more emphatic consideration of the election as a mandate. In the second paragraph, the president continued the theme of having to deal with "circumstances the most delicate and painful." But he left the referents obscure, stating that he would cover in the address only a "few leading considerations connected" with the general government.[10]

As in his Annual Messages, Jackson addressed foreign relations first. Consistent with previous administrations' practices, he described American foreign policy as "crowned with almost complete success" that had "elevated our character among the nations of the earth." The nation, he added, had done no wrong to any other nation and thus was "at peace with all the world."[11] On the domestic front, Jackson specified two objectives of the government deserving the nation's attention: "the preservation of the rights of the several States and the integrity of the Union." These "necessarily connected" goals, he stated, "can only be attained by an enlightened exercise of the powers of each within its appropriate sphere in conformity with the public will constitutionally expressed." Jackson used a milder tone and dignified phrasing to describe the necessary balance between foreign and domestic policies and the role of the Constitution in regulating both. After prevailing in the two primary crises of his first term, Jackson did not need to do more than highlight the will of the people within the constitutional framework. His election secured that. The president's key areas of focus were the government's conformity to the wishes of the people and the "duty of all to yield a ready and patriotic submission to the laws constitutionally enacted."[12] Jackson specified neither the crisis at hand nor the tension between states' rights and the federal government. For him, the Constitution's power to require Americans' obedience was sufficiently instructive.

References to some people's and states' "discontents" and "heartburnings" [sic], as well as to the need "to refrain from the exercise of even rightful powers" were also removed from the final Second Inaugural Address. Had they remained, these words would have been ill suited to the occasion. They would also have suggested that nullifiers had perhaps fought for a just cause but erred in using the wrong means. Instead, Jackson addressed his "experience in public concerns" such that "the destruction of our State governments or the annihilation of their control over the local concerns of the people would lead directly to revolution and anarchy, and finally to despotism and military domination."[13] The president believed the Nullification

Crisis and the threat of secession necessitated the most vivid description of their potential ramifications.

To offset this ominous projection, Jackson sought a balance between states' rights and the general government (the address contains many references to the general government and only one to the federal government): "In proportion, therefore, as the General Government encroaches upon the rights of the States, in the same proportion does it impair its own power and detract from its ability to fulfill the purposes of its creation." This astute phrasing allowed Jackson to express support for states' rights and the federal government by offering that any limitation on the former would injure the latter. Hence, he "solemnly"" promised that "[The nation] will never find me ready to exercise my constitutional powers in arresting measures which may directly or indirectly encroach upon the rights of the States or tend to consolidate all political power in the General Government."[14] With this astounding statement, the president attempted a conciliatory offering to those on the other side of the Nullification Crisis. He also a completely reversed the harsh pro-Union sentiments in his initial draft.

Lest some misconstrue his sentiments, Jackson complimented Americans for learning "to think and speak of the Union as of the palladium of [their] political safety and prosperity, watching for its preservation with jealous anxiety, discountenancing whatever may suggest even a suspicion that it [could] in any event be abandoned, and indignantly frowning upon the first dawning of any attempt to alienate any portion of our country from the rest or to enfeeble the sacred ties which now link together the various part." He added, "Without union, our independence and liberty would never have been achieved; without union they never can be maintained." Jackson did not deviate from his pro-Union rhetoric in the final speech. But he greatly improved on the accusatory references of his first draft, strengthening the overall argument and using more moderate phrasing. The president addressed the sentiments of a young nation wherein some citizens still doubted the experiment of federated states but were learning to think and speak as a unified entity "frowning" over any attempt at disunity. In Jackson's modified phrasing, the people are the driving force of the Union. It is they who are "watching for its preservation," and they who are indignant in the face of any attempt to undo the link.

These words would suffice for the nullifiers to understand Jackson's meaning about the strength of the Union and its popular and moral appeal. Jackson hammered on his earlier innovative point about the Union as principally made of people and not of states. Importantly, he provided another vivid description of what disunion could look like: a nation divided into twenty-four "separate communities," suffering from constrained trade, communities cut off from each other and "[whose] sons [were] made soldiers to deluge with blood the fields they now till in peace; armies and navies, and military leaders at the head of their victorious legions becoming our lawgivers and judges." This ominous state of disunion would end, Jackson projected, with "the loss of liberty, of all good government, of peace, plenty, and happiness, must inevitably follow a dissolution of the Union."[15]

There is no question where Jackson stood with regard to the Union. He believed in it, and he minced no words about its crucial importance to the federation of states. And though he spoke of a balancing act between the states and the federal government, he deemed the Union the anchor of the entire political system. Describing what the nation would look like without the Union was Jackson's rhetorical strategy for cementing that which was still fresh in many Americans' minds. That he would so accurately portend the reality of disunion speaks to his political acumen.

One of Jackson's best lines, "people [are] not best governed who have the most laws," was removed from the final version of his Second Inaugural Address. He and his aides calculated that, despite its strong, effective sentiments and phrasing, this speech was not the platform for arguing the merit of more or fewer laws. Neither would the address include references to "discontents," "murmurings," "dissention and revolution," "misguided men" responsible for the Nullification Crisis, and acts meant "to impair or overthrow" the government. Finally, Jackson's accusation of "madness or delusion" was judged too strong a reference and too easily attributable to key antagonists and removed as well. Yet the president still stated, "The eyes of all nations are fixed on our Republic," and "[The] event of the existing crisis will be decisive in the opinion of mankind of the practicability of our federal system of government." The Nullification Crisis, if anyone doubted what he referred to, was front and center. Jackson now called on the nation (keeping the "Let us" anaphora intact) to realize the enormity of what it stood to lose. He asked Americans to "realize the importance of the attitude in which [they stood] before the world," to "exercise forbearance and firmness," and to "extricate [their] country from the dangers which surround[ed] it."[16]

While the final address was shortened by two paragraphs, the introduction was expanded, allowing Jackson's presidential stature to shine through and in a dignified and solemn way. Jackson stated, "[I will continue] to exert all my faculties to maintain the just powers of the Constitution and to transmit unimpaired to posterity the blessings of our federal union." He promised to exercise for "the General Government those powers only that are clearly delegated," adhering to his long-standing position of the primacy of the federal government but acknowledging that entity's limitations as well.[17] If this statement was meant to send a conciliatory hint to the nullifiers, they could, indeed, have read it as such. More importantly, Jackson included no attack on any state or individual. Committing to the posterity of the federal union was a much more productive way for him to secure his objective than threatening to crush any attempt to destroy it.

Jackson's conclusion included a well-phrased principle: "Individuals must give up a share of liberty to preserve the rest." For the Union to prevail, Jackson believed that all Americans needed to adhere to this rule. In addition, by focusing on liberty, the president stressed his commitment to the Union in a more appealing way than voicing willingness to fight its dissolution and even be killed in the process. His task, he elaborated, was "to foster with our brethren in all parts of the country the spirit of liberal concession and compromise, and, by reconciling our fellow citizens to those partial sacrifices which they must unavoidably make for the preservation of a greater good, to recommend our invaluable government and union to the confidence and affections of the American people."

The Nullification Crisis remained Jackson's central focus, but it befitted the occasion for him not to address it directly in his Inaugural Address. The speech's distinct conciliatory and transcendent quality changed Jackson's tone. The very rhetorical quality of identification, of asking "brethren" for a few sacrifices necessary for recognizing the larger good of the Union, could diffuse the crisis rather than intensify it.

The Second Inaugural Address's final paragraph, devoted to a prayer to the Almighty, was also revised. References to those with "excited passions" and to "the misguided" were removed, along with Jackson's threat to exercise the "terrible powers which are vested in [him]" as president. Instead, Jackson made a request of the Almighty Being: "[I ask God] who has kept us in His hands from the infancy of our republic to the present day, that He will so overrule all my intentions and actions and inspire the hearts of my fellow citizens that we may be preserved from dangers of all kinds and continue forever a united and happy people."[18] Thus Jackson ended with the theme of the entire address: preserving the young nation from any threat to itself. He presented his "intentions and actions" in the last sentence of the speech, but with a twist—he hoped the Almighty would overrule his plan to take action to preserve the Union. A larger agent was thus inserted into the narrative, keeping Jackson as His humble servant. By leaving the decision to God, Jackson tamed the threat in his first draft to use force against an unspecified entity. The Second Inaugural Address concludes on a conciliatory tone but nonetheless reveals Jackson's determination. The president was bent on preserving the Union, even if he had to argue with the Almighty about it.

✳✳✳

Relative to the intense initial draft, the final version of Jackson's Second Inaugural Address is dignified. Yet it retains the president's earlier message of determination and hints of anger. Jackson alluded to the Nullification Crisis throughout the final speech, but he handled the subject more delicately, focusing on transcending states' rights and the federal union. Moreover, Jackson and his aides did not make the Bank War a central point in the address. Though related difficulties had just commenced, the conflict's end was decided. Subsequently, there was no reason to dwell on that which was essentially over. Jackson made preserving the Union the constant theme of his Second Inaugural Address. On that point Jackson did not compromise, though he moderated his tone and made his references clearer and more general.

Overall, the Second Inaugural Address, with its focus on a desirable resolution of the Nullification Crisis, is a superb document, the historical significance of which would be realized three decades later. Yet at least on the surface, there is something odd about this address. Jackson and his aides wrote this speech when the Nullification Crisis was almost over. The conflict had peaked and was on course for a resolution by March 1833, with South Carolina retreating from its initial threats of secession. Why, then, did Jackson make the Nullification Crisis the central theme of the Second Inaugural Address? Why would he risk antagonizing the opposition during the inauguration on March 4? And, relatedly, why did Jackson initially use such angry language? The likely answers lie with Jackson himself. He could see the dangers inherent in the Nullification Crisis, and he continued to worry that its culprits would somehow extend it or find another issue to circumvent the delicate compromise that had been arranged. Jackson's political sense and astute reading of the political map brought him to realize that he could not trust anyone who plotted this crisis in the first place. If the nation required additional warnings, the few rhetorical outlets available to the president during the early nineteenth century meant that an Inaugural

Address, with its wide audience, would be the opportune means of delivering them. Jackson stated as much in other addresses. And in his Second Inaugural Address, he issued a warning for the future, crafting his words for posterity, much as a president would in a Farewell Address.

Jackson was astute enough to realize that the Nullification Crisis was not truly over. Hard feelings remained, and nemeses would seek to act again. For the same reason of limited public rhetorical outlets available to presidents, and four years before thinking of a Farewell Address, Jackson quite possibly considered his Second Inaugural Address, unlike his Annual Messages to Congress, his last opportunity to warn the nation of what the Nullification Crisis portended. This was, after all, the main theme of the address—warnings about potential dissolution of the Union.

The Second Inaugural Address is also a watershed document in the evolvement of presidential power. Jackson sought to use the address strategically in this regard. The Nullification Crisis and his handling of it allowed Jackson to strengthen the presidency once more. He argued that he had all the authority granted to him as president to engage in military action, emphasizing the need for compromise guided by the federal government. These negotiations would reinforce some elements of states' rights but, above all else, keep the primacy of the Union unquestioned and necessary for securing the nation's freedom and independence. The Nullification Crisis afforded Jackson the opportunity to show the nation that he was its chief manager and the deciding authority over its destiny.

Finally, as the Nullification Crisis was a serious threat to the Union, Jackson used his Second Inaugural Address to rhetorically visualize the best course for the nation and the potential perils in case a different course was pursued. The editing of the First Inaugural Address produced a final version less powerful than Jackson's own draft. In contrast, close advisors' and speechwriters' revisions of the Second Inaugural Address secured a first-class speech after rejecting Jackson's more personal account and angry tone. At the same time, these changes eliminated the vitality and enthusiasm of Jackson's initial draft. The final address lacks a clear agenda, and in focusing on warnings Jackson revealed preoccupation with the lingering issues of his first term. Nonetheless, the Second Inaugural Address was well received when Jackson delivered it; many Americans considered it a great speech.[19]

FROM CHIEF MAGISTRATE
TO PRESIDENT

Jackson was determined not to wait for the Bank of the United States' charter to expire; he wanted to begin withdrawing its funds. His reelection made this decision easier, but it was not without risks. Treasury officials, including two secretaries and several bank presidents, cautioned Jackson against the move. Secretary of the Treasury Louis McLane cautioned the president that such withdrawals could hurt the bank's credit, and he also advised withholding all action until an investigation into the bank's practices was complete. Jackson did not appreciate these views. In writing his "Notes on Treasury Opinion," Jackson pointed to McLane's assertion that a new bank would be "more dangerous to the liberties of the people" because it would make new appointees dependent on the president. It would also, opined McLane, create a situation in which "the *monied prerogative* would be in effect transferred to the Chief Magistrate."[1] Realizing that McLane would not be supportive of finishing the bank, Jackson fired him and appointed William J. Duane to replace him. With the Bank Veto enjoying public support, Jackson was not going to change his mind in the face of new challenges.

When Secretary Duane raised his own concerns about the plans for a future national bank, Jackson sent him a lengthy letter detailing the "full development of the policy which he [Jackson] [thought] it is his [Duane's] duty to pursue in relation to the Bank of the United States, and the future arrangement of the public revenue so far as it depend[ed] on his action or authority."[2] The president detailed his past actions to justify his final move against the bank. He reminded Duane that he had addressed the bank's constitutionality and questioned its rechartering in 1829, while delivering his First Annual Message to Congress. In a message to Congress a year later, Jackson had then suggested a substitute to the bank, and in December 1831, he had asked that the bank be left to the consideration of the people and their representatives, hinting at the election of 1832. During that session of Congress, the president reminded Duane, the majority had approved the bank's petition for the renewal of its charter. Jackson had then issued a veto while campaigning for reelection. Presuming that Americans had supported the Bank Veto by electing him a second time, Jackson told the Treasury secretary, "By a decisive majority the people condemned the Bank to be both inexpedient and unconstitutional."[3]

In the president's narrative, the Bank War and the Bank Veto in particular had generated strong public support in the form of his reelection, thus proving the correctness of his policy. Beyond the arguments he presented to Duane, and to himself, Jackson added an important caveat and the seed of a significant change in American politics. He argued in private what he was yet cautious to state publicly, that elections and the mass support of the people were a mandate for policy, thereby adding a new and significant feature to the American polity.

With his justificatory narrative, Jackson instructed Duane to make "such arrangements as [would] enable the Government to carry on all its fiscal operations through the agency of the state Banks." Jackson reminded Duane of the bank's corruption, pointing to the loans it had extended "to gain power in the country and force the Government through the influence of the debtors to grant it a new charter." The Bank of the United States, he averred, had loaned "$28,000,000 in sixteen months, for the purpose of bringing the people within its power. It had secured to its interest editors and presses by extraordinary loans upon unusual terms," and it had "sought to procure the friendship and support of public men who might have [had] an influence or a vote upon the question of its charter."[4] The narrative Jackson sent to

Duane is significant, for it affords rare insight into how the president composed a cohesive account of the bank crisis, and how this account functioned relative to his policy and public pronouncements. In essence, Jackson listed arguments strengthening his overall charge of a Bank of the United States plot to circumvent the government, and strengthening his conclusion that he was correct to refuse the bank's recharter.

Jackson's narrative against the bank did not fully persuade Duane, who asked for further clarification. Jackson replied to the secretary of the Treasury's misgivings, especially his view that Congress should decide on a substitute bank lest the people think their representatives "[were] incompetent or corrupt." Rejecting this view, the president asked Duane to see the error of his view: "Can Congress make any provision for the deposit of the public money's [sic] until after they have been removed from the Bank of the United States by order of the Secretary of the Treasury?" The obvious answer was "Certainly not. This was the reply given on the floor of the house of representatives [sic] when an investigation was asked at the last session, and it would be renewed with vastly increased force at the next."[5] Duane remained unconvinced.

While preparations were under way for a formal letter announcing the withdrawal of bank deposits, the continued investigation into the bank's practices convinced Jackson more than ever of his actions' justness. On August 31, 1833, Jackson wrote James K. Polk, a member of the House Ways and Means Committee, a confidential letter detailing what he had learned about Biddle's expense account. The president stated that in two years some $80,000 had been used "to corrupt the people and buy a recharter [sic] of that mammoth of corruption [the Bank of the United States]." Jackson continued, "By an order of the board of directors, the whole funds of the Bank are placed at the disposal of Mr. Biddle to appro[priate] as he pleases without ac[counting] voucher, to [illegible word] of the Bank by the most bold specious [sic] of corruption ever practiced by any body of people in the most corrupt governments and in the most corrupt times—can any one really say, from this exposé that the U.S. Bank is a safe deposit for the peoples [sic] money?"[6] Jackson's frustrations were evident. He did not like having a second Treasury secretary question his motives, and he now had to convince the important congressional committee to agree with him. Importantly, the narrative quality of these exchanged letters provides context for Jackson's public rhetoric and the arguments therein.

Jackson also acted strategically, understanding the timing of his public statements. In a September 8, 1833, letter to Van Buren, he declared that any action regarding the bank should be taken before Congress convened. Jackson also stated his intention to utilize the *Globe* (the administration's newspaper, which Jackson established in 1830 in Washington, DC, with Francis P. Blair as its editor) to publish an unofficial exposé of the reason for the removal of bank deposits. Such action, suggested the president, would "prepare the minds of the people for a full and official exposure."[7] Jackson's immediate concern was protecting state banks from the Bank of the United States' retaliatory political attacks and financial pressure. For his part, Van Buren worried about citizens questioning his motives in the larger Bank War. Some believed the vice president had developed the scheme to substitute the federal bank with state banks in order to divert money to banks in his own state, New York.[8] Given his own presidential ambitions, Van Buren feared such a charge could hurt him politically.

On September 15, 1833, Jackson informed Taney that he had finalized the decision to remove deposits from the bank, and that the money had to be transferred to state banks as soon as possible. Jackson also opined that Congress had no say on the matter.[9] Three days later, the president read his cabinet a lengthy paper justifying his move regarding the bank. This widely published letter is listed as an official document in volume 3 of *A Compilation of Messages and Papers of the Presidents*. Jackson composed the lengthy message while he was in Rip Raps in late August, and, according to Van Buren, Taney edited the draft. This document became a watershed in presidential politics. Unlike his other official addresses, Jackson wrote it in the third person, lending his words weight, greater formality, and, most importantly, an authoritative flavor.

"The President," Jackson stated, "deems it his duty to communicate in this manner to his cabinet the final conclusions of his own mind and the reasons on which they are founded."[10] This phrasing reflects his decisive approach. Referring to "The President," "his duty," and "his own mind," Jackson introduced a new conception of the executive as commanding the sole, ultimate authority to render a decision, even vis-à-vis the cabinet. He elaborated further in the next sentence: "The President's convictions of the dangerous tendencies of the Bank of the United States, since signally illustrated by its own acts, were so overpowering when he entered on the duties of Chief Magistrate that he felt it his duty . . . to avail himself of the first occasion to call the attention of Congress and the people to the question of its recharter."[11] Here, the shift in tenses from present to past and the shift in titles from president to chief magistrate point to a changing conception of the nation's chief executive. If one takes *chief magistrate* as a term signifying an operative and adjudicative function, the president was presenting a chief magistrate's active, personal, and authoritative attributes.

Jackson mentioned his requests in three previous Annual Messages to Congress to consider the question of the Bank of the United States' charter. As he reminded his cabinet, he had even suggested some potential actions concerning the charter. But Congress had ignored his requests and his concerns over the bank's practices. And in 1831 and 1832, both houses had voted for a recharter, "upon which the President felt it his duty to put his constitutional veto."[12] Jackson provided the most significant part of the report in this statement: "There [were] strong reasons for believing that the motive of the bank in asking for a recharter at that session of Congress was to make it a leading question in the election of a President of the United States the ensuing November, and all steps deemed necessary were taken to procure from the people a reversal of the President's decision."[13]

Henceforth, the bank engaged in dubious loans, often with "insufficient security," in order "to bring as large a portion of the people as possible under its power and influence" during the election year. The bank, charged Jackson, also "warned of the ruin which awaited them should the President be sustained." He followed with a rhetorical question: "Can it now be said, that the question of a recharter of the bank was not decided at the election which ensued? Since individuals' positions on the bank had framed the election, Jackson therefore asserted, "The people have sustained the President." Now, he declared, "it is too late . . . to say that the question has not been decided." He then reiterated his point: "The President considers his reelection as a decision of the people against the bank."[14] And lest anyone still doubted his position, Jackson authoritatively announced, "The President considers it as conclusively settled that the charter of the Bank of the United States will not be renewed, and he has no reasonable ground to believe that any substitute will be established."[15]

As in the veto and related documents, Jackson spelled out numerous actions by the bank that cumulatively proved its corrupt practices, especially those in conjunction with the election and the manipulation of favorable press. He also blamed legislators for not heeding his earlier requests to deal with the bank, stating, had Congress "the wisdom . . . to decide upon the best substitute to be adopted in the place of the Bank . . . the President would have felt himself relieved from a heavy and painful responsibility if in the charter to the bank Congress had reserved to itself the power of directing at its pleasure the public money." Now, he added, "it is useless . . . to inquire why this high and important power was surrendered by those who are peculiarly and appropriately the guardians of the public money."[16] Jackson then followed with these profound words:

> While the President anxiously wishes to abstain from the exercise of doubtful powers and to avoid all interference with the rights and duties of others, he must yet with unshaken constancy discharge his own obligations, and can not allow himself to turn aside in order to avoid any responsibility which the high trust with which he has been honored requires him to encounter; and it being the duty of one of the Executive Departments to decide in the first instance, subject to the future action of the legislative power, whether the public deposits shall remain in the Bank of the United States until the end of its existence or be withdrawn some time before, the President has felt himself bound to examine the question carefully and deliberately in order to make up his judgment on the subject, and in his opinion the near approach of the termination of the charter and the public considerations heretofore mentioned are of themselves amply sufficient to justify the removal of the deposits.[17]

Jackson had just won the presidency with the opposition making the bank recharter its primary campaign issue. He could now consider his victory as providing the necessary mandate to remove funds from the bank. The president acknowledged that there were other reasons to oppose the recharter, including the Bank of the United States' "faithlessness," "interference in elections," and "flagrant misconduct."[18] But Jackson attached "sufficient"— the key word in the principle he pursued—to the election mandate warranting his policy. While this was a radical change in presidential politics, Jackson went even further. He stated that he was justified in his decision to remove the deposits. With strong words such as "unshaken constancy," "obligation," "duty," "responsibility," and "judgment," Jackson strengthened his office once more, asserting that the president could make decisions he considered justified. He acknowledged that future actions of the legislative branch could counter such decisions. But until that time, the president's decision would stand.

Jackson elaborated on this idea, stating that he did not desire "to interpose another body between himself and the people in order to avoid a measure which he [was] called upon to meet." With this artful phrasing, Jackson characterized the executive as answerable directly to the people, and not via Congress. The president, he added, "disclaims any design of soliciting the opinion of the House of Representatives in relation to his own duties," though he was always "ready to listen to the suggestions of the representatives of the people." Yet, Jackson continued, "whatever may be the consequences . . . to himself, he must finally form his own judgment where the Constitution and the law make it his duty to decide, and must act accordingly; and he is bound to suppose that such a course on his part will never be regarded by that elevated body as a mark of disrespect to itself, but that they will, on the contrary, esteem it the strongest evidence he can give of his fixed resolution conscientiously to discharge his duty to them and the country."[19]

In Jackson's opinion, the presidency was independent of Congress, and the president had a constitutional duty to make his own decision and render his own judgment. Though he would welcome consultation with legislative bodies, the president was not bound by congressional advice. Since Jackson chastised Congress for not doing its job, the constitutional argument interwove an article based on principle with an argument based on circumstance affording him the opportunity to strengthen the presidency one more time. This case also allowed him to argue that, had he not removed the deposits, he would have considered himself "almost an accomplice in a conspiracy against the Government which he ha[d] sworn honestly to administer."[20] The magnitude of these statements did not escape Congress, which suspected the president of being a despot in the making.

The drafting of Jackson's letter to his cabinet is important because gaps exist between the initial and final documents. Foremost, the lengthy draft of this letter includes no reference to the election and the mandate it generated. It must be assumed that this particular point—and it is a significant one—was strategically inserted during the editing process. Jackson dictated the draft, including a litany of accusations and charges against the Bank of the United States. But he made no attempt to ground his decision to remove deposits in the recent election results. Jackson came closest to assessing the needs of the nation in this statement: "The mass of people have more to fear from combinations of the wealthy and professional classes—from an aristocracy which thru' the influence of riches and talents, insidiously employed, sometimes succeeds in preventing political institutions however well adjusted, from securing the freedom of the citizens."[21] Yet this passage is too ambiguous to reference popular sentiments as justifying policy. Jackson, who was often ahead of his aides in arguing the popular appeal of his authority, used none of this reasoning in the draft letter.[22] The missing pages in this version may have included such a passage. However, it is important to note that the president did cite the mandate of the recent election in his response to Secretary of the Treasury Duane's misgivings.

In the formal letter, Jackson decisively changed the balance of power between the branches of government, specifically rejecting Congress's right to decide on the matter of the bank's deposits. The closest he approached such a view in the draft was in stating, "Congress, if it have any right to grant a new charter, can do so, only for the sake of the community, and not to satisfy any just claims which the corporation can assert."[23] Finally, Jackson's references to himself as "the President"—a new term for him—appear throughout the initial letter. Overall, the finalized document differs significantly from the draft. Initially, Jackson did not address the radical reconceptualization of the presidency. It is possible that a stronger justification was necessary for the president to argue his right to remove funds from the Bank of the United States relative to Congress. It is also possible that those working on the draft, primarily Taney and Van Buren, deemed it insufficient to repeat a list enumerating the bank's corrupt actions.

The exposé and the cabinet report did not coincide by chance. Their timing was a rhetorical move calculated to generate the greatest public support for the president's plan. When issued, Jackson's statement was a watershed in presidential politics, an assertion of presidential influence and a warning about corrupt practices that the president ought to correct. Executive power was once again transformed. With one statement, Jackson asserted formally what he had been thinking privately and had even written in drafts of earlier addresses: elections mattered, and they could provide the president support and authority for agenda and policies. With his reelection behind him, Jackson declared his mandate, once and for all, to eliminate the Bank of the United States. With that, his decision to remove deposits from the bank was finalized.

Though assuming that "the expose ha[d] put [him] on strong grounds, and ha[d] entirely presented the case in a new form to his mind," Secretary Duane still refused to remove deposits from the federal bank to state banks.[24] He also refused to resign. Jackson thus dismissed him and appointed Attorney General Taney the next secretary of the Treasury on September 23, 1833. (Jackson knew that Congress would not approve Taney's appointment. But with Taney as a temporary Treasury secretary, Jackson could proceed with the deposits transfer.) In the meantime, Van Buren reported that the exposé's "effect upon the public mind," had proved "equal to its merits" in informing the public of the bank's corruption.[25] The exposé was a public relations coup and a further blow to the bank and its allies.

In his Fifth Annual Message to Congress on December 3, 1833, Jackson announced, "The Secretary of Treasury has directed the money of the United States to be deposited in certain State banks designated by him." He detailed again the federal bank's corruption and misconduct, observing that a recent investigation had proved "beyond question" that it sought "to influence the elections of public officers by means of its money." The president further stated, per "the terms of the bank charter no officer but the Secretary of the Treasury could remove the deposits, it seemed to me that this authority ought to be at once exerted to deprive that great corporation of the support and countenance of the Government in such an [sic] use of its funds and such an exertion of its power."[26]

Jackson acknowledged a growing panic over the money supply, accusing the bank of seeking "to control public opinion, through the distresses of some and the fears of others." He was also quick to state, "The effort to set up a panic has hitherto failed," and he expanded on this point as follows, "No public distress has followed the exertions of the bank, and it can not be doubted that the exercise of its power and the expenditure of its money, as well as its efforts to spread groundless alarm, will be met and rebuked as they deserve."[27]

Though he hammered the bank's corruption for a while, Jackson now tied his rhetoric to the depressed economy. The economy had contracted for additional reasons, such as the opposition to paper money and the weakening of a strong central bank. But the president did not address these points. He stayed with his most successful rhetorical line, calling on Congress for a "serious investigation" of the Bank of the United States. Jackson said, "[I am] declaring it as my opinion that an inquiry into the transactions of that institution, embracing the branches as well as the principal bank, was called for by the credit which was given throughout the country to many serious charges impeaching their character, and which, if true, might justly excite the apprehension that they were no longer a safe depository for the public money."[28]

With Jackson on the path to winning the Bank War, political scrambling became evident, especially with Calhoun and Clay on the attack. In a December 23, 1833, letter to Jackson, James Polk asked whether he was authorized to answer a question by a House representative. McDuffie's question touched on information that Polk had learned privately from Jackson:

The initial draft of the Inaugural Address (Polk presumably meant the First Inaugural Address) had contained a section on the bank. In finalizing the address, had Jackson removed that section and decided to include it in his first annual message to Congress?[29] Jackson replied on the same day, confirming that he had indeed thought the passage in question more fitting for an Annual Message to Congress than an Inaugural Address. He rationalized the omission: "Every one that knows me, does know, that I have been always opposed to the U. States Bank, nay, all Banks."[30] Jackson gave Polk permission to reveal this information.

Though the specific reason for the above request was not spelled out, one can surmise that some in Congress were now accusing Jackson of concealing his plans for the bank. Jackson had not spelled out the specifics of his alternative mechanism for the national bank—not when he entered the presidency, and not when he issued his various charges of corruption. This debate over the differences between the initial and final versions of the First Inaugural Address suggests that the speech was taken as a primary document akin to an abiding contractual iteration of a president's agenda. Criticizing Jackson for supposedly being less than forthcoming was perhaps a counterattack on his tough line against the bank's corruption. Yet the president made explicit statements about the bank's recharter in every Annual Message. Targeting his First Inaugural Address was likely an act of desperation by the opposition that would now intensify the attack on the president.

Clay instigated the plan to politicize the Bank of the United States' recharter. He hoped that making the bank a major campaign issue would help him defeat Jackson. Having lost the election and not realized Jackson's assertion of presidential power and mandate, Clay introduced a resolution in the Senate on March 28, 1834, censuring the president for withdrawing the bank's deposits. That act was now described as unconstitutional, in keeping with the following statement from Clay: "We are in the midst of a revolution, hitherto bloodless, but rapidly rendering toward a total change of the pure republican character of the government, and to the concentration of all power in the hands of one man."[31] For Clay and other opponents of Jackson, the executive's outreach disrupted the balance between the three branches of government. Jackson strengthened the office of the executive to a tyrannical extreme.[32]

In response, Jackson wrote notes on the matter for potential use. He pointed to the fact that everything he had ever done was deemed by Clay and company as unconstitutional. Jackson pointed to the fact that when

Crawford, Treasury secretary under Monroe, "with the advice of the President removed the deposits whenever necessary for the public welfare," congressmen did not "proclaim these acts of Mr. Monroe and Mr. Crawford violation of the constitution and acts of usurpation."[33] Jackson's removal of a secretaries of the Treasury was also now under scrutiny. The opposition was looking for every possible way to attack the president. Jackson wrote to Amos Kendall in April 1834, noting that while his predecessors had removed cabinet secretaries from their posts, only his own removal of the Treasury secretary was considered unconstitutional.[34] Even so, the Senate approved the censure. It also rejected Taney's appointment as secretary of the Treasury on June 24, 1834, just as Jackson predicted.[35] Seeking another setback to a Jackson protégé, the Senate even rejected James K. Polk as Speaker of the House.[36]

As the Bank War intensified, Jackson devoted more time to addressing it in his remaining Annual Messages. In his Sixth Annual Message to Congress, delivered on December 1, 1834, Jackson stated, "The mischiefs and dangers which flow from a national bank far over-balance all its advantages." Noting that the bank also sought "to control the Government," the president averred, "The distresses it has wantonly produced, the violence of which it has been the occasion in one of our cities famed for its observance of law and order, are but premonitions of the fate which awaits the American people should they be deluded into a perpetuation of this institution or the establishment of another like it." Jackson now used intense rhetoric to prove that his accusations were correct all along. He was ready to kill the Bank of the United States once and for all.[37]

In his Seventh Annual Message, Jackson "confirmed the utter fallacy of the idea that the Bank of the United States was necessary as a fiscal agent of the Government." Seeking to prove that the nation's economy had functioned well "without its aid," the president proclaimed, "Despite of all the embarrassment it was in its power to create, the revenue has been paid with punctuality by our citizens, the business of exchange, both foreign and domestic, has been conducted with convenience, and the circulating medium has been greatly improved." He added that without the bank as "the agency of a great moneyed monopoly the revenue [could] be collected and conveniently and safely applied to all the purposes of the public expenditure."[38] Jackson praised the ability of state banks to replace a national bank: "Severed from the Government as political engines, and not susceptible of dangerous extension and combination, the State banks will not be tempted, nor will they have the power, which we have seen exercised, to divert the public funds from the legitimate purposes of the Government." Jackson acknowledged that he "was aware that there was in the act of the removal of the deposits a liability to excite that sensitiveness to Executive power which it is characteristic and the duty of free men to indulge; but [he] relied on this feeling also, directed by patriotism and intelligence, to vindicate the conduct which in the end would appear to have been called for by the interests of [his] country."[39]

As he neared the end of his presidency, Jackson reflected more on the Bank War and sought to justify his lengthy battle throughout it. Yet the need for vindication may also have functioned as a measure of concern, especially since the tightening money supply was beginning to hurt the nation's economy and distress its citizens. Employing a distinct rhetorical method of explaining his attitude toward the Bank of the United States, Jackson tied his actions to his reading of the people's sentiments. He took measures he believed were not only justified but also confirmed and vindicated by the nation's patriotism and intelligence. The president artfully referenced the 1832 presidential campaign centering on the Bank War and his reelection to a second term as proof of the justness of his cause.

Jackson attempted to allay concerns over his withdrawing deposits from the bank and the executive's influence over this issue, stating, "The public servant who is called on to take a step of high responsibility should feel in the freedom which gives rise to such apprehensions his highest security." Adding that his "constitutional obligations demanded the steps which were taken in reference to the removal of the deposits," he further declared, "It was impossible for me to be deterred from the path of duty by a fear that my motives could be misjudged or that political prejudices could defeat the just consideration of the merits of my conduct." Jackson's defense of his actions with appeals to his fearless character and constitutional duty was in reaction to the congressional censure, and to the criticism that he had made the presidency uniquely powerful and different from any previous conception of the office.

In his Eighth (and final) Annual Message to Congress on December 5, 1836, Jackson devoted more attention to the national bank and the consequences of moving its funds to state banks than he had in any other such address. While he acknowledged doubts about state banks' ability to assume their new responsibilities, he emphasized their efficiency: "It is now well ascertained that the real domestic exchanges performed through discounts by the United States Bank and its twenty-five branches were at least one-third less than those of the deposit banks for an equal period of time."[40] To substantiate this statement, Jackson cited the aggregate figure of some $59 million transferred at an exchange rate preferable to the federal bank's.

The president's optimism was probably more for obviating criticism than providing a realistic assessment, as he included a note of caution that would prove prescient later. He observed that "removal of the deposits [was] a step unquestionably necessary to prevent the evils which it was foreseen the bank itself would endeavor to create in a final struggle to procure a renewal of its charter." Jackson further elaborated, "It may be thus, too, in some degree with the further steps which may be taken to prevent the excessive issue of other bank paper, but it is to be hoped that nothing will now deter the federal and state authorities from the firm and vigorous performance of their duties to themselves and to the people in this respect."[41] The economic hardship citizens were already experiencing, partly due to the withdrawal of funds from the federal bank, were that bank's doings, Jackson stated. He was not responsible for Americans' present financial difficulties. With the endgame in sight, Jackson just hoped that Congress would finish removing deposits from the bank regardless of the hindrances it faced.

Jackson was not done; he displayed his hatred of the Bank of the United States one more time. He informed Congress of the institution's actions just prior to the expiration of its charter: "Instead of proceeding to wind up their concerns and pay over to the United States the amount due on account of the stock held by them, the president and directors of the old bank appear to have transferred the books, papers, notes, obligations, and most or all of its property to this new corporation, which entered upon business as a continuation of the old concern."[42] If Jackson needed to remind the nation once more of the bank administrators' corruption, he had the best evidence to put forward. Bank officials had taken "seven million of Government stock for their own profit, and [they had] refuse[d] to the United States all information as to the present condition of their own property and the prospect of recovering it into their own possession." Positing, "The lessons taught by the Bank of the United States can not well be lost upon the American people," Jackson also hoped that Congress "[would] adopt the modifications which are necessary to prevent this consequence" from recurring.[43] As the nation's economy showed signs of strain, the president's post veto rhetoric grew more defensive. He limited himself to identifying the bank's corruption as the primary cause of that strain. Jackson was not going to take any blame for difficulties caused by the removal of deposits.

THE AFTERMATH

While fighting with Jackson, the Bank of the United States tightened the money supply, deliberately causing panic. However, when the business community began to see this move as vengeful and economically unnecessary, Biddle, the bank president, quickly reversed course and increased the money supply. The sudden influx of funds brought inflation and land speculation, causing still more economic panic. As historian Schlesinger notes, Biddle "lost his grip on reality" and completely misunderstood the American people. In another foolish move, Biddle had ordered and distributed thirty thousand copies of Jackson's Bank Veto as supportive material for Clay's presidential campaign.[44]

Biddle's ill-advised actions following the Bank Veto made Jackson's quarrel with the bank more credible, especially once the bank began using its money to buy political support and favorable press. After that point, all Jackson had to do was present evidence of the bank's misdeeds and appeal for public support—and he did so very well. The president issued powerful, well-crafted public statements perfectly suited to his reputation as a popular, fearless leader. He centered his rhetoric primarily on appeals and simple arguments that attracted the support of the majority of Americans. People not fully versed in the mechanism of banking were thus willing to support Jackson in his battle against corruption and the moneyed elite. Once Jackson clothed the rhetoric of the Bank War in patriotic garb, his heroic image and anticorruption mantra carried the day.

The strength of the Bank Veto message lies in its straightforwardness and the simple logic of its arguments. Jackson emphasized two principles, the unconstitutionality of the Bank of the United States' charter and the corruption of its practices. He provided multiple examples illustrating these points in order to cement his objective of terminating the Bank. Jackson practiced "going public" some 150 years before the term was been coined and applied to a modern president. It is difficult not to label him a rhetorical president. He displayed his rhetorical acumen during the Bank War, pitting the public against the political elite and successfully issuing tried and true appeals to populism, patriotism, and fair play. During his first term, he had said very little on the subject, confining himself to oblique, mild statements often at the conclusion of his Annual Messages. Yet toward the end of his presidency, Jackson significantly increased his discussion of the national bank in his Annual Messages to Congress. Perhaps certain doubts crept into Jackson's rhetoric as he witnessed increasing economic panic over the tightening money supply. Perhaps he worried that he might be blamed for the panic after all.

The Bank of the United States ceased to exist in February 1836, when it was chartered as the United States Bank of Pennsylvania, a state bank. Biddle stepped down as the institution's president. Of the various state banks in operation, the Bank of New York became a center of economic and financial operations, returning to its original glory just as Alexander Hamilton founded it several decades earlier, and lasting as an economic center into the twenty-first century. Jackson misunderstood the advantages of a central bank for a growing nation with vast commerce and industry. Though he also advocated a national bank in Washington, DC, to be central to the operation of regional banks, nothing came of this plan.

Jackson brought to the presidency a rudimentary understanding of economics. He tended to view banks via the prism of ethics and relative to the needs of individual entrepreneurs, just as he had in his earlier days. The president's attacks on paper money and preference for specie likely reflected the views of Jefferson, his idol. These views on money probably did not reflect any particular economic sense of the industrially expanding nation.

Jackson did not appreciate losing any battle, military or political. He realized his last victory of the Bank War when his censure was expunged from the Senate's records in 1837. Jackson noted his appreciation for "this act of justice" against what he called an "odious sentence which . . . the voice of millions of freemen has ordered to be expunged."[45] Jackson's status as the people's president was central to his rhetorical calculations. He remained loyal to the millions who had voted for him and who felt that he did what they wanted—reform the corrupt government. Perhaps among his most decisive rhetorical acts, removing deposits from the federal bank was proof of Jackson's popular appeal. The president was censured over this act, not over any other policy statement or veto. This fact proves how much the withdrawals alarmed congressional leaders, and how decisively Jackson altered the role of the executive.

Jackson's own words over a span of eight years reflected his assessment of the expanding nation. His remarks also revealed his need to preserve a strong but limited federal government while not losing sight of Jeffersonian values. Jackson felt that these ideals were fading, and not always in a positive way. The president, then, looked forward but also to the past, seeking the best combination of both, precisely because the country was quickly expanding and advancing.

✳✳✳✳

Following his issue of the Maysville and Bank Vetoes, Jackson removed deposits from the Bank of the United States, expanding the power and reach of the executive once more. He made the executive branch first among the three branches of government. Moreover, he made the president an independent decision-maker. While there would no longer be an independent Bank of the United States, regional banks would operate under the authority of the Treasury and with directors appointed by the executive. However, such assertions of presidential power carried a price—the rise of intense partisan politics. Jackson's actions resulted in the rise of the Whig Party that sought to counter what it considered a usurpation of power. Yet in opposing Jackson, the Whigs also opposed the people and their popular support for him. The Bank War changed the American polity far beyond the confines of the national banking system. It also changed the presidency quite profoundly.

IMAGES OF OLD HICKORY
VISUAL RHETORIC IN THE SERVICE OF POLITICS

Notwithstanding the two presidents' differing ideologies, a steel engraving titled "The First Reading of the Emancipation Proclamation Before the Cabinet" depicts a portrait of Andrew Jackson on the wall of Abraham Lincoln's office.[1] Franklin D. Roosevelt considered Jackson "a man whom the average American deeply and fundamentally understood." In Roosevelt's opinion, "they [Americans] loved him well because they understood him well—his passion for justice, his championship of the cause of the exploited and the downtrodden, his ardent and flaming patriotism."[2] Harry S. Truman adorned his desk with a small bronze statue of Jackson on horseback, a small-scale replica of the statue Truman commissioned Charles Keck to create for the Jackson County Courthouse in Kansas City in 1935.[3] Throughout his life, Truman would cite Jackson as his hero. Most recently, Donald Trump put Jackson's portrait in the Oval Office and claimed him as his hero. Lincoln saw in Jackson a great leader determined to save the Union; Truman, a man of courage; and Trump, a strong president.

Political rhetoric is not limited to the purview of verbal utterances and their impact. Significantly, it is also the purview of visual framing, which is meant to enhance the verbal and at times override it. Visual framing must be understood as a rhetorical strategy that can effectively communicate sentiments, positions, and an overall ethos that many can identify with. History is replete with individuals who reached prominence via the manipulation of images that functioned persuasively for personal and national objectives. Historically, monuments, grand architecture, and statues have projected strong leadership or impressive national standing. Similarly, portraits and photographs have framed individuals in ways that highlight their positive attributes and enhance their reputation and standing. Image framing, then, is as rhetorical as verbal statements; both seek to communicate a message and a persona that is conducive to public consumption.[4]

For example, those who viewed a head shot photograph of Lincoln from the mid-1840s, discovered and published in McClure in 1895, were quite impressed by the president as a young man. Many of these individuals recorded their interpretations of the picture in letters. Those who saw this photograph tapped into myths that were already circulating, and they relied on their social knowledge of Lincoln to "see" him in a certain way. In their "image vernacular," they saw a character and expression via Lincoln's physiognomy. Viewers commented on his noble face and even read meaning into his mind and soul.[5] In this instance, the framed image functioned as a source of interpretation and judgment situated in existing myths about the person pictured.

Likewise, portraits of Jackson fit the overall hero narrative in circulation during his lifetime, especially the idea of the general as the nation's first hero after George Washington. Jackson's initial image construction, then, was a function of the America's search for a national icon. He became a hero instantly following the Battle of New Orleans in 1815. The fight ended three years of warfare with the United States' old nemesis, Great Britain, which was still sulking over its loss of the colonies. With the battle over, the nation felt secure and confident for the first time in a long while. The benefactor of this stability was a previously unknown military general who would be worshiped thereafter.

Jackson became a household name and a national hero via depictions of his military success and wide distribution of his image. He would be the focus of image makers from 1815 until his death thirty years later, inspiring hundreds of artworks including gamut of paintings, engravings, busts, statues, and cartoons. Many streets, towns, and counties would be named after Jackson in various states. No previous individual of prominence, save perhaps George Washington, had generated so much visual coverage. It is reasonable to suggest that this widespread visual rhetoric did much to propel Jackson to national importance and, subsequently, the presidency. This may be a novel idea for a nation inclined to associate image making with presidencies of the twentieth and twenty-first centuries.

In 1991, the National Portrait Gallery of the Smithsonian Institution in Washington, DC, published *Andrew Jackson: A Portrait Study*, edited by James G. Barber. This volume catalogues many known images of the president, including paintings, lithographs, engravings, busts, and cartoons. It was fitting for the Smithsonian to produce this work, as it was President Jackson who arranged for James Smithson's bequest to the US government to become a premier institution of arts and sciences named in his honor. The catalogues' images are accompanied by information about the artists and commentary concerning the circumstances surrounding each work. This chapter relies heavily on Barber's collection of images and annotations to provide unique insight into likenesses of Jackson through rhetorical assessment.

In the catalogue's foreword, National Portrait Gallery director Alan Fern writes of Jackson's "striking appearance." Coupled with his "military and political victories in fierce contests, and his enormous popular appeal as the first national leader to emerge from a modest background," the president's looks made him "an irresistible magnet for portraitists."[6] While most of his presidential predecessors had had their portraits made early in their lives, perhaps even as children, often to mark their prosperous upbringing, in contrast, Jackson's portraits came relatively late; his first depicts him at age forty-eight. While he did not make himself available to many artists, he sat for portraits enough times to ensure an assortment of renderings. One portraitist, Ralph E. W. Earl, would become a close friend of the president's, and even a member of his extended family. Earl lived in the White House and in the Hermitage in Tennessee.[7]

That Jackson was popular is an acceptable premise. But the extent of Jackson's popularity in the early republic is revealed in this 1833 statement by diarist Phillip Hone: "Talk of him as the second Washington . . . won't do now; Washington was only the first Jackson."[8] This was the context in which many sought portraits of the president. Americans wanted to see what the Hero of New Orleans looked like. Artists of the time knew a business opportunity when they saw one.

Several artists made the long trip to Tennessee to study Jackson, and the general quite reluctantly agreed to sit for their endeavors. He did not like to have his picture painted, but he understood the paintings' political impact. The earliest images of Jackson depicted him on on January 8, 1815, the day of the American victory at New Orleans, standing triumphantly on a battlefield littered with dead British soldiers.[9] This representation would capture the heart of many and make him a national hero within weeks. One such early rendering, an 1815 head portrait by Jean Francois de Vallee, is an ivory miniature presenting Jackson as younger than he actually was. One distinct feature of this engraving is Jackson's hair, which does not accord with his natural look. Instead, the artist has Jackson's hair fall down on his forehead in the style of the period, and in a manner likely influenced by images of Napoleon Bonaparte.[10] The portrait by Nathan W. Wheeler and John Wesley Jarvis is another distinct attempt to portray Jackson as Napoleon-like; the artists consciously ignored Jackson's rather impressive thick gray hair and imprinted the French emperor's hairstyle instead. Early images, then, were doctored to make Jackson fit the fashion of the day as well as resemble the hero of the age. Napoleon broke with conventions, and for a while, was considered the "champion of the people" and like Jackson, "a self-made man."[11]

Requests for portraits of Jackson increased a few years later, as several cities commissioned large paintings of him for prominent display. Charles Wilson Peale's 1819 portrait would become one of the more reputable ones. Jackson sat for Peale while in Washington for the congressional hearing concerning his incursion into Florida (Jackson sat for Peale three times and even had Peale's niece paint his portrait).[12] While Congress was debating Jackson's military campaign in Florida and alluding to his lack of restraint and savage character, the nation's capital was witnessing the future president's gentlemanly manners. Through Peale's portraits in particular, the public began to see a Jackson that did not cohere with the aforementioned negative portrayals, especially those made by the press. Instead of critical press coverage, Americans saw a subdued face with dreamy eyes. His military uniform carries no distinct decoration except for the shoulder epaulets. Any gap between crude and negative initial impressions of Jackson and subsequent more favorable ones began working to his advantage just as operatives began to contemplate and plan his presidential prospects. With the public approving of his actions in Florida actions, despite congressional criticism, his fame—and talk of his presidential potential—only grew.[13]

Another known portrait of Jackson by Thomas Sully, also painted in 1819, depicts a confident, heroic General Jackson in uniform, standing by his horse, and positioned centrally in the Battle of New Orleans.[14] Jackson, now with his known full head of white hair, appears sleepy and quite unassuming. He appears to be somewhere between standing upright and slightly leaning on his horse (even the horse looks a bit sleepy and is clearly not assuming any heroic pose). Overall, Jackson in this portrait does not resemble the hero that he was. Perhaps this very depiction made him popular; there are no allusions to grandeur or power in this painting. On April 19, 1819, the *Democratic Press* announced that this portrait would be on display in Philadelphia. The public then began to see Jackson, the nation's hero, as a humble and unassuming man.

The Sully portrait was good enough to be the model for several artists' engravings of Jackson. Also in 1819, while visiting Philadelphia, Jackson sat for sculptor William Rush, who created his bust. The *Nashville Gazette* described the finished work as possessing a striking likeness to Jackson,[15] and with this initial success, Rush was ready to produce plaster replicas upon request. A few days later, Jackson arrived in New York City for a triumphant public engagement; a standing painting of the general was commissioned for the city hall.[16] The growing requests and commissions for portraits of Jackson evidenced his popularity.

Ironically, John C. Calhoun asked the government to honor the Battle of New Orleans with a medal engraved with Jackson's portrait. In 1820, Calhoun, the secretary of defense, would seek to charge Jackson with not following orders. After numerous delays, the medal was finally issued in 1824, just in time for the presidential election.[17] Still another portrait, this one drawn in 1820 by John Vanderlyn, depicted General Jackson standing in combat position next to his horse and with his sword centrally featured. Jackson saw the portrait in New Orleans and reportedly liked it.[18] In 1828, Asher B. Durand completed an engraving of Jackson after Vanderlyn's work, and he then put a notice in the *National Intelligencer* that a subscription for prints of this portrait was available. Hoping to increase the engraving's value, Durand opted to issue and sell only 850 copies of the 21-by-15-inch portrait rather than the usual 2,000 to 3,000 copies.[19] The timing of this portrait was also ideal, as it coincided with the presidential election of 1828.

Collectively, a cohesive visual record of Jackson emerged in the 1820s, several years after the famous Battle of New Orleans. Images from this era depict him primarily, but not exclusively, as a military hero with few of the trimmings of a military general. These likenesses also reveal his true appearance, depicting him as a tall man with deep-set eyes, strong facial features, and an impressive head of wavy gray hair.[20] Yet, for the soldier to become a politician, Jackson's image had to change accordingly. As early as 1821, military depictions of Jacksons began a transformation—the uniformed soldier in a battle pose gave way to the farmer-gentleman wearing a black coat and white jabot.[21] The initial change was strategic and specific. It sought to dispel the rough and savage image borne of Jackson's military experience, battles with Indian tribes, and congressional hearing over his Florida campaigns. Jackson's new image coincided with his arrival in the nation's capital to assume his new position as senator from Tennessee. The transformation from a military general to a statesman was successful. Even Jackson noted the change in his public image, writing to a friend, "I am told the opinion of these whose minds were prepared to see me with a Tomahawk in one hand and a scalping knife in the other has greatly changed and I am getting on very smoothly."[22]

A transitional image construction can be observed in Vanderlyn's 1824 portrait. Here, Jackson is still in military uniform, but the uniform is dark and not markedly different from nonmilitary dress, except for the epaulets on his shoulders and the sword in his hand. Significantly, most military insignia are absent in this portrait. A cannon is partially visible in the background, but it does not occupy a central position in the image.[23] In the same year, Robert Street produced a portrait of Jackson as a politician in civilian attire. Street depicts Jackson sitting in front of a Greek column and gesturing with one hand, much as a statesman would during a speech. His other hand rests on a paper bearing the strategic title of "Fortification of New Orleans." A sword's handle in the shape of an eagle is depicted next to Jackson's left hand.

Produced during Jackson's senatorial period (1823–25), Street's portrait assumes a political setting yet contains significant allusions to his subject's military history.[24] Political and strategic, this image seeks the advantage of visual rhetoric. It is a persuasive depiction of a new persona that merges the military and the political and assumes viewers would observe the richness of Jackson's experience. Jackson's military experience is reduced to his service in Battle of New Orleans, indicated by a partial sword and the papers carrying his military plans. The political setting is much richer here. It dominates the background, and Jackson's attire and the physical features of the polity in the form of Greek columns seek to enhance his political viability. The strategic framing makes Jackson's military secondary and places his political persona center stage. This merging of his military and political experience would dominate many portraits hereafter, and it would function as the metonymy for his political persona.

Though other factors contributed to Jackson's 1824 campaign, it is hard to disprove that his image as a military hero with presidential timber brought it about. We do know that Jackson's portraits were commercially successful. Subsequently, many citizens were exposed to his image in a short period of time, getting their first inkling of what he looked like. The public was also "instructed" on how they should read Jackson's image. The circulation of his numerous portraits, then, cannot be discounted as a factor propelling him into the presidency.

After his bitter loss in 1824, Jackson left Washington and the Senate. On his way back to Tennessee, he stopped in Cincinnati and sat for Aaron H. Corwine, who produced one of the more impressive portraits of Jackson. The *Cincinnati Advertiser* complimented the artist for creating an "excellent likeness of our hero" and that would surely "give satisfaction to every one who ha[d] seen the original, and who admire the character of the man." As the newspaper suggested, Corwine had created more than an artistic depiction. He had produced one of the better representations of a character, and a heroic one at that.[25] As befitted a nineteenth-century audience, portraits of that era gave license to a rich story of character and impression. Viewers were at liberty to develop their own insights into the subjects' character and intentions. In Corwine's work, Jackson looks distinguished. The general is dressed in a fur collar and a white jabot. His full white hair is pushed back from his forehead, and his gaze is slightly sleepy, as it is in most portraits. As noted in the review of this portrait, Jackson also exudes confidence with a bit of peevishness, a likely allusion to his unjust presidential loss.[26] This image, then, carries a flexible interpretation including sympathy and lament of an unjust political setback.

Back at the Hermitage, Jackson's friend and portraitist Earl produced several renderings of Jackson. Earl also commissioned James Barton Longacre, who had earlier produced engravings of Jackson after portraits by Sully, to create additional engravings. The new ones were completed in to Earl's satisfaction in 1828; he ordered some five hundred copies. The Jackson of this engraving is different from previous portraits. Though he still wears a black coat and white jabot, the image is sharper. Moreover, Jackson's increasing age is distinct. According to the Nashville *Republican and Gazette*, Jackson appears in the Longacre engravings as a "hospitable, benevolent and philanthropic farmer, surrounded by a happy domestic circle, not to be disturbed by the calumnies of faction or the infamous detractions of political demagogues."[27] A writer for the Nashville *Whig and Banner* made a similar observation, stating, the portrait "exhibits the

General in the costume of a private citizen, enjoying the comforts of domestic life, and will preserve the recollection of him, amongst his neighbors and friends, in the character in which they most value and esteem him—that of a kind, affectionate and benevolent citizen."[28] In the post-1824 narratives concerning Jackson, viewers read deep meaning into the new engraving and suggested how it should be interpreted. The effects of the 1824 loss were now covered in image commentaries and in additional material reflecting the spillage of Jackson's resentment over this setback and into public sentiment.

Clearly, the press took license in allowing politics to determine how the visuals should be interpreted. It also assumed a defensive tone to explain Jackson's unjustified presidential loss and rationalize his return home following the "corrupt bargain." Such commentary about his happy family and domestic life is pure fiction, as there is nothing in the portrait besides Jackson's upper body. The background of Jackson's "head shot" is a gray curtain of sorts, devoid of any hint or suggestion. The reference to Jackson as a "farmer of Tennessee" is a likely attempt to distinguish him from the eastern professional politicians whose machinations prevented him from winning the presidency as he deserved. It is also an attempt to appeal to northern farmers. Gearing up for the next election, the opposition countered these images with references to Jackson's expensive taste. Yet, the farmer framing fit the new era; portraying Jackson as returning to nature and toiling the land supported his image as a self-made man. Of course, Jackson was not a farmer in the sense of working the land with his own hands. His slaves did the work.[29]

The portraits that presented Jackson as a "farmer," would become a political asset for the next election and an important element in the construction of Jackson's persona. The completion of Longacre's portrait in 1828 was timely. During his successful quest for the presidency that year, Jackson's primary campaign issue was the denial of his win in 1824. Also in contrast to other politicians of the day, Jackson was described as philanthropic and benevolent, kind and affectionate. In short, he was said to possess the very characteristics his opponents presumably lacked. Now, the artistic and the political coincided. The Longacre portrait proved commercially successful, and its wide distribution was an added asset during the presidential campaign.

Even a rare printed portrait of Jackson by Orramel Hinckley Throop, issued in 1828, proved successful; it was extensively recorded in letters and newspapers of the time. Throop traveled to Nashville to ask Jackson sit for him, and the resulting engraved print was like no previous portrait. Wearing civilian attire, Jackson is seated in a library. Behind him are bookshelves, and to his left is a desk bearing writing instruments. Jackson's right hand is positioned inside his jacket, perhaps in a suggestive allusion to Napoleon, and his left hand, half resting on the desk, holds a paper titled "Plan—8th of January 1815."[30] Overall, the portrait resembles a cartoon more than a full-pledged artistic painting. It is clearly not an attempt at an accurate portrayal, as Jackson's features are a bit exaggerated but in an appealing way. On May 17, 1828, the *United States Telegraph* (a Jackson newspaper) attested to the print's success: "Most, if not all of the portraits heretofore published, have represented him [Jackson] as a military character. This engraving presents him as a civilian, both in employment and costume, a character which he deservedly acquired as that of the citizen soldier."[31]

Jackson's new and modified portraits clearly benefited his presidential campaign, promoting his intellectual prowess and his distinguished military career. As had other portraitists, Throop strategically inserted a military artifact into a nonmilitary scene. Yet in this instance, the allusion to Jackson's military is much reduced. It is limited to the plans for the Battle of New Orleans, marked only by the date of the decisive engagement on the papers in Jackson's hand. During the campaign, the portrait argued Jackson's merit for the highest office in the land. It was also enthymematic, assuming that viewers would fill in the gaps in the information presented (as many knew and celebrated the date of the US victory in New Orleans).

Surprisingly, once Jackson was elected president, portraitists resumed depicting his military career. Artists fulfilled the demands of many who wished to own a presidential portrait highly suggestive of military success. A flurry of new paintings circulated, many of them featuring a full-length, canvas-size image of Jackson as either a general at a battle scene or a man of presidential stature. Some of them present General Jackson at the age he was in 1815. Others depict President Jackson at his contemporary age.

In 1833, Earl, Jackson's live-in portraitist, portrayed the president as he appeared during his second term. Earl painted Jackson as an aging general wearing the uniform of the 1830s, not the uniform of fifteen years prior, which Jackson had actually worn. In several other portraits painted between 1833 and 1835, Earl rendered Jackson's facial features to reflect his true age. At the same time, Earl depicted Jackson as wearing a military uniform and holding a sword in his left hand. In several instances, the sword's scabbard is inscribed with the president's famous toast to the Union.[32] Jackson's military exploits, then, continued to be a rich source of imagery even some eighteen years after the Battle of New Orleans. The convergence of the political and the military had appeared in several earlier portraits. But such depictions were now clearly out of time. The addition of the third variable—Jackson's famous toast to the Union during the Nullification Crisis—became in the second term metonymic of the president's character, depicting him as a military hero and a determined president. Disparate features from Jackson's career framed his image for both biographical and ideological purposes.

Much later, Jackson's image as a military hero was again coupled with his toast to the Union in plans for a monument in Lafayette Park, in front of the White House. This monument portrays Major General Jackson riding his horse in battle. The inscription on the base of the monument reads, "The Federal Union: It Must Be Preserved." Like numerous portraits, this monument, the ultimate honor to Jackson, integrates his military successes in 1815 and his strong advocacy for the Union during the Nullification Crisis. Jackson's monument is a rhetorical visual emphasizing his determination and courage for a posterity that would forever combine the military and the political.

JACKSON IN PERIOD CARTOONS

Cartoons and caricatures of Jackson offer an entirely different perspective on presidential image construction, and they provide important insight into his particular political imagery. On the face of it, these likenesses correspond to the increasing volume of portraits and engravings of Jackson starting around 1819. Initially, both types of images emanated from Jackson's troubles with Congress and the Monroe administration concerning his actions in Florida.

The first known cartoon depicting Jackson, drawn by James Akin and finally issued in 1824, criticizes the "preposterous proceeding" against him in Congress over his Florida excursion. Likely assisted by portraitist Ralph E. W. Earl, the cartoonist depicted Jackson as the Hero of New Orleans "standing resolute against the congressional caucus" supporting William H. Crawford for the presidency. The image shows Jackson wearing his military uniform and holding a sword inscribed with Caesar's famous line "Veni, Vidi Vici" (I came, I saw, I conquered"), a statement of ultimate decisiveness and determination.[33] In front of Jackson are several dogs representing various presidential candidates, each uttering an appropriate political statement. This cartoon was timed perfectly for the 1824 presidential election, depicting Jackson as an honorable person manipulated by Washington politicians. However, this supportive cartoon of Jackson is an exception, for it preceded his presidency.

"A Foot-Race," a cartoon drawn by David Claypool Johnson and issued in Boston on the eve of the 1824 election, marked "a new trend in American political caricature"—using sports competition to explain politics. Whether depicting boxing, foot racing, horse racing, or card playing, this sort of cartoon proliferated and signified something new—"unpredictable competition—as a metaphor for the democratic campaigns."[34] This metaphor for politics introduced a new notion to the American policy. If presidential elections had been predictable, often involving a sitting president giving the nod to the secretary of state to be the next chief magistrate, they were henceforth open to competition. When it was published, Johnson's cartoon signaled a significant change in the American democratic polity, one "channeling that egalitarian experience into partisan fervor rather than radical challenges to the social and political order."[35] Scholar John Sullivan contends a cartoon is "enthymemic in nature," as it relies "on the audience to participate in the process of persuasion by supplying the 'factual' information upon which it is based." He further states, "In time such symbolic representations come to stand for arguments which voters cannot reconstruct but nonetheless believe."[36]

In "A Foot-Race," Johnson drew four candidates racing to the White House. Adams is slightly ahead, William Crawford is running second, and Jackson, in military uniform, is coming in third. Clay is placing fourth, ready to quit rather than finish last. The footrace resembles a horse race—a bag containing $25,000 (standing for the president's salary) is the competitors' tempting goal. The most distinct feature of the cartoon is the assortment of people pictured in the background. Spectators of the race include African American boys, immigrants, frontiersmen, and veterans, all joining and encouraging one candidate or another.[37] The age of populism was under way with no class distinctions separating the audience.

"Symptoms of a Locked Jaw," another early cartoon, depicts Clay sewing Jackson's mouth shut. Jackson is seated in a chair and wearing his military uniform. As Clay plies his needle and thread, he also pushes his knee into Jackson to force him to sit still. A note reading "cure for calumny" protrudes from Clay's pocket, and the caption written on the wall reads, "Plain sewing done here."[38] This 1827 cartoon is a reaction to Jackson's accusation that Clay had arranged the 1824 election for Adams and himself, and to Clay's wish that Jackson would stop accusing him of brokering a "corrupt bargain." The cartoon was likely published in response to the Carter Beverley article concerning Jackson's renewal of his charge against Clay. It likely also reflected Clay's July 12, 1827, speech defending himself against Beverley's exposé.[39] Having Clay sew Jackson's mouth shut suggests that the latter's accusation of intrigue had stuck and disrupted the Adams-Clay ticket. Clay wanted Jackson to shut up. Depicting Jackson in military uniform tellingly demonstrates that his image was fixated on his military credentials, even a decade after the Battle of New Orleans.[40] Cartoons would continue to depict Jackson in uniform during his presidency and beyond.

The most infamous cartoon of the period was the "Coffin Handbill," published in 1828 by John Binn of the Philadelphia *Democratic Press*. This image sought to depict Jackson as a cold-blooded murderer for upholding a death sentence for six soldiers who protested their length of service during the Creek War (1814). Part of the opposition's campaign material, this cartoon was most likely issued once it became clear that Jackson would win the election. Yet this "vicious attack ultimately backfired on the pro-Adams forces."[41]

Considered the "most notorious poster of all times," the "Coffin Handbill" was deemed "the first national smear campaign."[42] A military court condemned the soldiers to death. Jackson's involvement in the case was indirect; he allowed the military court's ruling to stand. The court-martial took place in the midst of military action in New Orleans, when Jackson served as major general of the Tennessee militia and, shortly thereafter, as a major general in the US Army. The poster attacks Jackson's character, portraying him as a cruel military chieftain whose battle background, behavior, and actions made him unfit for the presidency. The "Coffin Handbills" were issued in six different groups, each depicting coffins under the heading "Monumental inscriptions," skulls and bones on the top of each coffin, and a poem titled "Mournful Tragedy" at the bottom of the poster. While several of the handbills depict six coffins, others have more than six. One cartoon titled "An Account of some of the Bloody Deeds of Gen. Jackson" displays 234 coffins.[43]

"Richard III," another campaign cartoon published by Binn, depicts Jackson as the evil English king, and as a presidential candidate attempting to cash in on the corpses of his past military career. This cartoon also appeared in the *Democratic Press* during the campaign for the 1828 presidential election. Like the "Coffin Handbill," "Richard III" presents Jackson as unfit to be president. In this cartoon, Jackson's face is made of dead Indians, and his hair is made of swords. His right epaulet is comprised of the six hanged militiamen, his collar is made of cannons, and his head is a military tent. The military theme was thus a signifier, precisely because many Americans made Jackson's service record a measure of his suitability to be president.[44] Even so, both posters failed because the public could not accept "such a vicious attack" on a presidential candidate. The "Coffin Handbills" were never reissued, not during the 1830 midterm election or the 1832 presidential election. Binn would close his newspaper in 1829 due to lack of subscriptions.[45]

The first national smear campaign failed, but it opened the door to the use of cartoons as political weapons based on exaggeration and falsehood. Binn's cartoons also taught many Americans a lesson—the public was neither blind nor ignorant enough to buy into every caricature the press issued. As the aforementioned portraits of Jackson have already indicate, the Hero of New Orleans became a cherished national treasure. This heroic image would carry him into the White House, and attempts to tarnish it would not only fail but also impart an important lesson. Political insiders were slow to catch on to the growing public interest in political matters and presidential politics in particular.

"A Political Game of Bragg," a cartoon published during the 1832 presidential election, pictures several individuals playing cards. In this image, Henry Clay, the candidate of the National Republican Party, holds cards labeled "internal improvements," "domestic manufactures," and "U.S. Bank" cards; Jackson holds cards reading, "Intrigue," "Corruption," and "Imbecility"; and Calhoun clutches "Nullification" and "Anti-tariff" cards. William Wirt of the Masonic Party is also among the players. Jackson is portrayed as having the worst cards, while his opponents are depicted as skilled players.[46] This partisan cartoon failed in its goal of influencing voters by engaging in comparative argument—Jackson won the presidential election decisively. It was an ill-conceived plan on the cartoonist's part to have Jackson's opponents in this image consider his cards weak. Jackson had won the 1828 election by making a case against intrigue and corruption. In 1832, he attached the same issues to the Bank War and with similar effect. Read differently, the opposition had bad cards. It could not point to any damaging information about Jackson, and it thus resorted to the primary issues he had raised in 1828.

The Bank War as the primary campaign issue of 1832 prompted several cartoons from both parties. One of the more prominent ones is titled "General Jackson Slaying the Many Headed Monster." With the aid of Maj. Jack Downing, Jackson and Vice President Van Buren are fighting the Bank of the United States monster in this image. The beast's many heads include that of the bank's president, Nicholas Biddle.[47] Inabinet argues that the illustrator depicted the bank as a monster since it "could not be dealt with rationally and . . . reasonable compromise would be impossible." Only a general with military skill could "slice each head of the 'hydra.'"[48] Another cartoon from the Bank War period, "The Model of a Republican President," shows Van Buren giving Jackson a pillow to fatten him up so that he looks like the French dictator.[49] This cartoon seeks to portray Jackson as a megalomaniac, just like Napoleon was a few years earlier (although in 1832, French events of 1815 and earlier were rather outdated). The image suggests that the only difference between the two leaders is the president's lack of physical resemblance to the emperor—hence the need to fatten him up. These cartoons mock Jackson and tie his powerful presidency to megalomania.

Yet another cartoon, titled "Office Hunters for the Year 1834," mocks Jackson's reform policy and intent to replace corrupt officeholders by depicting him as the devil "tantalizing the people with the fruits of victory."[50] This drawing references Jackson's entry into office in 1829, as well as his promise to enact major reform by dismissing many incompetent officeholders and affording more qualified candidates to seek opportunities not available to them before. Depicting Jackson as the devil probably reflects the anguish of many Americans who lost jobs. Yet such demonization presents an extreme version of what for many was a democratic and much warranted reform. While the caricature "A Grand Functionary" has Jackson locking up Tobias Watkins of the Treasury Department for fraud, the president is the one coming under fire from the cartoonist. Jackson is being depicted as a sinister sailor preventing Watkins from getting due justice. He double-locks the jail door and proclaims, "I'm acting in my Magisterial Capacity!!!! D—n the fellow he opposed my election and if he is released he'll set up a Newspaper against me. Here let him rot!!!!"[51] Jackson is thus portrayed as a thin-skinned president and a vengeful one. But above all else, he is depicted as a dictator who tolerates no opposition to his rule. The specific accusation of fraud, one of Jackson's central reform policies, is altogether ignored in this cartoon.

A prominent cartoon titled "The Rats" criticizes Jackson for reshuffling his cabinet. As drawn, the president is seated sloppily with outstretched legs, and he is trying to step on the tails of several rats representing his cabinet members. When Van Buren's son asks him when he will return to New York, Van Buren replies, "When the President takes off his foot."[52] This cartoon, which sold thousands of copies, condemned Jackson for demanding an agreeable cabinet. At the time, much turmoil followed several cabinet secretaries' resignation. Yet the line Van Buren's son utters in this cartoon is inconsistent with his father's presidential ambitions and his overall loyalty to Jackson. Another prominent cartoon, "King Andrew the First: Born to Command" (1832), unflatteringly portrays the aging Jackson in royal regalia, including a crown like that of a British royal. The president is shown abusing his power by trampling on the Constitution during the Bank War and with his frequent vetoes. The imperial presidency was under way, or so thought the opposition, and it was hence material for critical view.[53]

Jackson's 1833 tour of New England inspired "The Grand National Caravan," a cartoon rendering Jackson on horseback at the head of the procession and uttering, "I've kissed & I've prattled to fifty fair maids." This image mocks Yankee girls who lined up to watch the tour. It also ridicules Van Buren, who sits sideways on the same horse as Jackson. Here as elsewhere, Van Buren is portrayed as a petty politician doing the bidding of his master. At the end of the touring caravan, akin to a circus arriving in town, are five Black Hawk warriors in a caged wagon. Defeated by federal troops a year earlier during an uprising in northern Illinois (indeed, five warriors were imprisoned before they were released), these combatants are Jackson's war spoils. The caption attached to the imprisoned Black Hawks—"Home! Sweet home!"—mocks the president for forcing the tribes off their land and moving them to a faraway territory.[54]

While most cartoonists ignored the issue of Indian removal altogether, one drawing focuses exclusively on the tribes' fate. Seated in a large, ornate chair, Jackson appears oversized relative to the undersized American Indians around him. He holds two Indians on his lap, and several others stand at his feet and look up to him.[55] The domineering Jackson looking down at the submissive Indians ironically alludes to a father figure holding his babies. A framed picture of Lady Justice hangs on the wall in this seemingly compassionate and intimate setting. The rather small framed image is meant to contrast with Jackson's harsh treatment of the tribes. Lady Justice argues "justice" against a patronizing Jackson and Indian children. Size, as in the oversized Jackson and the undersized Indians, is the trope of the cartoon, symbolizing Jackson mistreating the tribes with paternalism, determination, and injustice.

A cartoon challenging Jackson's actions during the Bank War and his resistance to paper currency depicts him riding a donkey while Van Buren walks behind him. This image depicts the vice president's intention to follow his master against his better judgment. Titled "The Modern Balaam and his Ass," this cartoon is based on the Old Testament story of Balaam, who was hired to curse ancient Israel while his ass stopped three times because an angel of God stood in front of him. While the ass could see the angel, Balaam could not see what was before him. This rather sophisticated cartoon takes Jackson to task for pushing hard against paper currency without realizing how quickly the economy would experience distress in the event of a shortage. The president failed to realize the advantages of paper currency and the credit it would bring to the expanding nation.[56]

Collectively, Jackson has been depicted in cartoons as a king, the devil, a lion, a cat, an eagle, an old lady, and—cartoonists' favorite choice—a jackass, as a take on his name. It is due to this last depiction that the donkey would later become the symbol of the Democratic Party.[57] Ironically, an image designed for ridicule—Jackson was a "jackass" for advocating the astonishing position of a populist government whereby the people rule—did not stick. Out of mockery, an iconic image emerged as symbolic of Jackson's Party.   The majority of the cartoons published during Jackson's presidency center on his political fights. Drawings cover the primary issues of the day, including the Bank War and Jackson's quarrels with opposition leaders. Only few images concern the Indian Removal Act or the Nullification Crisis. For the most part, these cartoons mock Jackson's administration. The large number of critical cartoons speaks to the growing importance of party politics and the increasing use of the partisan press as a political weapon. Yet what is distinct about these cartoons is their focus on specific episodes, with Jackson as the central figure with the key political players of the time, such as Biddle, Clay, Webster, Van Buren, and Calhoun, the supporting figures. In line with political cartoons of the period, the words uttered by those depicted are meant to ridicule and exaggerate.

The critical point here, however, is that the aforementioned cartoons are no different from those covering Jackson's predecessors. These cartoons are generally consistent with other period cartoons lampooning politicians. Yet, the criticism of Jackson and his administration follows the political scene of his predecessors, not the scene of his administration. Whether by design or due to ignorance, these cartoons, with very few exceptions, lack any depiction of Jackson's populism. There are no "people" in them. The cartoons collectively misread Jackson's elevation to the presidency via the popular vote, depicting instead the politics of the past—the gamesmanship of specific individuals and the maneuvering of the political elite.

Put differently, the cartoons and those who drew them were stuck in the political commentary of the pre-Jacksonian era. They missed the new politics the Jacksonians had ushered in. Though studies of cartoons depicting Jackson argue that their proliferation was a democratic form of the time, they missed the very change Jackson brought to the presidency.[58] If cartoonists were critical image makers seeking to argue a point, their attempt at influence failed. The renderings mock and criticize issues and events in which Jackson oftentimes triumphed: the Bank War, political reforms, the Maysville Road improvement plan, and the Nullification Crisis. Even the consistent mockery of Vice President Van Buren did not yield the results it sought, as he won the presidency following Jackson. The political cartoons featuring Jackson, as Inabinet points out, are rough and base relative to the expectations of his era, "when the truly honorable still were supposed to rise to rule naturally."[59] Yet, becoming the first people's president, Jackson brought honor to the American polity by fighting every issue and soliciting the people's support in political struggles through rhetorical means. Ostensibly, several cartoons suggest interpretations inconsistent with facts on the ground—for example, Van Buren seeking to escape Jackson's cabinet or many Americans opposing Jackson's political reforms. It is plausible, that most cartoon images failed for the same reason the "Coffin Handbills" backfired. The cartoons presented unconvincing images to a populace increasing its political involvement and becoming better informed about the issues of the day.

Jackson's correspondence provides no evidence of his thoughts on these cartoons. He never mentioned them, even in letters dating from his presidential terms.[60] As a consummate letter writer attuned to the press of the day, Jackson was most likely aware of these images. Since he tended to be rather harsh toward his opposition, his lack of comment is rather surprising. We are left, then, to surmise that he did not give the cartoons much credence. Perhaps their mockery did not bother him; he triumphed on almost every issue the cartoons sought to expose and criticize. After all, Jackson had learned during the campaigns of 1824 and 1828 not to react publically to vicious public attacks.

Yet, notes John Sullivan, Jacksonians in 1828 took a literal view of satirical material. They were unable to see anything "imaginative" in anti-Jacksonian attacks, and they were not imaginative enough themselves to comprehend the sophisticated arguments in the cartoons. In a larger sense, Jacksonians were people of action and not "of words of the brush." They did not appreciate attacks on the man whom they admired. Despite their limited appreciation for critical cartoons, they were able at the same time to construct a larger-than-life image of Jackson.[61]

�֍֎֍֎

In all, images of Andrew Jackson are rather plentiful, including paintings, portraits, and engravings depicting him as a general and president. A quick survey of Google Images reveals literally hundreds of portraits of the seventh president. A few daguerreotype images of Jackson, taken a few months before his death in 1845, are the first photographs of a president. Most images of Jackson focus on his sharp-featured face. Several full-size portraits depict him in heroic and commanding ways, whereas others portray him as a gentleman-farmer. Scenery, garb, and insignia aside, however, the actual portrayals of Jackson are tamed. His eyes, the central feature of his image, often appear sleepy, and this portrayal is very much in line with his early portraits. That several artists over a span of two decades depicted Jackson similarly indicates the accuracy of their renderings. He looked like a gentle person with a friendly gaze. Though his political opponents did not, many Americans saw Jackson as a kind person, and in that sense his image was a political asset.

The images' consistent depiction of Jackson as a heroic military leader first and a president second is also notable. There are several reasons for this consistency, all emanating from his victory in New Orleans and that event's quick popular impact on the nation. This triumph and the nation's need for a hero following the War of 1815 significantly developed Jackson's image, an image that subsequently elevated him to the presidency. In image as well as in politics, Jackson differed from his predecessors. Public knowledge of Jackson's appearance, military success and character preceded his political career. Cumulatively these circumstances produced a new style of politician, an outsider with a different biography who was depicted frequently and most crucially as the people's president. Indeed, Jackson's style must be taken as a significant rhetorical asset and an integral part of his presidential prospects. He proved to be the president that his image revealed.

The durability of Jackson's image can be attributed in part to immediate efforts to enshrine it following his death. Only eight years later, in 1853, a bronze statue of Jackson riding a horse in battle was erected in Lafayette Park, in the nation's capital. This statue stands prominently across from the White House, which Jackson occupied for eight years, and it is closer to the

White House than any other presidential monument in Washington, DC. This location is symbolic at several levels, standing for the president who significantly expanded the power of the executive. Yet the statue has Jackson riding into battle, a scene taken not from his presidential period but from his military career. The statue's engraved statement "Our Federal Union; It Must be Preserved" interjects the metonymy of Jackson's entire presidency and as it sums up his stance as defender of the Union. In conflating his military and presidential success, the monument is consistent with many images produced some twenty years earlier. Jackson's presence in front of the White House must have been a symbolic reminder, especially during the tense years leading up to and after the Civil War, that the Union must be preserved, and that the White House was the seat of the chief magistrate of the entire United States. Replicated throughout the nation, this monument is often centrally located in various towns and cities.

Today, the most enduring and prominent image of Andrew Jackson graces the US twenty-dollar note, among the widest in distribution and use (and now quite controversial). This bill, first issued in 1928, exactly a century after Jackson became president, bears an image based on Thomas Sully's oil-on-canvas portrait, painted around 1824.[62] Like the monument in Lafayette Park, the portrait on the twenty-dollar bill dates from Jackson's pre-presidential period.[63] It is part of a head shot from Sully's larger portrait, and it repeats earlier images of Jackson that merged military and political features and contexts. Jackson would have likely been quite upset to see his image on paper currency, the very monetary item he vehemently opposed. He would probably support efforts to remove his portrait from the twenty-dollar bill.

Jackson's visual images must be understood as an integral part of his rhetorical presence and his political success. Though Jackson did not encourage the creation of his likeness, he appears to have understood these images' importance during a period when most people did not know what their president looked like. Jackson brought a new style of politics to America, and he radically changed how presidents are elected. He indeed benefitted from the widespread circulation of his picture. Perhaps intuitively, Jackson understood that the nation was yearning for another kind of politician. Since memories of George Washington were still fresh in Americans' minds, he had an anchor on which his own image could be constructed.

Jackson introduced a new way of campaigning; persuading the masses became necessary in a system that no longer relied on internal political caucusing. Now, a presidential candidate had to communicate with the entire nation and its growing regional differences and tensions. Image making was a natural outgrowth of this development. Contenders required wider name recognition, and they sought to appeal to the masses with a new rhetoric that depended on visual narratives and verbal statements. When considering the various paintings, engravings, and busts, as well as the image he conveyed in his verbal utterings, Jackson's persona was rather uniform and tightly constructed. He presented himself as commanding but gentle, as a determined man who was also a people's president. The political cartoons of the day took almost the opposite approach, depicting Jackson mostly negatively and zeroing in on his king-like character, his roughness, and his aggression. These cartoons reflect the overall anti-Jackson press of the time.[64] If, as Inabinet argues, Jacksonian democracy brought about the irony, satire, and allegory displayed in various political cartoons, the incongruity between them and the multiple images of Jackson in lithographs and engravings did little to diminish his growing standing in the American polity.[65]

Though initial images of Jackson were for the most part the creative expressions of others, Jackson and his aides took a more active role in his image formation in the early 1820s. This greater activity coincided with the improvement in his presidential prospects. In relation to the Battle of New Orleans, Jackson was portrayed early on as a reluctant hero. There are no portraits of an arrogant or vain Jackson. However, this is not the case with period cartoons, clearly instruments of the opposition and those who simply did not like the president and his political reach. Collectively, the many images of Jackson are the rhetorical embodiment of his era—diverse, colorful, and rough.[66] But images are also fluid and temperamental. While Ward considers the image of Jackson as "the sentimental hero"[67] a likely fit for the 1950s, this image is no longer operative. Instead, Jackson has more recently acquired a counter image—that of a cruel warrior and a harsh slave owner—more in line with the intertextuality paradigm of the early twenty-first century.

11

PARTING COUNSEL

ANDREW JACKSON'S FAREWELL ADDRESS

On October 13, 1836, some five months before ending his second term, Jackson sent a letter to Chief Justice Roger Taney, writing, "I have turned my thoughts to the subject of a Farewell Address, as a means of rendering a last service to my country." The president said he was too busy with affairs of state to compose such an address, and he asked Taney to draft the final version. In framing the Farewell Address and guiding its approach, Jackson hoped that a speech delivered near the end of his presidency would garner a positive reception: "[I want these remarks to]be more impartially considered than any communication made at a time when my anxiety for the success of my measures might be suspected of warping my opinions, and when the interests of an opposing party produced an inclination in all under its influence, to judge most uncharitably any intentions."[1] This is eloquent phrasing about an endgame that Jackson hoped would be devoid of political tension and would promote a more objective account of his presidency. Yet with the words "my anxiety," "my measures," and "my opinions," Jackson added an interesting feature to his final presidential address. He made the speech a personal account describing his personal stake in the nation's polity.

According to his instructions, Jackson wanted a Farewell Address that would be taken as an objective, unbiased account of his experience and any advice he could provide thereof. In issuing a final address, Americans would know that he had nothing to gain politically from such a reflection. He understood how opinions expressed in the midst of political tensions were often slanted and biased. Somewhat distanced from the heated arguments of the day, Jackson was now hoping for an address indicative of his pure motives. This was clearly the move of a president attuned to the rhetorical.

Jackson also asked Taney to suggest appropriate timing for such an address, as well as "the mode of presenting it to the nation, if one [was] delivered at all."[2] Jackson was experimenting again with the role and function of the presidency. He wondered whether the address should be presented to Congress at the start of a new session, perhaps as an attachment to his last Annual Message to Congress,[3] which he would be expected to give in early December. Alternatively, Jackson contemplated delivering the speech at the conclusion of the session, when Congress would inquire whether he had "any further communication to make to them."[4] The president told Taney he preferred the latter option, and he asked him to suggest the best course of action. Concerning the substance of his speech, Jackson instructed the chief justice as follows: "Throw on paper your thoughts as to the topics which you would consider most appropriate for the address, and your views generally of the range it should take."[5] This elaborate request of his "speechwriter" provides clear evidence that presidential speechwriting is a continuous practice as old as the republic. Jackson's wishes also demonstrate that he gave his departure careful thought and planned ahead.

Typically, however, Jackson, could not avoid suggesting to Taney several preferred topics for the address: "our *glorious Union* [italics in the original]," the schemes of those who wished to dissolve it, and how to instruct the public "with an adequate aversion to the sectional jelousies [sic], the sectional parties, and sectional preferrences [sic] which centuring [sic] on mischievous and intrigueing [sic] individuals gave them power to disturb and shake our happy confederacy." Jackson also added the "dangerous power of the United States Bank" and the corrupting nature of paper currency as topics for consideration.[6] In short, he outlined all the big battles of his presidency as potential main points of the Farewell Address. In so doing, Jackson abandoned the distance and impartiality of his initial request. His accumulated anger and frustrations from eight years of presidential battles clouded his own guidance to Taney. Even so, Jackson grasped the essence of the Farewell Address before there was a clear genre of such speeches to consult. He sought a review of his accomplishments and a departure from the executive with warnings for future generations.

Jackson concluded his letter by apologizing to Taney for asking him to write the address. He reiterated his busy schedule and noted that he was also deprived of the assistance of his nephew and longtime aide, Major Andrew Jackson Donelson.[7] In essence, the president forwarded a rough outline of his Farewell Address. The letter's spelling errors are strong evidence that the speech's outline and the entire plan were Jackson's own, and that he wrote them in a hurry. This point is significant. Jackson's letter to Taney is consistent with earlier addresses that he initially outlined and in several cases also drafted. When he created these documents, Jackson's spelling errors increased in proportion to the pace of his writing.

Taney replied two days later, complimenting Jackson on his decision to give "a parting address" and stating, "It should be the last act of your political life and not form a part of your annual message." Taney also opined, "Your farewell address should be exclusively devoted to those great and enduring principles upon which our institutions are founded, and without which the blessings of freedom cannot be preserved."[8] In other words, the chief justice suggested that one clear theme should undergird the Farewell Address. For Jackson, the theme was to be found in the "enduring principles" of the Constitution, especially its manifestation in the sacredness of the Union and the fight against corruption and the privileged elite. Taney wrote to Jackson again on October 27, 1836, noting his progress on the Farewell Address and providing his opinion on the growing crisis over paper currency.[9] The confluence of these two topics was not accidental, as it would greatly influence the address.

Though fully cognizant of the other presidential Farewell Address—that of George Washington—neither Jackson nor Taney mentioned it when planning for the speech. The prevailing understanding was that such an address was unique to the nation's founding president. No one expected any other president to complete his term in such a way, but Jackson thought otherwise. Harry Truman would be the next to resurrect the Farewell Address, perhaps as his own tribute to Jackson, whom he greatly admired. Jackson understood Washington's Farewell Address intuitively and took it for what would become an acceptable genre and tradition: a speech bringing to an end that which a president's Inaugural Address had commenced. Seeking a symbolic departure, presidents used these remarks to convey lessons and warnings learned during their time in office. Executives sought to impart knowledge to future generations without self-interest.[10] Fully aware of Washington's Farewell Address and its lesson to posterity, Jackson demonstrated this knowledge when drafting his "Paper Read to the Cabinet" on withdrawing deposits in the Bank of the United States. He raised the issue of foreign involvement and foreign-owned stocks in the bank, stating, "It has always been a favorite maxim with the American people, to form no 'entangling alliances' to draw them within the vortex of European policy."[11] Ironically, as a young congressman, Jackson refused to endorse Washington's Farewell Address on the grounds that it appeared too much like King George III's address to Parliament.[12] In 1826, however, Jackson opposed President John Quincy Adams's sending a delegation to a Panama Congress, citing Washington's warning of "entangling alliance."[13] In short, at several junctures, Jackson had taken special note of the enduring quality of Washington's Farewell Address. Now, he sought to produce his own address for posterity. It is also noteworthy that Jackson had earlier given a farewell address to his troops. Thus, Washington's precedent may not have been the only one he considered.[14]

When he suggested ending his term with a Farewell Address, Jackson knew he took a liberty. This act could be construed as breaking with Washington's tradition. But Jackson being Jackson, he felt otherwise. He felt strongly about informing Americans of his experiences and warning them of potential dangers. Jackson had already included many cautions in his Second Inaugural Address, and he was doubtless considering the nation's future and worrying about specific scenarios. That Washington left the presidency with his own warning may have been the connecting line between the two addresses. Jackson saw his two terms in office as different from his those of his predecessors; he knew his ascendancy marked a major transition in the nation's polity. He brought upon the Union a new form of presidential election, and he expanded the function of the presidency. Jackson's vetoes particularly increased the power and reach of the executive despite his claims to supporting a limited federal government. Finally, his endurance of eight years involving several acute crises rendered him worthy of offering advice. At the half-century mark of the confederate Union, Jackson wished to dwell on that confederation's critical importance and on several looming dangers to it.

The timing of the Farewell Address, delivered on March 4, 1837, was important. It was issued on the last day of Jackson's presidency, and it was his last official act in office. Taney wrote the entire address; the document appears in his handwriting, with Jackson's signature and remark of praise affixed to it.[15] Jackson submitted his Farewell Address in written form to Congress rather than orating it, as was the case with most major addresses of the time. However, in a departure from his practice with important speeches, he did not draft the Farewell Address, not even in part. Neither did he review the remarks before their formal submission. Taney did all the work. Martin Van Buren would take the oath of office on the same day.

PRESERVING THE UNION

Jackson commenced his lengthy Farewell Address by recalling "difficult and trying situations" that required "prompt and energetic action," situations that, given the "interest of the country," also required him to act "fearlessly."[16] The nation's confidence in him had sustained him "in every trial." Acknowledging his long public life and recognizing that he was not always "free from errors," Jackson nevertheless hoped that the mistakes he had made "[had] not seriously injured the country." Now, upon leaving the presidency, he was secure in his knowledge of the nation's prosperity and its citizens' happiness. Americans were happy and "in the full enjoyment of liberty and peace, and honored and respected by every nation of the world." Possessed of an "advanced age and a broken frame," Jackson could only hope that he had somewhat contributed to these circumstances. As he left the nation's service, he stated, "[I want] to offer to you the counsels of age and experience."[17] In this introduction, Jackson touched on the contrasting points of energy and courage on the one hand and advanced age and frailty on the other. He employed the narrative poles of a hero reaching the end of his life and reflecting on his time. For Jackson, his pure motives of courage, determination, and popular support transcended his errors. The hero was now ready to leave the scene, and he was confident in his actions and the nation's well-being.

Declaring, "We have now lived almost fifty years under the Constitution framed by the sages and patriots of the Revolution," Jackson marked the nation's progress by surveying the period when "we encountered these trials with our Constitution yet in its infancy." Yet upon reflection, "our Constitution [was] no longer a doubtful experiment" but a stable system that "preserved unimpaired the liberties of the people."[18] In sum, Jackson contended that the United States had neared the end of its experimental phase and been transformed into a stable political system. Given Jackson's battles inherently based on the Constitution, he could now claim successes that reassured the nation that the experiment in democracy would not fail. Ever so subtly, Jackson also inscribed himself as the agent of these many changes.

Jackson devoted a few awkwardly positioned words to the removal of the Indian tribes, stating, "[Several states are now] relieved from the evil, and this unhappy race—the original dwellers in our land—are now placed in a situation where we may well hope that they will share in the blessings of civilization and be saved from the degradation and destruction to which they were rapidly hastening." This was not a very charitable thing for the president to say, but his long history of fighting American Indians left him with little sympathy for their plight. He considered his actions benevolent. He also believed he did the best he could with a paternalistic and caring federal government.[19] Jackson opined in the name of civilization, "The philanthropist will rejoice that the remnant of that ill-fated race has been at length placed beyond the reach of injury or oppression."[20] He hoped the overall conditions of the removal would satisfy whites who advocated for and sympathized with tribes. The rhetorical distance Jackson put between his views and philanthropists', as well as the ways in which he demonized Indians left no room for doubting how he felt about the tribes.

Since the Constitution grounded most of Jackson's battles, it was only fitting that he complimented the Founding Fathers for their "wisdom and foresight" in creating it. The Constitution had foundational value in securing the freedom and happiness of the Union. Yet he issued this caution: "At every hazard and by every sacrifice this Union must be preserved." This warning would constitute a major portion of the address, with the president calling for "the necessity of watching with jealous anxiety for the preservation of the Union," as it was "earnestly pressed upon his fellow-citizens by the Father of his Country in his Farewell Address."[21] Jackson acknowledged Washington's own Farewell Address and the specific message it carried, thus connecting two presidencies nearly fifty-years apart. He quoted the first president, who stated, "There will always be reason to distrust the patriotism of those who in any quarter may endeavor to weaken its bands." Jackson also emphasized Washington's warning "against the formation of parties on geographical discriminations, as one means which might disturb our Union and to which designing men would be likely to resort."[22] The Nullification Crisis was now contextualized in Washington's prescient warning. And by implication, Jackson's actions during the crisis were taken in the spirit of Washington's Farewell Message.

Jackson considered Washington's quote apt for the major crisis he faced:" "When we look upon the scenes that are pressing around us and dwell upon the pages of his parting address, his paternal counsels would seem to be not merely the offspring of wisdom and foresight, but the voice of prophecy, foretelling events and warning us of evils to come."[23] Washington, continued Jackson, considered the Constitution an experiment and was willing "to lay down his life" for it. The experiment had succeeded "beyond the proudest hopes of those who framed it." At the same time, Jackson noted the "seeds of discord between different parts of the United States" that had "excited the *South* against the *North* and the *North* against the *South*," bringing to the fore "the most delicate and exciting topics—topics upon which it [was] impossible that a large portion of the Union [could] ever speak without strong emotion."[24] Washington's warning grounded Jackson's own departing thoughts, hitting hard on regional tensions that threatened to break the Union apart. The primary issue—slavery—was the unnamed cause of exciting and emotional topics that began to tear the nation apart.

Jackson asked tersely, "Has the warning voice of Washington been forgotten, or have designs already been formed to sever the Union?" He did not deny the right of people to express the "honorable feeling of State pride and local attachment," but he also believed they must acknowledge their brethren in other states. Festering suspicions would soon bring hostility, thus inflaming feelings and causing "fatal divisions" in "different sections of the country." Jackson went as far as criticizing constant attempts "to influence the election of the Chief Magistrate, as if it were desired that he should favor a particular quarter of the country instead of fulfilling the duties of his station with impartial justice to all."[25] Presidential politics and regional tensions conjoined to tilt the executive's favor toward one region or another, further pointing to the growing regional rift.

The Nullification Crisis, then, would prompt most of the references in this address to securing the Union and warning against local sentiments seeking its dissolution. As Washington was the first to advice against weakening the Union over regional tensions, Jackson could argue a continuous line of reasoning that preceded him. He followed a path agreed upon at the very foundation of the United States as a Union. If Washington was the agent of warning, Jackson positioned himself as the person accomplishing the first president's mission. Past and present conjoined to send a powerful message about the future of the nation. In stating as much, the seventh president also narrated a Washington-Jackson view that was foundational and unique, and that warranted heeding advice about dangers to come.

The Nullification Crisis was the first major threat to the Union. Though Jackson crushed this dangerous precedent, he made several references to the possibility that secession was not dead. Significantly, in his Farewell Address, he portended the Civil War over regional economic tensions. He saw how the tariff issue grew out of deeper sentiments, and he genuinely feared for this Union on this account. Though it took Jackson a while, he also came to realize that slavery was the institutional marker of southern sentiments upon which secession was possible. Instead of arguing against the advocacy of any given issue because it disrupted the Union, he took a different tack, pointing out the futility of any cause for secession. "What have you to gain by division and dissension?" he asked, presaging what could happen after division and dissension. "If the Union is once severed," he continued, the separation would grow wider, and division in legislative chambers would end on the battlefield "and determined by the sword."[26] And if a different union were formed, it too would end in division, disrupted by new local sentiments and individuals' ambition.

If memories of fighting for the United States' independence from a common foe were not enough to maintain the Union, asked Jackson, "What tie will hold united the new divisions of empire when these bonds have been broken and this Union dissevered?" The first line of separation, he predicted, would clearly not be the last one. The new republic would "be broken into a multitude of petty States." With limited commerce and credit, taxes would increase to build an army to defend these new entities. Foreign powers' competition for allies among foreign powers would result in the "petty states" being "insulted and trampled upon by the nations of Europe until, harassed with conflicts and humbled and debased in spirit, they would be ready to submit to the absolute dominion of any military adventurer and to surrender their liberty for the sake of repose." Jackson insightfully posed a critical question: "[If memories of past glories, prosperity and happiness] under the present Constitution . . . are not strong enough to bind us together as one people, what tie will hold united the new divisions of empire when these bonds have been broken and this Union dissevered?"[27] Jackson's apt questions were meant to wake people up so they could see the error of preaching regional interests at the expense of the entire nation.

Jackson visualized secession's potential destructiveness to those seeking it. Though disunion might satisfy the immediate objectives of some, any new political system would be even weaker than the one destroyed. The result would be perpetual conflict eventually involving the same European powers that had only recently sought a foothold in the Americas. Jackson hoped this rationalization would be sufficient to dissuade some states from pursuing secession. With this powerful, vivid projection of what might happen, the president accurately prophesied what would transpire some twenty-four years later.

Jackson contended that the Union's future must rest on the principle of an "unimpaired" obedience to the Constitution, and on the need for "every good citizen" to "stand ready to put down, with the combined force of the nation, every attempt to unlawful resistance, under whatever pretext it [might] be made." As in his previous point, Jackson warned that the "victory of the injured would not secure to them the blessings of liberty; it would avenge their wrongs, but they would themselves share in the common ruin." He understood the South's sentiments and its inclination to engage in a ruinous course of action. The Farewell Address provided him a final opportunity to warn southerners of their shortsightedness. Even so, Jackson carefully did not explicate the means of putting down insurrection, using instead the more careful phrasing of "the combined force of the nation," and preferring to display the effect of moral force rather than the threat of military actions.[28] Crucially, the president believed that secession would not be allowed under any condition or pretext if obedience to the Constitution as the grounding of the Union remained "unimpaired." For Jackson, the Union's strongest foundation was the constitutional argument, and hence the legal one, which he hoped would trump any other consideration.

The president argued that the Constitution could be maintained and the Union could be preserved only if supported by the public's feeling and affection. Appealing to Americans' better judgment, he acknowledged that force alone was insufficient. Jackson thus asserted, "The citizens of every State should studiously avoid everything calculated to wound the sensibility or offend the just pride of the people of other States, and they should frown upon any proceedings within their own borders likely to disturb the tranquility of their political brethren in other portions of the Union." He told the nation that wisdom, foresight, and the ability to see beyond each state and its unique feelings were crucial to the Union's survival. In a confederation of states, considering self and others secured the whole. Jackson acknowledged that in a country "so extensive as the United States," varied interests, some of them rooted in colonial times, were unavoidable. But he also asserted, "Each State has the unquestionable right to regulate its own internal concerns . . . while it does not interfere with the rights of the people of other States or the right of the Union."[29]

Jackson sought not only to emphasize the separation between the two entities—the federal government and the states of the Union—but also to emphasize the responsibilities of each. Echoing his earlier Maysville Veto, he contended that the states could regulate their own internal improvements, and that the federal government had no right to interfere in the affairs of a given state. Likewise, states could not interfere with the authority of the Union. This balance of power must be maintained, and the Constitution and the Union must be preserved along with it. Yet the Constitution always came first for Jackson. It was the basis for the Union, and it would be sustained only as long as the public—people and not states—supported it. This, then, was Jackson's foundational principle, echoing the very notion he developed during the Nullification Crisis. This crisis and the hard feelings it left no doubt informed a large portion of his Farewell Address. Expressed four years after the Nullification Crisis ended, the sentiments in Jackson's final address echo those in his initial draft of the Second Inaugural Address, the one he did not deliver.

Jackson's experience allowed him to suggest that "motives of philanthropy may be assigned for this unwarranted interference, and weak men may persuade themselves for a moment that they are laboring in the course of humanity and asserting the rights of the human race; but everyone, upon sober reflection, will see that nothing but mischief can come from these improper assaults upon the feelings and rights of others." This was his great concern—some individuals' tendency to exploit state pride or philanthropic sentiments to assault the Union under false pretenses. Jackson directed this charge at both the leaders of the Nullification Crisis and the opponents of slavery, telling his audience, "[Those] found busy in this work of discord are not worthy of your confidence, and deserve your strongest reprobation."[30] From the outset, Jackson saw in antislavery sentiment and activism attempts to disrupt the Union, both from those who acted in the name of philanthropy and from those who opposed them. The president considered such efforts interference in states' rights. In stating as much in addition to criticizing those keen on assaulting the Union, he presented a pro–states' rights view while performing a balancing act. On this point, Jackson missed the dynamic of the antislavery movement. But, then, his priority was safeguarding the Union from both states' rights advocates and antislavery activists.

Jackson warned, "No free government can stand without virtue in the people and a lofty spirit of patriotism, and if the sordid feelings of mere selfishness shall usurp the place which ought to be filled by public spirit, the legislation of Congress will soon be converted into scramble for personal and sectional advantages." With this lofty call, he asked the nation to assume a spirit of patriotism instead of selfishness, and he criticized those bent on regional interests. To those fearful of an enlarged general government (a euphemism for the federal government), Jackson offered this reassurance: "Its legitimate authority is abundantly sufficient for all the purposes for which it was created." He espoused a limited but strong federal government balancing states' rights, and he denied any claim that the federal government had assumed more power than the Constitution allowed. This was the president's counterargument to the nullifiers and others who charged the opposite—that the general government had grown too powerful and Jackson had strengthened its executive branch. Jackson asked the nation "to maintain unimpaired and in full vigor the rights and sovereignty of the States and to confine the action of the General Government strictly to the sphere of its appropriate duties."[31] The Union's survival depended on this balancing act. Any break in the balance would be detrimental to America's future. Jackson spoke prophetically, but he did not admit that he had indeed strengthened the executive—impressively so.

PUBLIC MONEY

On the issue of public revenue, Jackson stated his long-held opposition to the general government's imposition of taxes and retention of surpluses. He said it all in his opening line: "There is, perhaps, no one of the powers conferred on the Federal Government so liable to abuse as the taxing power." Jackson opined that taxes from commerce tended to conceal themselves "from the real payer in the price of the article." They often went unnoticed since they amounted to smaller sums. Yet they "enhance[d] by so much the price of the commodity to the consumer," and they were so frequently used on items of necessity, and that they subsequently drew large sums of money from people's pockets. "Congress," Jackson stated, "has no right under the Constitution to take money from the people unless it is required to execute some one of the specific powers intrusted [sic] to the Government." And when more money is raised than needed, "it is an abuse of the power of taxation, and unjust and oppressive." When the government collects more than it needs, taxes should be reduced "for no circumstances can justify it in assuming a power not given to it by the Constitution nor in taking away the money of the people."[32] Throughout his two terms Jackson paid special attention to the nation's finances and budget. He adopted a simple, practical economic perspective, siding with hardworking individuals who needed to save every penny and often got cheated of their hard-earned money. Jackson did not adopt a governmental perspective, instead considering himself the people's champion.

The context for Jackson's point about taxes was based on his experience with the "constant effort to induce the General Government to go beyond the limits of its taxing power and to impose unnecessary burdens upon the people." It was for this reason that tariffs were considered oppressive and various internal improvement schemes were believed to cause an "unjust and unequal system of taxation." Jackson reminded the nation of his Maysville Veto, issued because the scheme was unjust and beyond what the Constitution prescribed. His objection to such taxation resulted in a "rapid extinguishment of the public debt." The surplus of revenues incurred in the Treasury was used to reduce tariff rates. Yet, the design of "corporations and wealthy individuals," the president warned, constantly sought high tariffs and increased profits.[33] Jackson tied the Nullification Crisis to his opposition to the federal government's practice of overtaxing. He reminded the nation that the crisis was supposedly over tariff rates, which he had opposed and even reduced.

Yet Jackson had concerns about the future: "Efforts will be made to seduce and mislead the citizens of the several States by holding out to them the deceitful prospect of benefits to be derived from a surplus revenue collected by the General Government and annually divided among the States." He could see how such a practice would be the hope of several states. He could see how quickly expenditures would exceed income, and how a national debt would subsequently be incurred to the detriment of all Americans. As in all other cases, the solution lay in the Constitution's principles. That document stated, the "Federal Government can not collect a surplus for such purposes without violating the principles of the Constitution and assuming powers which have not been granted."[34]

THE BANK AND THE CURRENCY CRISIS

The lengthiest part of the Farewell Address concerns the Bank War and its lingering effects in the form of widely distributed paper currency and the economic depression it had supposedly brought. In describing paper currency as a "deep-seated evil," Jackson signaled his resentment toward this new commercial device. Here, too, the Constitution was the principal perspective from whence he could render a public judgment. Jackson stated, the "Constitution of the United States unquestionably intended to secure to the people a circulating medium of gold and silver." He acknowledged that paper money was a complex matter; even honest and enlightened individuals were misled by this new medium. For Jackson, paper currency was wholly "founded on public confidence." By itself, this is an insightful observation about the invisible hand of the economy, as well as the rhetorical force of confidence, or uncertainty, in the nation's economy. But such confidence, Jackson iterated, "is liable to great and sudden fluctuations," and paper currency's use could result in unstable property values and uncertain wages.[35]

Jackson's specific concern was that fluctuations in currency value could trigger false confidence and a sudden depression: "These ebbs and flows in the currency and these indiscreet extensions of credit naturally engender a spirit of speculation injurious to the habits and character of the people." In his view, speculation in public lands had already exhibited paper currency's tendency to cause "hardship upon the class of society least able to bear it." This money's ability to become "appreciated or worthless" and to be counterfeited would increase overall fraud and manipulation.[36] Jackson continued, "The Government is emphatically the Government of the people, and where this respectable portion of our citizens are so proudly distinguished from the laboring classes of all other nations by their independent spirit, their love of liberty, their intelligence. . . . Their industry in peace is the source of our wealth and their bravery in war has covered us with glory; and the Government of the United States will but ill discharge its duties if it leaves them a prey to such dishonest impositions."[37] Paper currency, then, had put the general government in an unfortunate position. It could not fully protect the people, especially the laboring class, from such fraud "unless silver and gold [were] restored to circulation."[38] Ever projecting himself as the people's president, Jackson once more offered himself as the defender of the working class that could not protect itself from unscrupulous interests.

Jackson fought the last battle of the Bank War in his Farewell Address, extending his criticism of paper currency to the larger issue of the Bank of the United States and his refusal to recharter it. The bank, stated Jackson, "asserted (and it undoubtedly possessed) the power to make money plenty or scarce at its pleasure." Subsequently, other banks fell in line and "became obedient instruments, ready at all times to execute its mandates." The legislation that allowed this monopoly was "ill-advised," allowing manipulation and control "under the direction and command of one acknowledged head."

In "the hands of this formidable power, thus perfectly organized, was also placed unlimited dominion over the amount of the circulating medium." The bank had the power "to regulate the value of property and the fruits of labor in every quarter of the Union, and to bestow prosperity or bring ruin upon any city or section of the country as might best comport with its own interest or policy."[39]

Jackson sought to tie the current economic downturn to the bank's policy, not to his opposition to paper currency. After all, the bank fought him, and he, in turn, would not let the bank get away with what he considered to be corrupt practices. "The distress and alarm," he said, "which pervaded and agitated the whole country when the Bank of the United States waged war upon the people in order to compel them to submit to its demands can not yet be forgotten." And this was the point—not to forget the Bank of the United States' corrupting effect on the nation. Jackson followed with a description of the "ruthless and unsparing temper with which whole cities and communities were oppressed" by the bank. He also noted the bank's practice of ruining individuals by causing "gloom and despondency," which "ought to be indelibly impressed on the memory of the people of the United States."[40] Twice in one paragraph, Jackson made the address personal and immediate by asking Americans not to forget what the bank did. The warning stipulated in the address now covered the bank's abuses and its insistence on paper currency. The president suggested that the Bank War was not over and that it might resume after he left office.

The Farewell Address was not just a lesson imparted on future generations; it was also a narrative account of Jackson's bitter fights with and his anger at the bank. As Taney was his chief advisor throughout the bank crisis, the president and his speechwriter held the same views on this subject. The inconclusive end to the Bank War bothered Jackson. So did the country's severe economic distress, which could not be attributed solely to his struggles with the bank. The president thus sought to deflect any responsibility for the conflict and to defend any related charge to that effect. Jackson acknowledged as much, telling the nation, "Distress and sufferings inflicted on the people by the Bank are some of the fruits of that system of policy which is continually striving to enlarge the authority of the Federal Government beyond the limits fixed by the Constitution." Jackson suggested that the nation abide by "the Constitution as . . . written, or amend it[s] [flaws] in the constitutional mode if it is found to be defective," but not allow "temporary circumstances" to dictate government policies. "It behooves you," he sternly advised the nation, "to be watchful in your States as well as in the Federal

Government" not to repeat the mistake of concentrating "under a single head" the financial affairs to the country.[41] He implied that he was justified in closing the bank because it managed the nation's finances independently of the government and allowed "one head" who was not answerable to the people to dictate the nation's economy at will.

Jackson reminded the nation that the struggle with the bank was not yet over: "Defeated in the General Government, the same class of intriguers and politicians will now resort to the States and endeavor to obtain there the same organizations which they failed to perpetuate in the Union; and with specious and deceitful plans." No doubt, the Bank War left Jackson concerned, seeing a devious plot at every corner designed to undo his successful end to the bank. Jackson did not fully trust that the new mechanism would be sustained after his departure, seeing new devices ready to abuse the nation, stating that "the money power would in a few years govern the State and control its measures," and that he would no longer be in a watchful position to heed such attempts. He resented bankers as a class, as evidenced by his frequent use of the word "evil" to describe them. This description also captures Jackson's loathing of what he called "our present system of banking that . . . enables one class of society . . . by its control over the currency, to act injuriously upon the interests of all the others and to exercise more than its just proportion of influence in political affairs."[42]

As the advocate of the poor and those of moderate means, Jackson spoke for an entire "laboring class" of farmers and mechanics. This class of Americans, he said, "have little or no share in the direction of the great moneyed corporations, and from their habits and the nature of their pursuits they are incapable of forming extensive combinations to act together with united force."[43] This astute popular appeal was consistent with Jackson's long-term rhetoric advocating for the working class and empathizing with farmers and laborers, who tended to work individually and who were not inclined to join forces to form powerful economic interests. He resented the moneyed elite and the advantages they sought for themselves at the expense of others unable to resist financial schemes. Jackson's rise to the presidency from the working class of people and from a remote part of the nation made him sensitive to the plight of hardworking people, particularly their difficulties in financing their enterprises.

Bogged down in details, Jackson's account of the Bank War borders on a diatribe against all things financial rather than a delineation of key issues from the conflict. Clearly, Jackson did not see any problem with expounding on the wealthy class and its financial dealings—this section of the address is its longest. His aversion to the "paper-money system and its natural associ-ations—monopoly and exclusive privileges—have already struck their roots too deep in the soil, and it will require all your efforts to check its further growth and to eradicate the evil." Jackson was practical enough to realize that he might have lost his battle over paper currency. All he could do now was warn the nation to check this expanded use of the new currency.

Jackson's specific concern, hence his advice, was to watch how those abusing the nation's financial system would "besiege the halls of legislation in the General Government as well as in the States, and . . . seek by every artifice to mislead and deceive the public servants." He provided a clear recommendation: The people were the sovereigns of the country, and it was their responsibility to guard their rights. If they did so, the government would be safe "and the cause of freedom [would] continue to triumph over all its enemies." But the task ahead, he added, was a difficult one: "So many interests are united to resist all reform on this subject [paper currency] that you must not hope the conflict will be a short one nor success easy."[44] Jackson understood how commercial and financial blocks coupled with a growing bureaucracy could manipulate and defeat a government of laws.

Toward the end of the Farewell Address, Jackson took the rare step of addressing a military topic. Indeed, the ex-general said little about military affairs during his presidential terms; the many battles he fought during those years were of a different sort. Yet at the conclusion of his presidency, Jackson declared, "No nation . . . desirous of peace, can hope to escape occasional collisions with other powers, and . . . soundest dictates of policy require that we should place ourselves in a condition to assert our rights if a resort to force should ever become necessary." Jackson was particularly concerned with the nation's long and intricate geographical coastline. He advised strengthening the navy, America's primary means of defense, during a time of peace and surplus revenues. Reemphasizing a point from his First Annual Message to Congress, Jackson noted that a strong navy could protect the nation and meet "danger at a distance from home."[45]

In addition, Jackson suggested protecting ports and important cities by promptly strengthening fortifications. He noted the benefits of a strong navy and fortified ports in key cities: "We need not fear that any nation will wantonly insult us or needlessly provoke hostilities," and "[We] shall more certainly preserve peace when it is well understood that we are prepared for war."[46] Jackson understood that America's expansion, land acquisition, and growing clout and prosperity would eventually provoke enmity and tensions that only a strong, well-defended nation could withstand. The president had consistently emphasized the nation's growing influence. He now assessed the need for a potential world power to prepare accordingly. Furthermore, Jackson was aware of Great Britain's continued meddling in North America, and he especially feared its interest in preventing Texas from joining the United States. Texas was of great importance to Jackson, but he consistently stated nothing about it in any public address.

PARTING COUNSELS

Jackson conceived his Farewell Address as a way to offer "parting counsels" based on principles that guided his two terms in office. He sought to repeat what George Washington started, and he succeeded on his own terms. While Washington's Farewell Address is often cited for its warnings against "permanent alliances" and "foreign alliances," Jackson focused his remarks on the benefits of the federal Union.[47] He asserted, "Knowing that the path of freedom is continually beset by enemies which often assume the disguise of friends, I have devoted the last hours of my public life to warn you of the dangers." This is how Jackson rationalized his final address—by projecting enemies and identifying lurking dangers that needed to be guarded against.

Shifting from dangers and risks to the most positive descriptors, Jackson then summed up his view of his presidency. He outlined the nation's rapid growth "beyond all former example [sic] in numbers, in wealth, in knowledge, and all the useful arts," observing, "Never have been thirteen millions of people associated in one political body who enjoyed so much freedom and happiness as the people of these United States." In other words, the experiment in republican democracy had succeeded. Like a dying parent imparting his final words of wisdom, Jackson told the nation, "You have no longer any cause to fear danger from abroad; your strength and power are well known throughout the civilized world." The dangers, he warned, were only from within: "Among yoursel[ves]—[it is] from cupidity, from corruption, from disappointed ambition and inordinate thirst for power—that factions will be formed and liberty endangered. It is against such designs, whatever disguise the actors may assume, that you have especially to guard yourselves."[48] The Farewell Address ended where Jackson had begun eight years earlier, when he outlined his First Inaugural Address and emphasized eradicating corruption. His warning about the dangers from within was the overarching theme of his final address in office. However, Jackson also projected a stabilizing idea—that of the United States as a growing, powerful nation, a nation confident and secure on the international scene.

Jackson saved personal remarks for the address's final sentences, telling the nation, "[My] own race is nearly run; advanced age and failing health warn me that before long I must pass beyond the reach of human events." He thanked God for a life "spent in the land of liberty and that He has given me a heart to love [his] country with the affection of a son." He continued, "Filled with gratitude for your constant and unwavering kindness, I bid you last and affectionate farewell."[49] Knowing he had done his duty, the son of the Revolution and liberty was ready to depart. Jackson ended on a dramatic metaphorical note, citing his nearing physical end and the happiness and freedom of the American people, his children whom he would leave. In the final paragraph of the address, he turned the paternal metaphor he had used on numerous occasions during the past eight years upside down. Jackson, the son of liberty, looked back at the nation's beginning and accounted for its success. As president, he had often seen himself as the father of the nation. Upon departing the White House, he could not claim to continue the paternal metaphor. Neither could Jackson be a son to anyone else, but he could be a literal and metaphorical son to an idea—liberty. The past and the future were united to strengthen the lessons Jackson imparted to the nation in his final hours in office.

Jackson's long Farewell Address is insightful and exhaustive in its coverage. Despite the warnings therein, it at times reads more like an Annual Message to Congress. Jackson understood Washington's Farewell Address as it was intended—a warning and advice to future generations. Yet, he did not fully establish this generic purpose in his remarks.

Reasonably, the Farewell Address covers all the issues of Jackson's day, with the Nullification Crisis and the Bank War as the key concerns. The Nullification Crisis is not named; Jackson artfully dealt with it from a constitutional perspective and merely hinted at culprits. In contrast, the longest portion of the address is devoted to the Bank War. One is left with the impression that this lengthy coverage stemmed from the conflict's inconclusive end. In his remarks, Jackson fully addressed his bitter struggle with the Bank of the United States. He also emphasized the bank's negative impact on the nation's economy toward the end of his presidency. The institution's limiting of the money supply caused inflation and hardship, and this circumstance may explain why Jackson felt the need to defend his actions. He reserved his most acute and elaborate criticism for the usage of paper currency. The address contains an extensive diatribe against the transformation of currency from coins to paper. It is here that the Farewell Address becomes a defensive tract, perhaps because Jackson wanted to influence the next administration's policy as well as defend his own.

Jackson had composed initial drafts of most of his previous major addresses. His closest aides had then edited them, producing effective speeches. Though a strong speech, the Farewell Address did not benefit from such careful revisions. It was written and finalized essentially by one individual, Roger Taney, and this fact may explain some of its limitations. Jackson made his concern for the Union the central focus of his Farewell Address. He tackled the subject in his unique way, seeking to preserve the Union while limiting its power and operating within the framework designated by the Constitution. Jackson worried that his careful oversight of the government—especially of its overreach of what the Constitution allowed, as displayed in his numerous vetoes—would dissipate with future administrations. Hence, he heavily dosed the Farewell Address with warnings about the need for a balanced approach between states' rights and the importance of a central government. It was for this reason that the Nullification Crisis caused Jackson more apprehension than any other issue. If doubts remained about what motivated Jackson's rhetoric during the crisis, the Farewell Address made it clear that preserving the Union and balancing federal authority and states' rights were his paramount concerns.

The Nullification Crisis was the first test of the Union since the establishment of the United States as a confederation of states. Jackson made it clear that he would not let the Union rupture under his administration. Ultimately, he called for restoring "constitutional boundaries and warned against violating such limits in the future."[50] As Campbell and Jamieson astutely note, Jackson's phrasing in his Farewell Address supports this central argument. He talked of the government's limited sphere, its "legitimate authority" and constitutional boundaries. He chastised those who assumed "a power not given" and a "usurping power," and he criticized those with "a wild spirit of speculation," "monopoly and exclusive privileges," and "despotic sway."[51]

The Washington-Jackson analogue, then, goes only so far as taking the first president's Farewell Address as a speech for parting counsel. The analogue provides much flexibility in developing a final presidential speech reflecting a unique context and time. If presidents developed parting counsel around a specific concern—for Washington, this was primarily international alliances—Jackson issued a purely domestic warning. More than any of his aides, Jackson understood the flexible nature of the speech as modeled after Washington's caution. The document that resulted from Jackson's understanding commenced a tradition of separate Farewell Addresses that would not be resumed until the mid-twentieth century.

An earlier assessment of Jackson's influence appears in the first issue of the *Political Science Quarterly*, wherein Anson Morse argues that the president sought to distinguish between states' rights, which he supported, and sectionalism, which he opposed.[52] Indeed, Jackson's warnings about how such a challenge could disrupt the Union were on the mark. But this is only the case when one assesses his Farewell Address in hindsight, recognizing how state-centered sentiments and regional calculations would break the Union. Read in light of the experience of 1860, when America was on the brink of the Civil War, the speech is indeed powerful and prophetic. Writing some twenty years after the Civil War, Morse argues that "the greatness of his [Jackson's] service was hidden for a time. Sectionalism, under the influence and agitation against slavery, developed rapidly in the North as well as in the South; but when the doubtful struggle began, it was in obedience to the teachings of Jackson that the Northern Democrats put aside their scruples against 'coercion,' and resolutely engaged in the war for the Union. Were it not for him, the issue of the conflict between '61 and '65 might well have been other than it was."[53] Though it may contain hyperbole, this statement is significant nonetheless. Jackson's obstinate stand regarding the Union was considered his ultimate gift to the generation that fought the Civil War. Jackson's rhetorical influence was more fully understood and appreciated only a few decades later, as he had enjoyed immediate success in stopping secession sentiments.

Jackson knew that behind sectional sentiments stood powerful individuals who wished to disrupt the Union. For this reason, he used his final presidential address to lash out at those who initiated the struggles in the first place, admonishing them as a lesson to others who might follow their example. While Jackson left the Union more secure by quelling any attempt at secession, at least for now, he accurately portended well the conditions under which the Union would be broken. That among his warnings George Washington's Farewell Address also cautioned against sectional tension was ideal for Jackson. The seventh president is credited for developing this address and modeling it after the first president's such that later executives would turn it into a genre focused on counselling the nation about potential dangers and forwarding advice for posterity.

12

JACKSONIAN DEMOCRACY
AND RHETORICAL ENTITY

"The age was not his. He was the age's."[1]

Andrew Jackson effectively and skillfully used his rhetoric as a political tool during his two campaigns and later for governing purposes. He was a formidable president who left his mark on the nation at its fiftieth year. He expanded the executive's power and reach, changed the presidential election process, and stabilized a political structure that had remained tenuous since the early years of the American republic. Crucially, Jackson privileged the Constitution as foundational and sacred, and thus the ultimate guide to the nation. The Constitution was Jackson's warrant. It afforded him the lever he needed whenever he sought a principle and a justification for a political stance.

Jackson was the first popular president, elected by the people because he appealed directly to their sentiments, aspirations, and concerns. His extensive popular appeals also made him the first rhetorical president. He insisted that he was the representative of the entire nation, especially the larger population that felt estranged relative to the moneyed and privileged elite. With that, Jackson changed the United States from a republic to a democracy. Much of what Jackson accomplished was recognized in hindsight assessment. Even so, he and a few of his contemporaries had insight into the changes he brought.

Jackson came into office with a clear set of principles and objectives—he was determined to change the American polity he saw as corrupt and corrupting. He did so by outlining his overall plan in key addresses formulated around the narrow perspective of the Constitution's and the Union's primacy. Jackson communicated extensively, often expressing his views for wide distribution even before he entered the White House. Once in office, he issued more vetoes than any of his predecessors and many future presidents, well understanding how they enhanced his presidential power. Indeed, he left the executive more powerful than ever before. In addition, the structural changes he introduced to the American political system would serve the nation for decades to come. Yet much of what Jackson accomplished was not necessarily the result of planning specific steps. Rather, it was the result of taking advantage of controversies or crises that presented opportunities to advance the people's causes. Jackson promoted these causes despite the difficult challenges and harsh invectives thrown at him.

Jackson was not sure, though, how the reforms and changes he introduced would fare after his two terms. Toward the end of his presidency, he worried much about the future of the nation, and for good reasons. He did not foresee a Jacksonian era built over his accomplishments, as he had followed the ideal of his time—a Jeffersonian democracy—in seeking "to rescue and restore the moral values of an Old Republican way of life."[2] Jackson saw in Jeffersonian democracy the values and principles that needed restoration so that the nation could move forward during the progressive era of the 1830s. Jackson accomplished this goal by emphasizing and exercising public persuasion in the service of politics. His rhetoric often functioned like a compass, focusing on key principles and displaying "leadership, particularly through its moral and psychological symbolism."[3] His public discourse resonated with the nation despite much political strife and antagonism in Congress, and his populist appeal worked for him at every juncture during his eight years in office.

Great leaders are often great simplifiers, and Jackson was a great simplifier. In attacking the Bank of the United States, one of his most intense and lengthy crises, he reduced complicated political issues to a rich-poor rhetorical equation many could empathize with. Jackson spoke for many who had had similar experiences with the class divide. Thus he ushered in a popular movement of democratic reforms that opened the floodgates of entrepreneurial spirit. Jackson's popular rhetoric was simple and straight-forward; he talked about the people's virtue and good sense, and, above all else, he trusted their judgment. Belohlavek notes that Jackson truly believed in the capacity of the people. The president figured that, "if left to their own reason, they [would] always decide right."[4]

Jackson's rhetorical presidency was not an exclusively verbal accom-plishment. He also understood the importance of image construction and public relations, attributes seemingly more characteristic of the presidency in the mid-twentieth century and beyond. Jackson succeeded early on in constructing an image of a viable politician, transforming his primary ex-perience as a military general into qualifications for being a strong and determined president. Significantly, his rhetoric constituted "the people" as a new political force comprised of laborers, shopkeepers, mechanics, and farmers. In so doing, he changed the face of political campaigns by bringing with him a new class of politicians skilled in public relations, image making, and even demagoguery. Jackson displayed campaign practices not seen before, including the construction of an appealing image broadcast effectively by state-based campaign operatives and the partisan press. He complemented this construct with verbal rhetoric that spoke the language of the masses. Jackson referred to being the people's president and to caring and fighting their battles. And he meant it. Historian M. J. Heale contends that no person "ever again commanded the Democratic party as Jackson did." The initial formation of the party coalesced around his persona. He set the agenda for his administration, and the party deferred to him.[5]

Jackson's lively, rich correspondence was a significant variable in his at-tunement to public sentiments. Through letters, he advocated and received advice and commentary from across the country. The "epistolary public sphere" that Gerard Hauser attributes to Franklin D. Roosevelt was widely practiced a century earlier, with Jackson constructing a rhetorical space for extensive correspondence with political operatives, friends, associates, clergy, and private citizens that carried a significant influence on his public address.[6] And though Jackson did not receive hundreds of thousands of letters as Roosevelt did, extensive letter writing was often the initial phase for public communication. As such, it functioned as a special space for rehearsing rhetorical expositions as well assessing the effect of delivered speeches. Indeed, Jackson indicated throughout his correspondence that he knew what Americans were thinking and was aware they supported his policies.[7]

French jurist and reformist Alexis de Tocqueville's visit to the United States in 1832, just as Jackson was upon his second term, was propitious. Tocqueville's epitome *Democracy in America*, published only three years later, while Jackson was still in office, was very much written in the spirit of Jacksonian democracy. The author observed and reflected on the young nation as it underwent a major shift in geographical spread and the resulting significant political realignments. *Democracy in America*, in a sense, is a testimonial to the effects of Jacksonian influence. Its very theme—the sovereignty of the people—echoes Jackson's long-standing political principle. Jacksonian democracy privileged the common person against the political elite that had governed since the nation's founding. Jackson's reforms were the manifestation of the new emphasis on majority rule whereby suffrage was expanded, officeholders were no longer selected using property-based criteria, and terms of appointment were set for office seekers.[8] With these changes, a larger number of the population began to feel that they had a stake in the nation's polity. A new cadre of people who lacked an aristocratic and landed background could be professionally elevated. The advent of this egalitarian society allowed Tocqueville to observe the passionate ways in which Americans publicly argued their equality and, by implication, ushered in a new popular rhetoric.

In Jackson's polity, there was ostensibly no room for political manipulation and undue influences, especially when they contradicted the principles outlined in the Constitution and the Bill of Rights. Jackson would take this approach with issues of minor and major significance. When Philadelphia reverend Ezra Stiles Ely sought in 1828 to interject religion into politics, Jackson rebuffed him. The president objected to Ely's "sectarian rhetoric," saying that it ought not to disrupt the nation's great principle of religious freedom. And though the issue was primarily one of evangelical quality— Ely called on people to elect Jackson—the separation of church and state was critical for Jackson. Accordingly, he wrote Ely and was even willing to offend a supporter.[9] Jackson was a principled politician on the matter of separating church and state, repeating his stance when Clay suggested a day of prayer and fasting after a cholera epidemic killed thousands of Americans on the East Coast. As Clay was moving legislation in the House, Jackson prepared a veto. The House tabled the motion, making the veto unnecessary, but Jackson's statement is revealing nevertheless. Though he believed in the "efficacy of prayer in all times," Jackson pointed to constitutional provisions that had "carefully separated sacred from civilian concerns."[10] The president's rhetoric began and ended with the Constitution. His principles were clear, even if they cost him votes or the support of key individuals.

Jackson loved being president. He saw himself as an activist executive, and he recognized his time in office as affording him a unique opportunity to reflect on the American experiment in republican democracy. Subsequently, Jackson functioned as the agent of the country's transition from its founding period to its new era of expansion. He understood the changes he created, but he did not fully assess all new arrangements for policy and economy. The president did not entirely appreciate the transition from specie (coins and hard currency) to paper currency. This change benefitted a growing nation that needed to rely more and more on credit and on efficient and manageable currency transfer. Though Jackson spoke frequently about the growing tensions between various regions of the nation, especially between the North and the South, it took him a while to understand that the crux of the matter was slavery, especially as it related to tariffs, the Nullification Crisis, and states' rights issues. However, once he saw the issue more clearly, he was prescient enough to predict that the South would eventually blow up the Union over slavery. It seemed that Jackson was a strong president precisely because he was unlike his predecessors; he was an outsider and therefore not of an established party. The party he established coalesced around his persona so that his character and image carried rhetorical qualities. Jackson could thus talk credibly about the restoration of virtue and liberty to the people.[11]

As an activist president, Jackson expanded the power of the office and set a precedent for future executives like Abraham Lincoln, Teddy Roosevelt, and Harry Truman. Jackson was a strong president because he was a skilled politician—much shrewder than many thought—and rather insightful about human beings and their motives. He was also a skilled administrator; though aided by able advisors, he was in charge of the executive. Moreover, Jackson understood the games of politics quite well, and this acumen allowed him to preempt others' moves or calculate how an issue would evolve and thus plan accordingly. His method of preparing public speeches made his advance planning apparent. Jackson often drafted his own addresses, messages, and vetoes, and his aides and close advisors incorporated improvements, additions, and deletions into his initial thoughts. In some instances, such as his initial draft of the First Annual Message to Congress or of the Bank Veto, Jackson and his aides followed an outline of key points or principles that he created as a guideline for composition. To manage key issues and battles as well as other rhetorical duties, Jackson assigned drafting duties to specific individuals. Some of his aides shared these responsibilities, while others focused on specific tasks. For example, Amos Kendall dealt primarily with the bank and Treasury matters, and Edward Livingston helped Jackson with the Nullification Crisis. Yet with the exception of the Farewell Address, Jackson would write most of his important addresses. Though good editing was often necessary at key junctures in his presidency, it was more for strategic reasons than stylistic ones. His staff sought caution in his remarks, and they constrained statements that were politically risky.[12]

A survey by Robert K. Murray and Tim H. Blessing rates Andrew Jackson as a "near great" president, together with Teddy Roosevelt, Woodrow Wilson, and Harry Truman. (The "great" presidents are Abraham Lincoln, Franklin D. Roosevelt, and Thomas Jefferson.) A similar ranking by top historians also places Jackson in the "near great" category, accompanied by the same presidents as in the Murray-Blessing ranking. In another study, Jackson places second to Franklin D. Roosevelt in the use of metaphors, which, according to one researcher, is characteristic of charismatic presidents.[13] Rhetorical scholar Walter Fisher groups Jackson together with Washington, Jefferson, Lincoln, and Franklin D. Roosevelt as presidents who share a "romantic strain" in their character. All the men exhibited selfless love for the people, possessed "an idealistic vision," and were known for being "visionary and mythic, a subject for folklore and legend."[14] Though one can quibble with such ranking and grouping, these disparate studies consistently include Jackson among the top presidents. This categorization is significant, as all these leaders were known for their strong rhetorical skills.

Jackson activated his primary rhetorical tools in the forms of vetoes, statements to the press, and announcements guided by his short list of key principles. His rhetoric and his strong popularity carried the credibility necessary for his presidential impact. This presidential style was unknown to the more insular Washington elite, who sought to handle issues within the nation's capital and the halls of government. Jackson expanded his rhetorical reach by using the press as a public relations tool and connecting with the larger population that was quite attuned to the political. The vetoes in particular added to the weight of Jackson's decisions. They went beyond the traditional Annual Messages to Congress as dramatic acts that caught the nation's interest.

Jackson tended to initially downplay most significant policy agendas. In most formal addresses, he covered issues of great concern such as the Bank War and the Nullification Crisis only slightly. When he did mention them, he did so at the end of speeches, as if to signal their lesser status and his preference for a quiet resolution. Yet as Jackson's private correspondence reveals, these matters were in reality most crucial to him. The president hoped that a milder public approach would advance this issues' solution. Once he realized that his sought solution was not in the offing, he settled for a decisive move such as the Bank Veto or the Proclamation to the People of South Carolina. He moved in the opposite direction with such measures, issuing the strongest public statements—lengthy, detailed, and determined—and working diligently to shape the rhetorical tone he desired. Like the military strategist that he was, Jackson utilized the skills of evasion and timing, lying low to confuse the opposition, and then lashing out at the opportune time.

One can observe a militant slant in Jacksonian rhetoric that affected Democratic and Whig politicians, describing the party and its agenda as a "'Spartan band' which stood militantly between civilization and barbarism," or likening the Kitchen Cabinet during the Bank War to military officers. Jackson himself often referred to his opposition as the "enemy," telling Francis Blair that Democrats "ought like faithful soldiers to unite and die on their posts and pass the Independent Treasury Bill."[15] Jackson's rhetoric and followers tended to take a Manichean world view in which the opposition was the enemy and every struggle was similar to a military battle. As Perry M. Goldman notes, this style is likely the result of the partisan discipline necessary to hold together the loose Democratic coalition of Jackson's day.[16]

Jackson had an innate understanding of all things rhetorical. He constructed rather sophisticated messages, and he brought into his public address a keen understanding of how to present and argue an issue in an effective and appealing way. He preferred forceful rhetorical lines. But he always turned a keen eye to how he should address his primary audience—the people. Though Jackson did not mind disagreeing with his listeners, he did not offend them. Nor did he present himself arrogantly and display poor rhetorical sense, as his intellectual predecessor John Quincy Adams had. If anything, Jackson often took the humble style in his public remarks. His approach was more modern than appreciated, focusing on key issues and simplifying them, sounding positive and optimistic, and often empowering the people by appealing to their best judgment as the true holders of political power. Jackson also listened to his aides and accepted modifications that strengthened what he intended to say. He would argue against changes in the text only if he felt that they weakened or subverted his intentions.

Jackson's persuasive strategy was to argue from authority—specifically, the authority of the Constitution and the related authority of the executive. When he had to, as in his address to South Carolinians at a critical moment in the Nullification Crisis, he engaged in direct appeals to the people. On most other issues, Jackson's persuasive, and hence rhetorical, approach was to engage in indirect appeal by addressing the generic farmer or mechanic. Constitutional precepts allowed him to argue in favor of the Bank Veto and the Maysville Veto. Likewise, the Indian Removal Act was reasoned as consistent with the clear separation of federal and state jurisdictions. The scarcity of personal appeal is indicative of Jackson's logical and even legal investment in an issue. In these cases, he preferred to confine his personal views on specific issues and individuals to private letters. On rare occasions, Jackson would resort to paternalistic or familial metaphors for an added personal perspective. The paternalism in his rhetoric is perhaps unique in the sense that it came from an emotional and sensitive side of his character. He employed the paternalistic when addressing difficult matters, as in his appeal to South Carolina or his discussion of treatment of the Indian tribes, or even in his Farewell Address, which he did not draft but entrusted to his last speechwriter, Roger Taney.

Toward the end of his presidency, Jackson made his rhetoric reflective. He devoted a lengthy portion of his Annual Message of December 7, 1835, to the Bank War, which was for all intents and purposes over. The Bank of the United States had closed, and only a few lingering issues of corrupt practices were still being revealed. Growing economic distress was the primary issue of the day. The bank's punishing constriction of the money supply was largely to blame, as was its reversal of course by flooding the markets with money. Jackson elected in this context to address first principles as instructive for correct policies, and his discussion is insightful and revealing of his world view. He urged the following for Congress and the nation: "Recur to first principles and see what it is that has prevented the legislation of Congress and the States on the subject of currency from satisfying the public expectation and realizing results corresponding to those which have attended the action of our system when truly consistent with the great principle of equality upon which it rests, and with that spirit of forbearance and mutual concession and generous patriotism which was originally, and must ever continue to be, the vital element of our Union."[17]

Jackson's basic tenets of the polity were in these first principles. Equality was the primary rule, coupled with willingness to engage in mutual concession and generous patriotism. For Jackson, these basic values formed the foundation of the nation and stood for its creed. With such a straightforward and simple perspective, Jackson approached politics as bound by key ideas that all could understand and accept. Talking about these principles and implementing them relative to issues of the day was likewise simple and straightforward. Subsequently, there was nothing complicated in Jackson's rhetoric; it was bound by the same basic, foundational, and logical principles. He was the first people's president, and he appealed to the masses because he understood their plight and their struggles with a system that was neither equal nor fair. He abhorred unethical and manipulative practices and saw the dangers such practices posed to the nation. Therefore, rectifying the polity was Jackson's straightforward objective.

In a subsequent passage in the same Annual Message, Jackson further developed the notion of first principles, referring to the Bank of the United States as "one of the fruits of a system at war with the genius of all our institutions—a system founded upon a political creed the fundamental principle of which is a distrust of the popular will as a safe regulator of political power."[18] The people and their popular will were foundational to the nation's success. In addition, the people's inherent distrust of political power was the guarantor of American democracy. Jackson had a knack for focusing on the nation's suspicion of power as essential to its democratic principles, and he expressed this idea with great rhetorical economy and clarity.

Overall, Jackson was a strategic communicator who consciously decided whether a given issue merited public pronouncements. When silence was the preferred strategy over a key issue such as the acquisition of Texas (an issue of great importance to Jackson), he stuck to it. Indeed, Jackson stated nothing in publicly about Texas throughout his eight years in office, and he cautioned others to be vigilant about their public rhetoric on the matter. Even so, he considered Texas crucial to the defense of the United States. He worried about losing this territory to Great Britain and subsequently exposing a weak part of the nation's frontier. All attempts to negotiate Texas with Mexico were handled in secrecy. Ostensibly, the covert handling of Texas displayed Jackson's understanding of the importance of public rhetoric when grand principles and values were at stake. Public remarks could generate public sentiments. Yet, when expediency was warranted that the public might suspect, Jackson opted for the secretive.

With hindsight, the president proved correct, sensing that public statements about Texas could weaken if not ruin his presidency. When his protégé Van Buren sought the presidency again in 1844, his somewhat cautious public statements about Texas disrupted his chances for reelection. Jackson's other protégé, James Polk, would become president in 1844 and acquire Texas. Yet it was Jackson who made this gain possible—he continued his secret negotiations and offered guidance some eight years after leaving the White House. Polk stated as much and even visited Jackson at the Hermitage ten days after his own election to discuss Texas.[19]

Jackson also brought the model soldier-politician to the presidency, setting a precedent that would repeat itself time and again, often at critical junctures in the nation's history. George Washington's status as a soldier-politician was not a precedent but a unique founding moment. Jackson changed all that with his quick rise in popularity following the United States' final victory over Great Britain in 1815. That he won the popular presidential vote only nine years later demonstrated the phenomenal transition in presidential politics. And that the nation chose a candidate who espoused no clear political agenda or policies marked this transition. Jackson succeeded in 1828 by making his loss 1824 the primary issue of the campaign. Yet, this campaign cannot be discounted as lacking direction, as it allowed Jackson to focus on political corruption and enter the presidency as an outsider bent on restoring honesty, fairness and ethical practices. Four years later, Jackson ran for the presidency again, making the corrupt bank as a populist theme of his campaign.

The campaign rhetoric Jackson and his aides developed appealed to the masses precisely because it addressed the sentiments of many. His audience-centered political appeals kept him popular and receptive to numerous Americans' experiences. Attacking the wealthy and their corrupt practices resonated with the masses, and this phenomenon was a measure of the new political rhetoric.

A MODERN PRESIDENT

Three months after his second inauguration, on June 6, 1833, Jackson embarked on a grand tour. Winning the Bank War and seeing the end of the Nullification Crisis, he decided to travel through New England, an unusual move for an early president. The tour would take him to major cities in northern states: Baltimore, Philadelphia, New York and Boston. Jackson encountered overwhelming support that energized him and gave him confidence. No previous president to date was able to establish such a warm relationship with the people. What the tour established was Jackson's intuition that his presence was as important as press accounts of his addresses and statements. The tour brought out Americans' affection for him; thousands awaited his passing entourage, shouting and screaming their support. Jackson's travels also involved many parades, banquets, handshakes, and even kisses for babies. The signs welcoming him to numerous cities and towns were displays of his effective rhetorical signature and images translated metonymically into "The Hero of New Orleans," "Ask Nothing not Right—Submit to Nothing Wrong," and "The Union Must be Preserved."[20]

What was not visible but was significant nonetheless was Jackson's consummate political acumen. The tour also carried political objectives; Jackson wished it and his presence to strengthen support for the Democratic Party in New England. While Jackson carried no state in the northeast in 1828, he carried only Maine and New Hampshire in the 1832 election.[21] Even so, the momentum was on his side, and he thought it wise to cash in on this growing support and strengthen Van Buren's prospects as his heir apparent.[22] The tour came after Jackson's election. It was thus meant to strengthen his party's hold in New England, not to promote his own self-interest. Today, this tour would likely take place prior to the election and for the purpose of securing votes. But Jackson was thinking of his party and the candidate he had picked to follow him.

The grand tour also included a short patriotic speech that summarized many of Jackson's political views. A short excerpt from those remarks delivered at the monument in Bunker Hill illustrates his modern approach to popular appeal: "And when to all these are added your moral, social, literary, and religious institutions—your happy equality of condition—the general diffusion of knowledge—your industry and enterprise—and when we reflect that most of this is common to the New England states, you may well be proud of your native land, and your country may well be proud of New England."[23] Jackson understood the entrepreneurial spirit of New England and the growth of its industrial and academic institutions. Though Jackson was an aging leader, youthful and progressive thinking was the hallmark of his presidency—he was optimistic and confident. He appreciated the interdependence of industry and education as foundational to the nation's growth. It was a given that these empowering statements could also build his political cachet. The heroic past enshrined in Bunker Hill allowed a special scene to double as patriotic and motivating rhetoric. Jackson's words could move various parts of the nation to take the Union as given if not an altogether sacred entity.

The masses whom Jackson considered foundational to his policies and actions came out to cheer him. He, in turn, was quite taken by the show of enthusiastic support. Jackson wanted to be seen, and he made every effort to allow as many well-wishers as possible that opportunity throughout the grueling tour. In all, the president was pleased with his reception, for he commented, "Suffice it to say that it surpassed any thing I ever witnessed."[24]

Ultimately, Jackson read the American people rather well, campaigning extensively via local political networks and employing a favorable press that emphasized his character and image. The very fact that Jackson developed national campaigns, an anathema to the political elite of his days, was a sign of changing times. This, Jackson understood perfectly, as evidenced by the key arguments of his public addresses, which were often based on developing popular appeals. With hindsight, those who concocted the 1824 presidential choice and ignored the popular vote might have wished that they had not. Their actions gave Jackson and many Americans the perfect justification for painting the nation's politicians as corrupt, and for agreeing on the need for serious reforms. His 1824 loss clearly gave Jackson a heavy dose of rhetorical ammunition from whence he formed arguments and charges grounded in clear principles of fairness and justice.

Yet an important caveat is needed here. Despite his growing reliance on popular appeals, Jackson did not look to adjust his views to the sentiments of many in the nation. He followed key principles that he strongly believed in. It was advantageous that these ideas corresponded to those of numerous Americans. But the arguments and the reasoning behind these ideas were all Jackson's. When the president's values did not accord with those of many Americans, he pursued them regardless of the consequences. The most difficult issues of the day, the removal of the Indian tribes and the withdrawal of deposits from the bank, were such cases. Jackson believed in and adhered to the course he pursued, and he did so despite opposition from his supporters and, in the case of the Removal Act, despite a very close vote in the House. The president had his blind spots. Tribal removal and increasing tensions over slavery put him squarely in opposition to any moral sentiment and just policies. The two issues were not similar, and Jackson's approach to each differed, but the net effect of his actions left a stain on his presidency.

On several fronts, Jackson carved a path that differed from any of his predecessors'. The marked change was not just political but rhetorical as well. He changed the presidency by raising new insights and convictions that his opponents misunderstood. Moreover, the changes Jackson introduced were reasonable and timely. Several considered radical at the time were actually rather simple and straightforward. Jackson grounded his reforms in basic principles: the people ought to elect the president; the president was the chief representative of the people; the presidency was above Congress, not its equal; the president had the right to appeal directly to the people in advocating policies; the government belonged to the people, and not to the few elite; and that the Union was of people, not of states. With all these principal changes, Jackson could construct the presidency as the symbolic embodiment of the nation.

Jackson believed in expanding the role and reach of the president while at the same time espousing a strong but limited federal government. With his First Annual Message to Congress, he set up a productive agenda for tackling all anticipated major issues as well as formulating the balancing act between the federal government and the states. Almost every issue Jackson faced was outlined in his First Annual Message. Ultimately, the important issues of the day, such as the Maysville and Bank Vetoes and the Nullification Crisis, afforded Jackson the opportunity to strengthen the executive office by postulating that it could also legislate and adjudicate. Thus he exerted power previously held in the balance between the three branches of government.

The rise of party politics of the late 1820s evolving around the character of Andrew Jackson was a loose coalition of northerners, southerners, and those who prompted his candidacy in Tennessee. This loose party centered on Jackson primarily for image and stature to unify disparate economic and regional interests. This coalition would be short-lived, and several controversies, especially the Bank War, would bring a realignment of partisan forces emanating from Jackson's growing image as a tyrannical president. The Whigs in particular, comprised of Clay, Calhoun, Webster, and some of Jackson's Tennessee supporters, such as Hugh Lawson White and John Bell, would unify around their opposition to "King Andrew I."[25] Jackson's character, then, carried rhetorical currency that helped form the Democrats. But it also sharpened partisan politics over major conflicts that were shaped critically as constitutional and thus foundational to the United States.

This rhetorical currency shaped Jackson's candidacy and presented him as the first to develop a presidential campaign tour and make public appearances in several states. Jackson's campaigns relied on an efficient organization that initially promoted his candidacy in "Hickory Clubs." These clubs hosted parades and barbecues, and they promoted an overall party atmosphere meant to bring politics to the people. Jackson also relied heavily on the partisan press to promote his causes. The early nineteenth century was often described as "a dark age of American journalism," primarily for its partisan media. But this description obscures the reason for that media's rise.[26] When presidential elections changed from an inside-the-beltway affairs to matters of popular rhetoric, a change owing significantly to Jackson, the press criticized such unbecoming self-promotion. Monroe's preference "for a government by consensus" ended after the presidential election of 1824. When popular aspirants found the press unhelpful, they began to create their own presses in which the editors often functioned as de facto party and campaign chairs. The partisan press became a public relations tool that rallied people and indicated growing reliance on officeholders' popularity.[27]

Such was the case with the Bank Veto, presented in the 1832 campaign as part of Jackson's fight for the people. At the same time, Clay was tipped as the candidate of the privileged.[28] Jackson himself traveled to several states as a presidential candidate, a feat not seen before. The presidential tours even included one to Kentucky, Clay's state. The shock of such a visit is well illustrated in this commentary from the pro-Clay *National Intelligencer*: "We do not recollect before to have heard of a President of the United States descending in person into the political arena."[29] Jackson understood the rhetorical advantage of visual presence, and he incorporated it into his unconventional approach to politics.

Late in his presidency, Jackson also had to tackle the growing voices of abolitionists. Successful distribution of abolitionist newspapers in the South caused much strife. Via Amos Kendall, his postmaster general and trusted advisor, Jackson sought a solution to what was taken as incendiary. Mercieca considers this episode an escalatory phase in the rhetorical war between abolitionists and slaveholders. The Jackson administration opted not to prohibit the newspapers' distribution, and by default the president's stand was interpreted as siding with the abolitionists. Jackson, however, sought to let the states resolve this issue without federal government intervention. He did not seek to prohibit people from reading the newspapers, arguing that it was their right to do so. In fact, he assumed that so few people would request them that they would cease distribution. Mercieca also notes that, though Jackson erroneously said abolitionist material had been sent to many who had not requested it,[30] he took a noteworthy principled approach to free expression—one of the thorniest and volatile issues of the day. As a slaveholder himself, Jackson opposed abolitionists and sought to limit the distribution of their material in the North and the South. But as president he took a cautionary approach that deemed a constitutional principle more important than the issue at hand.

The rhetorical perspective taken here explains much of Jackson's success. Early on and with the aid of astute advisors, he figured out how to present himself as a viable challenger and a people's president. He also determined how to manage presidential campaigns the like of which the nation had not experienced. High-level populism, often targeting "the people," became a condensed metaphor that gave Jackson the ethos and the motivation for great appeals without requiring too many elaborations. A straightforward but foundational principle, such as the people's right to appoint those who would govern them, or the Bank of the United States' responsibility to the entire nation and not just a selected few, was all that was needed to get Jacksonians going.

Jackson's rivals underestimated him, often ridiculing his backward upbringing, lack of education, and rough style. While vying for the presidency in 1832, Clay thought himself smarter than Jackson and believed he would win the election.[31] Nothing could have been further from the truth, as Jackson was a calculating and astute politician. He thought through every issue, assessed the various strategies available, predicted the moves others would make, and acted accordingly. He was patient when needed, silent when others expected the opposite, and threatening when it suited him. His opponents, such as Calhoun and Clay, were formidable politicians in their own right. But both men misunderstood Jackson and committed numerous errors of judgment that cost them politically.

Congressional leaders, especially Clay and Calhoun, considered the removal of the bank's deposits a despotic move that circumvented the Constitution. But they overlooked Jackson's new practices of going public. Calhoun even stated that the president could communicate with the people in two ways—by sending messages to the two houses of Congress or by issuing a proclamation. Any other methods were considered "alarming signs of the times which portend[ed] the overthrow of the Constitution and the approach of despotic power."[32] For these two presidential contenders, Jackson's communicating his view to the nation via the press was a gross violation of constitutional as well as traditional practices. They disregarded Jackson's status as the people's president and his practice of this perspective throughout his presidency.

Jackson also brought to the presidency new ideas and processes that were more democratic than those of his predecessors. His opponents could not fathom an organic presidency that responded to changing times. Older than most key politicians of his time, Jackson had a better sense of the need to reform politics such that it corresponded to significant changes effected by the masses' entry into the political arena. For example, while senators were still elected by their respective state legislatures, Jackson was signaling serious challenges to old practices. His rhetoric was part and parcel of appealing to the public at large and generating their assent to his reforms. Jackson did not mind appealing to the people emotionally. He spoke of himself as a father on several occasions, projecting paternal references in which America seemed to replace the biological family that he lacked. Jackson fretted about the care and future of the larger nation just as a father would with his own children.

Jackson faced one setback during his two terms: Clay's initiated Senate censure over his removal of deposits from the Bank of the United States. This vengeful move stung Jackson, and since he did not let any affront go unchallenged, he planned to react. In a letter to his friend Gen. John Coffee on April 6, 1832, Jackson rehearsed his principal argument: "In a protest I intend to present to them [the Senate], protesting against their usurping the impeaching power of the House and their daring violation of the constitution [sic] in the attempt to encroach upon the constitutional powers of the executive."[33] Jackson responded officially on April 15, 1834, with his lengthy "Protest," which countered all the charges against him. He challenged the censure as a personal attack, saying that he was charged "with [the] high crime of violating the laws and Constitution of [his] country."[34]

Masterfully, the president turned the attack on him into an attack on the entire nation. He warned that such a precedent was dangerous for him and for future presidents because the threat of censure would move the center of power from the executive to the legislative branch. The president as the "direct representative of the American people," argued Jackson, was attacked by a body that was not fully the representative of the people.[35] Even in anger over a petty Senate revenge, Jackson took another opportunity to assert presidential authority. He defined the executive as elected directly by the people, and he declared a power no previous president had asserted.[36] By implication, Congress was not as formidable as it thought—clearly not equal to the executive. This point did not escape Senator Calhoun, who sarcastically noted that Jackson had been voted into office by electors and not by the masses. Yet this was a narrow reading of the presidential election especially since senators were further removed from the masses because they were elected by state legislatures and not directly by the people of a given state.[37]

The "Protest" was much anticipated by the public at large. Jackson's team of speechwriters labored for about two weeks before he was satisfied that his statement advanced his political philosophy. He approached the "Protest" not as an argument but as a statement that needed no defense. Jackson stated that, as the censure was "wholly unauthorized by the Constitution, but in many respects repugnant to its provisions and subversive of the rights secured by it to other coordinate departments," he "deemed it an imperative duty to maintain the supremacy of that sacred instrument."[38] "It [the Senate] assumed," he charged, "that a single branch of the legislative department may for the purpose of public censure, and without any view to legislation or impeachment, take up, consider, and decide upon the official acts of the executive."[39] Jackson rejected this stance: "In no part of the Constitution is the President subjected to any such responsibility, and in no part of the instrument is any such power conferred on either branch of the Legislature."[40]

As with the Maysville and the Bank Vetoes, Jackson found another opportunity to strengthen the executive, this time by challenging the Senate for operating as judge and jury and in a manner not prescribed by the Constitution. The fact that the Senate did not impeach him, Jackson contended, pointed to the erroneous nature of the censure. As for the charge of dismissing the secretary of the Treasury, Jackson argued that he was within the jurisdiction of the executive. A constitutional provision specified that the president had to ensure "that the laws be faithfully executed." The censure suggested that the Senate had a vested role in "appointing" or "nominating," which it did not.[41] To the contrary, Congress had decided in 1789 that "the President derived from the Constitution the power of removal" of departmental officials.[42]

In the "Protest," Jackson also tackled the specific charge that he was unauthorized to remove deposits from the bank. He argued that when the Bank of the United States was established, its affairs were under the supervision of the secretary of the Treasury, including the right to direct deposits elsewhere. If such was the case, then the president clearly had authority over the actions of cabinet secretaries. The censure and "the doctrine which denie[d] to the President the power of supervising, directing and controlling the Secretary of the Treasury" were described in the "Protest" as "dangerous" and an affront to the president, who was directly responsible to the people.[43]

The conclusion of the "Protest" is vintage Jackson. He stated,

> *I do hereby solemnly* protest against the aforementioned proceedings of the Senate as unauthorized by the Constitution, contrary to its spirit and to several of its express provisions, subversive of that distribution of the powers of government which it has ordained and established, destructive of the checks and safeguards by which those powers were intended on the one hand to be controlled and on the other to be protected, and calculated by their immediate and collateral effects, by their character and tendency, to concentrate in the hands of a body not directly amenable to the people a degree of influence and power dangerous to their liberties and fatal to the Constitution of their choice.[44]

Turning personal at the conclusion of the "Protest," Jackson voiced the following desires: "To serve my fellowmen . . . to return to the people unimpaired the sacred trust they have confided to my charge; to heal the wounds of the Constitution and preserve it from further violation; to persuade my countrymen, so far as I may, that it is not in a splendid government supported by powerful monopolies and aristocratical establishments that they will find happiness or their liberties protection, but in a plain system, void of pomp, protecting all and granting favors to none."[45] Jackson's populist appeal framed his "Protest" but it also made serious inroads into constitutional interpretations that further changed the balance between the executive and the legislative branches. He had another opportunity to strengthen the presidency, and he pushed this point with the Constitution as the premier grounding document.

Significantly, Jackson spoke of his presidential role as that of a persuader. This, too, is an insightful statement by an early president who understood his role as rhetorician or advocate in chief. Though hurt by such a slight, Jackson left a significant precedent for future presidents: the executive was answerable only to the people, the Constitution was supreme, and the Union as a confederation of united states would be prosperous and free. With Jackson, the executive was no longer under the control of Congress or equal to Congress. Instead, the executive was under the control of the people. True democracy was finally seen and practiced.

In 1837, the Senate, through the able work of Sen. Thomas Benton, expunged Jackson's censure. Those who advocated the censure in the first place now criticized its reversal, clinging to the Constitution as the principle grounding their action. Their charge was that Jackson was a despot. He ignored the Constitution and usurped presidential power that belonged to the legislative bodies. In the end, the matter was that of constitutional interpretation, and Jackson proved that a presidential interpretation is more powerful than the interpretation of others.

Ultimately, Jackson found the best grounding for his public arguments in simple principles and reasoning that resonated with the masses rather easily. Benton made this very point while arguing for expunging the censure. Benton stated, "[Jackson]came into office the first of generals; he goes out the first of statesmen. . . . He always said the people would stand by those who stand by them; and nobly have they justified that confidence! That verdict, the voice of million, which now demands the expurgation of that sentence, which the Senate and the bank then pronounced upon him, is the magnificent response of the people's hearts to the implicit confidence which he then reposed in them."[46] The censure was expunged from the Senate's records. Jackson won the final battle, reminding his opponents again just how popular he was.

❊❊❊❊❊

Jackson came to Washington to change the nation, and he did. His path to the presidency was not the way he planned or wished it, as he was ready to take office in 1824. Yet, with hindsight, the individuals in Congress who wielded a different outcome that year might have wished they had not. They gave Jackson the rhetorical grounding for an impressive and accomplished presidency. Had he taken office in 1824, it is doubtful Jackson would have been able to accomplish what ultimately he did later. In 1824, he did not win the majority of the popular vote and the majority of the Electoral College. The "corrupt bargain" gave Jackson the material rhetoric for his next campaign and a moral grounding for a restorative administration and an era.

Jackson conceived the American democracy in rather simple but foundational terms. He did so by fighting one large battle (containing different versions of the same battle) during his two-term presidency, strengthening the Union and the executive branch against those who sought a weak federal government and a president with limited powers. Jackson triumphed over every issue, crisis, or controversy he met. He did not initiate crises to benefit a scheme or a plan; he had to respond to crises others constructed. He invariably succeeded because of his principled approach to governing. He was of the people, and his responsibility was to the people. Jackson's addresses, messages, vetoes, and proclamations were well-crafted appeals to the public outlining clear beliefs. His administration mastered the arts of politics and rhetoric, and he himself was the chief architect of his presidency. In all, Jackson wielded strong credibility and the ethos he needed to succeed.

Jackson was an activist president, as exemplified by the solid agenda he put forward in his First Annual Message. Activist presidents, note Campbell and Jamieson, are "more likely to remind Congress in subsequent State of the Union Addresses that parts of that agenda remain to be enacted, and more likely to veto acts that threaten to alter their agenda. Activists are more comfortable using rhetoric to achieve their ends," as well as "more inclined to break new grounds in the use of the veto."[47] Indeed, Jackson's vetoes, more than any of his other rhetorical acts, shaped a new relationship between the executive and legislative branches. His vetoes presented the executive as independent of the legislative branch, formulating a presidency that belonged to the entire nation and was thus answerable to the populace.

Not insignificantly, Jackson's presence was a political asset. His numerous travels—including trips to and from his home state of Tennessee and campaign tours—allowed him to receive the cheers of thousands and converse jovially with many along the way, thus expanding his popularity and his own political views. Perhaps more inadvertently than deliberately, the democratizing enterprise Jackson espoused also gave rise to numerous popular sentiments. These included abolitionists' and philanthropists' opposition to his Indian removal policy. At the time, Jackson saw these individuals as agitators who were intent on disrupting the fragile Union. His democratic appeals served him well, but they spread further than he anticipated. Jackson has been hailed as a great president, but he was also controversial primarily for his authoritative consolidation of executive power, which often relied, in the words of Mercieca, "upon the republican analysis of liberty, which does not include equality."[48]

Upon reflection, Jackson's presidency and the issues he confronted sound rather familiar and similar to the issues presidents have faced in the late twentieth and early twenty-first centuries. One is struck by the consistency between the issues he tackled throughout the life of the republic and contemporary issues such as public money, budget surpluses, pet projects, and deficits. Jackson sounds very much like a modern president, a leader keenly aware of the corrupting influence of deficits and the invisible force of the economy on public confidence.

Yet Jackson's approach, crisis management, and overall attitude are refreshing for their principles and convictions. Jackson "talked" more than his predecessors, arguing passionately over critical issues and, for better or worse, winning every battle. He accomplished much by projecting what Remini considers "the most honest and least corrupt administration" during the early years of the nation."[49] Though Jackson's military success in the Battle of New Orleans propelled him to the presidency, he devoted his two terms in office largely to economic issues, covering budget deficits, unwarranted expenditures, tariffs, and banking. Indeed, the economic flavor to Jackson's rhetoric merged populist appeals with the experience of the underprivileged.

Jackson conceived the presidency as a popular office and the executive as an independent entity more elevated than the other two branches of government. A strong character and an effective rhetorical presence were needed to actualize these ideas. He possessed both, and the people displayed their affection for him in turn, considering him serious and principled.

Despite many years of frequent illnesses and physical pain, Jackson did not depart from Earth as early as he thought or his opponents wished. He would live eight more years after leaving the White House, seeing the full term of his handpicked successor, Martin Van Buren, and even the successful election of a long-standing Tennessee family friend and ally, James K. Polk. His time in office would become an era, known since as Jacksonian democracy.

NOTES

PREFACE

1. Robert V. Remini, *The Course of American Democracy, 1833–1845*, vol. 3 of *Andrew Jackson* (New York: Harper & Row, 1984), 3:6. Throughout this study I have favored the term American Indian to designate the Indigenous peoples of America. Scrupulous readers will notice, however, that I have also retained the less precise terminology of "Indian" and "Indians" in many places. This is to preserve economy and minimize confusion in the discussion of texts replete with references to the Indian Removal Act, "Indian tribes," "Indian lands," and the like.

2. Danielle Allen, *Our Declaration: A Reading of the Declaration of Independence in Defense of Equality* (New York: Liveright, 2014), 243.

3. Ibid., 245.

INTRODUCTION

1. James Parton, *The Life of Andrew Jackson* (New York: Mason Brothers, 1860), 1:66.

2. Marvin Meyers, "The Jacksonian Persuasion," *American Quarterly* 5 (Spring 1953): 4–5.

3. Ibid.

4. David Zarefsky believes Jackson's election to a second term brought the pivotal change in focus from the personal to policy. I contend that Jackson's very candidacy in 1828 already focused on issues such as corrupt politics and the need for election reforms. Both problems emanated from the 1824 election. See Zarefsky, "Presidential Rhetoric and the Power of Definition," *Presidential Studies Quarterly* 34 (2004): 614.

5. Ronald H. Carpenter, "America's Tragic Metaphor: Our Twentieth-Century Combatants as Frontiersmen," *Quarterly Journal of Speech* 76 (1990): 1–4. Carpenter points to the myth created around the frontiersmen's sharpshooting successes, which in truth were minimal. Jackson had low opinions of his sharpshooters, and he defeated the British primarily by the use of cannons.

6. John William Ward, *Andrew Jackson: Symbol for an Age* (London: Oxford University Press, 1955), 16–17. Belohlavek puts the number of American soldiers killed at around one hundred. See John M. Belohlavek, *Andrew Jackson: Principle and Prejudice* (New York: Routledge, 2016), 31.

7. Mark R. Cheathem, *Andrew Jackson and the Rise of the Democrats* (Santa Barbara: ABC-CLIO, 2015), 48.

8. Robert V. Remini, "Winning the Presidency," in *Andrew Jackson: A Profile*, ed. Charles Sellers (New York: Hill & Wang, 1971), 94.

9. Cheathem, *Andrew Jackson and the Rise of the Democrats*, 58–59.

10. Cited in Arthur M. Schlesinger, "An Impressive Mandate and the Meaning of Jacksonianism," in Sellers, *Andrew Jackson: A Profile*, 121.

11. Ibid., 124.

12. Charles Sellers, introduction to Sellers, *Andrew Jackson: A Profile*, xii.

13. Remini, "Winning the Presidency," 94.

14. Marvin Meyers, *The Jacksonian Persuasion: Politics and Belief* (Stanford University Press, 1957), 4.

15. Remini, "Winning the Presidency," 83.

16. Quoted in ibid., 85–86.

17. Ibid., 89.

18. John William Ward, *"Andrew Jackson, Symbol for an Age,"* in Sellers, *Andrew Jackson: A Profile*, 215.

19. Ibid.

20. Ibid.

21. Ibid., 217.

22. *Illinois Gazette*, January 15, 1825, cited in ibid., 219.

23. "Address of the Republican General Committee of Young Men of the City and County of New York Friendly to the Election of Gen. Andrew Jackson," New York, 1828, p. 38, cited in Sellers, Andrew Jackson: Symbol for An Age, 219.

24. *Ohio State Journal*, November 29, 1827, cited in Sellers, *Andrew Jackson: A Profile*, 220.

25. Jeffery K. Tulis, *The Rhetorical Presidency* (Princeton: Princeton University Press, 1987).

26. Meyers, *The Jacksonian Persuasion*, 6.

27. Richard B. Latner, "The Kitchen Cabinet and Andrew Jackson's Advisory System," *Journal of American History* 65 (1978): 369–73. Sen. George Poindexter of Mississippi, an ardent advocate for southern states and an opponent of Jackson, was the first to use the term Kitchen Cabinet, and he meant it derogatorily. See Latner, 376.

28. Ibid., 378.

29. Henry A. Wise, *Seven Decades of the Union* (Philadelphia: J. B. Lippincott, 1881), 117.

30. Cheathem, *Andrew Jackson and the Rise of the Democrats*, 94–98.

31. Belohlavek, *Andrew Jackson: Principle and Prejudice*, 16.

32. See examples of Jackson's editorial work in which he struck out words and preferred economy in language. Andrew Jackson, "First Annual Message to Congress," in *The Papers of Andrew Jackson*, vol. 7, 1829, ed. Daniel Feller et al. (Knoxville: University of Tennessee Press, 2007), 601–3, 608.

33. Quoted in Remini, *Course of American Democracy*, 216–17.

34. John Sergeant to Henry Clay, June 25, 1830, in *Papers of Henry Clay. Candidate, Compromiser, Whig*, vol. 8, *March 5, 1829–December 31, 1836*, ed. Robert Seager II (Lexington: University Press of Kentucky, 1984), 230.

35. Henry Clay to Thomas Speed, June 25, 1830, in Seager, *Papers of Henry Clay*, 8:230.

36. James Jasinski, "Liberty and Power in Nineteenth Century Public Argument: A Foucaultian Analysis," *Argument and Critical Practices: Proceedings of the Fifth SCA/AFA Conference on Argumentation*, ed. Joseph W. Wenzel (Annandale, VA: Speech Communication Association, 1987), 515–17.

CHAPTER 1

1. Robert V. Remini, *The Course of American Freedom, 1822–1832*, vol. 2 of *Andrew Jackson* (New York: Harper & Row, 1981), 13.

2. Ibid., 37.

3. Andrew Jackson to H. W. Peterson, February 23, 1823, in *The Papers of Andrew Jackson*, vol. 5, *1821–1824*, ed. Harold D. Moser, David R. Hoth, and George H. Hoemann (Knoxville: University of Tennessee Press, 1996), 253.

4. Remini, *Course of American Freedom*, 49–50.

5. M. J. Heale, *The Presidential Quest: Candidates and Images in American Political Culture, 1787–1852* (London: Longman, 1982), 48.

6. Remini, *Course of American Freedom*, 60.

7. Heale, *Presidential Quest*, 49–51.

8. Donald Ratcliffe, *The One-Party Presidential Contest: Adams, Jackson, and 1824's Five-Horse Race* (Lawrence: University Press of Kansas, 2015), 7.

9. Heale, *Presidential Quest*, 54.

10. Remini, *Course of American Freedom*, 58–60.

11. Andrew Jackson to Littlejohn Coleman, April 26, 1824, in Moser, Hoth, and Hoemann, *Papers of Andrew Jackson*, 5:399.

12. Ibid.

13. Remini, *Course of American Freedom*, 70.

14. Robert P. Hay, "John Fitzgerald: Presidential Image Maker for Andrew Jackson in 1823," *Tennessee Historical Quarterly* 42 (1983): 138–41.

15. Ibid., 143–48.

16. Cheathem, *Andrew Jackson and the Rise of the Democrats*, 78–79.

17. Remini, *Course of American Freedom*, 76. Heale claims that Jackson was unaware of its authorship until a year later. See Heale, *Presidential Quest*, 51.

18. "Letters of Wyoming to the People of the United States on the Presidential Election, and In Favour of Andrew Jackson," Philadelphia: S. Simpson & J. Conrad, 1824, accessed May 9, 2015, http://www.forgottenbooks.com. Inconsistent capitalizations in the original.

19. Ibid., 2.

20. Ibid., 2–3.

21. Ibid., 4.

22. Ibid.

23. Ibid., 5.

24. Ibid., 6. The Latin phrase literally means "the voice and disregard nothing," which flexibly translates to considering delivery as the sole quality of speech and, colloquially, style above substance.

25. Ibid., 9.

26. Ibid.

27. Ibid., 10.

28. Ibid., 14.

29. Ibid., 23. Capitalizations in the original.

30. Ibid. Capitalization in the original.

31. Heale, *Presidential Quest*, 57.

32. *Letters of Wyoming*, 47.

33. Ibid.

34. Ibid., 51.

35. Ibid., 53–54.

36. Ibid., 58.

37. Ibid.

38. Ibid., 59.

39. Ibid.

40. Ibid., 62.

41. Ibid., 63–65.

42. Ibid., 66.

43. Ibid.

44. Ibid., 87.

45. Ibid., 88.

46. Ibid.

47. Ibid.

48. Ibid., 89.

49. Ibid.

50. Ibid., 92–93.

51. Ibid., 93.

52. Ibid.

53. Ibid., 97.

54. Ibid.

55. Ibid., 97–98.

56. Ibid., 103–4.

57. In a reply letter to John Calhoun, Jackson used the phrase "coalition intrigue & management." Jackson to Calhoun, ca. August 12, 1823, in Moser, Hoth, and Hoemann, *Papers of Andrew Jackson*, 5:286.

58. Remini, *Course of American Freedom*, 78.

59. Heale, *Presidential Quest*, 59–62.

60. Cheathem, *Andrew Jackson and the Rise of the Democrats*, 82.

61. Ibid., 84–87.

62. Remini, *Course of American Freedom*, 97.

63. This and other letters Jackson exchanged with Swartwout were published in 1922, by Henry F. Depuy in a volume titled *Some Letters of Andrew Jackson* (under the American Antiquarian Society and printed by Davis Press in Worcester, MA). The exchange of nine letters began while Jackson was in Washington, DC, and continued after he had returned to the Hermitage in Tennessee.

64. Henry F. Depuy, introduction to *Some Letters of Andrew Jackson,* by Andrews Jackson, ed. Henry F. Depuy (Worcester, Mass: American Antiquarian Society, 1922), 5.

65. Ward, *Andrew Jackson: Symbol of an Age*, 186–90.

66. In early 1825, Tennessee nominated Jackson as a candidate for the next presidential election. This move was intended to keep Jackson's name front and center for the duration of the Adams administration, and to slight Adams for the way he gained the presidency.

67. Depuy, *Some Letters of Andrew Jackson*, 14.

68. Ibid., 14.

69. Ibid., 15.

70. Ibid.

71. Ibid., 17.

72. Ibid.

73. Ibid.

74. Ibid., 18–19.

75. Andrew Jackson to John Coffee, April 24, 1825, in *The Papers of Andrew Jackson*, vol. 6, *1825–1828*, ed. Harold D. Moser and J. Clint Clift (Knoxville: University of Tennessee Press, 2002), 65.

76. John Quincy Adams, "First Annual Message," December 6, 1825, in *A Compilation of the Messages and Papers of the Presidents*, ed. James D. Richardson (New York: Bureau of National Literature, 1897), 2:882. Overall, Adams's First Annual Message was rhetorically awkward and intellectually arrogant.

77. Andrew Jackson to James Buchanan, January 29, 1827, in Moser and Clift, *Papers of Andrew Jackson*, 6:271–72.

78. Andrew Jackson to Carter Beverley, June 5, 1827, in Moser and Clift, *Papers of Andrew Jackson*, 6:330–31.

79. Cheathem, *Andrew Jackson and the Rise of Democrats*, 94–95.

80. Not to be confused with the Republican Party of the 1850s. See ibid., xxi.

81. Ratcliffe, *One-Party Presidential Contest*, 237.

82. Heale, *Presidential Quest*, 38.

83. Remini, *Course of American Freedom*, 114.

84. Ibid., 131, 135. In 1787 the nation's Founders were "not interested in establishing the rule of the majority." To the contrary, they wanted to check popular will. They established the Electoral College, whereby senators are elected by state legislatures with few having the right to vote. As ironic as it may seem, by 1828, the number of white men who voted for president increased from 27 to 57 percent. See Jon Meacham, *American Lion: Andrew Jackson in the White House* (New York: Random House, 2008), 43. For a detailed view of voter participation during the early years of the nation, see Donald Ratcliffe, "The Right to Vote and the Rise of Democracy, 1778–1828," *Journal of the Early Republic* 33 (Summer 2013): 248–54, especially pp. 248–52 covering Jackson's presidential campaigns.

85. James Hamilton Jr., to Andrew Jackson, February 16, 1827, in *Correspondence of Andrew Jackson*, vol. 3, *1822–1828,* ed. John Spencer Bassett (Washington D.C.: Carnegie Institution of Washington, 1928), 344. The letter does not appear in *The Papers of Andrew Jackson*, vol. 6.

86. Martin Van Buren "to Andrew Jackson, September 14, 1827, in Moser and Clift, *Papers of Andrew Jackson*, 6:392.

CHAPTER 2

1. Heale, *Presidential Quest*, 70.

2. Ibid., 70–71.

3. Ibid., 74.

4. Ibid., 75.

5. Ibid., 62.

6. Remini, *Course of American Freedom*, 116–44, especially p. 150.

7. Andrew Jackson to Littlejohn Waller Tazewell, [undated], in Feller et al., *Papers of Andrew Jackson*, 7:42. Senator Tazewell chaired the joint congressional committee that issued the official election results whereby Jackson won 173 electoral votes to 83 for John Quincy Adams.

8. Andrew Jackson to Richard Keith Call, May 3, 1827, in Moser and Clift, *Papers of Andrew Jackson*, 6:315.

9. Wise, *Seven Decades of the Union*, 116.

10. Remini, *Course of American Freedom*, 157, 175–80

11. Ibid., 116–42.

12. Richard J. Ellis and Stephen Kirk, "Jefferson, Jackson, and the Origins of the Presidential Mandate," in *Speaking to the People: The Rhetorical Presidency in Historical Perspective*, ed. Richard J. Ellis (Amherst: University of Massachusetts Press, 1998), 40–41.

13. Quoted in ibid., 41.

14. Quoted in Remini, *Course of American Freedom*, 147, 156–57.

15. Karlyn K. Campbell and Kathleen H. Jamieson, *Presidents Creating the Presidency: Deeds Done in Words* (Chicago: University of Chicago Press, 2008), 30–31.

16. Ibid., 30–31.

17. Jackson, "Memorandum on Administration Policy," [undated but likely after February 28, 1829, and prior to the inauguration day of March 4], in Feller et al., *Papers of Andrew Jackson*, 7:69–70.

18. Andrew Jackson, "Rough Draft of the First Inaugural Address," [undated but around March 4, 1829], in Feller et al., *Papers of Andrew Jackson*, 7:74–77. All citations from this draft are from the same source.

19. Andrew Donelson, "Donelson's draft of the First Inaugural Address," [undated], in Feller et al., *Papers of Andrew Jackson*, 7:77.

20. Ibid., 77.

21. Andrew Jackson, "Rough Draft of the First Inaugural Address," [undated], in Feller et al., *Papers of Andrew Jackson*, 7: 76.

22. Andrew Donelson, "Donelson's draft of the First Inaugural Address," [undated], in Feller et al., *Papers of Andrew Jackson*, 7: 78.

23. Ibid., 78.

24. Ibid., 78 and Andrew Jackson, "Rough Draft of the First Inaugural Address," [undated], in Feller et al., *Papers of Andrew Jackson*, 7: 76.

25. Ibid., 79.

26. Andrew Jackson, "First Inaugural Address," March 4, 1829, in Richardson, *Compilation*, 3:999–1001. All quotes from this address are from this source.

27. Pres. John Quincy Adams's Inaugural Address includes a short statement about the need "to promote the civilization of the Indian tribes." Adams, "Inaugural Address," March 4, 1825, in Richardson, *Compilation*, 2:864. Pres. James Monroe's First Inaugural Address also includes this short statement: "With the Indian tribes our duty [is] to cultivate friendly relations and to act with kindness and liberality," and "to extend to them the advantages of civilization." Monroe, "First Inaugural Address," March 4, 1817, in Richardson, *Compilation*, 2:578. In his Second Inaugural Address, Monroe included a lengthy paragraph

describing the sad affair of American Indians and put responsibility on the US government to manage tribal affairs humanely and justly. Monroe, "Second Inaugural Address," March 5, 1821, in Richardson, *Compilation*, 2:661.

28. Ellis and Kirk, "Jefferson, Jackson, and the Origins of the Presidential Mandate," 42.

29. James K. Polk to Andrew Jackson, December 23, 1833, in *Correspondence of Andrew Jackson*, vol. 5, *1833–1838*, ed. John C. Bassett (Washington, DC.: Carnegie Institution, 1931), 236. Jackson replied on the back of Polk's letter; hence it is documented as such. This account is corroborated in Cheathem, *Andrew Jackson and the Rise of the Democrats*, 188.

30. Remini, *Course of American Freedom*, 178.

31. Ibid., 180.

CHAPTER 3

1. Campbell and Jamieson, *Presidents Creating the Presidency*, 139.

2. Ibid.

3. Adams, "First Annual Message," 879–82.

4. Andrew Jackson to Anthony Butler, October 10, 1829, in Feller et al., *Papers of Andrew Jackson*, 7:488. Jackson would remain silent on the acquisition of Texas throughout his presidency and beyond. Yet he worked diligently behind the scenes to accomplish this objective, persisting in his efforts until a few weeks before his death in 1845, some nine years after leaving office.

5. Secretary Samuel Delucenna Ingham, November 26, 1829, in Feller et al., *Papers of Andrew Jackson*, 7:576–77.

6. John M. Berrien to Andrew Jackson, November 27, 1829, in Feller et al., *Papers of Andrew Jackson*, 7:578.

7. Ibid., 579.

8. Jackson wrote an earlier draft. Though Donelson, Kendall, Van Buren, Berrien, Eaton, and Hamilton all contributed drafts of their own, Jackson's final version retained much of what he had initially written. Andrew Jackson, "Draft of the First Annual Message," [ca. December 7, 1829], in Feller et al., *Papers of Andrew Jackson*, 7:601.

9. Ibid, 7:602.

10. Ibid.

11. Ibid., 7:602–3.

12. Ibid., 7:603.

13. Ibid.

14. Ibid.

15. Ibid., 7:604.

16. Ibid.

17. Ibid.

18. Ibid., 7:605.

19. Ibid.

20. Ibid.

21. Ibid., 7:606.

22. Ibid.

23. Ibid.

24. Ibid.

25. Ibid.

26. Ibid., 7:607.

27. Ibid.

28. Ibid., 7:609.

29. Ibid. Inconsistent capitalization in the original.

30. Ibid.

31. Ibid.

32. Ibid., 7:610.

33. Martin Van Buren, "Draft by Martin Van Buren on the tariff," [ca. December 7, 1829], in Feller et al., *Papers of Andrew Jackson*, 7:618–19.

34. Ibid., 618.

35. Ibid., 619–30.

36. "Draft by James Alexander Hamilton on the Bank of the United States," [ca. December 7, 1829], in Feller et al., *Papers of Andrew Jackson*, 7:628.

37. Ibid.

38. Andrew Jackson, "First Annual Message to Congress," December 8, 1829, in Richardson, *Compilation*, 3:1005.

39. Ibid., 3:1006.

40. The primary issue with Great Britain related to the border between Maine and Canada. Ibid., 3:1006–7.

41. Ibid., 3:1007.

42. Ibid., 3:1007–8.

43. Ibid., 3:1010.

44. Ibid., 3:1010–11.

45. Ibid., 3:1011.

46. Robert W. Merry, *A Country of Vast Designs: James K. Polk, the Mexican War and the Conquest of the American Continent* (New York: Simon & Schuster, 2009), 28.

47. Jackson, "First Annual Message to Congress," *Compilation*, 3:1013.

48. Ibid., 3:1014.

49. Ibid., 3:1015.

50. Ibid., 3:1016–18.

51. Ibid., 3:1019.

52. Ibid., 3:1020.

53. Ibid., 3:1020–21.

54. Ibid., 3:1022–23.

55. Ibid., 3:1023–24.

56. Ibid., 3:1024.

57. Ibid.

58. Ibid., 3:1025.

CHAPTER 4

1. Andrew Jackson, "Maysville Road Veto Message," [ca. May, 27, 1830], in *The Papers of Andrew Jackson*, vol. 8, *1830*, ed. Daniel Feller, Thomas Coens, Laura-Eve Moss (Knoxville: University of Tennessee Press, 2010), 279. Several drafts are included.

2. Cheathem, *Andrew Jackson and the Rise of the Democrats*, 149.

3. Campbell and Jamieson, *Presidents Creating the Presidency*, 189.

4. Jackson, James K, Polk, and Martin Van Buren drafted the Maysville Veto. Andrew Jackson Donelson revised Van Buren's draft, which comprised most of the final version. Jackson's second draft was inserted between the second and third paragraphs of Van Buren's draft. *Papers of Andrew Jackson*, 8:279–300.

5. "Draft by Andrew Jackson," in Feller, Coens, and Moss, *Papers of Andrew Jackson*, 8:280–82.

6. Ibid., 280.

7. Ibid.

8. Ibid., 281.

9. Ibid.

10. Ibid.

11. Ibid., 282.

12. Ibid., 280.

13. Ibid., 280–81.

14. Ibid., 281.

15. Ibid.

16. Ibid.

17. Cited in Campbell and Jamieson, *Presidents Creating the Presidency*, 177.

18. Ibid.

19. "Draft by Andrew Jackson," in Feller, Coens, and Moss, *Papers of Andrew Jackson*, 8:281.

20. Jackson may have left the sum of money blank because he planned a later addition as a separate draft detailing the Treasury balance. This information is also included in Jackson's papers and is part of the collection of drafts in preparations for the Maysville Veto. Ibid., 297–99.

21. "Draft by James Knox Polk," in Feller, Coens, and Moss, *Papers of Andrew Jackson*, 8:282.

22. Ibid., 284.

23. "Draft by Martin Van Buren," in Feller, Coens, and Moss, *Papers of Andrew Jackson*, 8:285, 295–300.

24. Andrew Jackson, "Veto Messages," in Richardson, *Compilation*, 3:1046.

25. Ibid.

26. Ibid., 1047.

27. Ibid.

28. Ibid.

29. Ibid.

30. Ibid., 1048.

31. Madison cited in ibid., 1049.

32. Monroe cited in ibid., 1049.

33. Ibid., 1050.

34. Ibid., 1050–51.

35. Ibid., 1052–53.

36. Ellis and Kirk, "Jefferson, Jackson, and the Origins of the Presidential Mandate," 45.

37. Jackson, "Veto Messages," in Richardson, *Compilation*, 3:1053.

38. Ibid., 1054.

39. Ibid.

40. Ibid.

41. Ibid. Italics in the original.

42. Ibid., 1055.

43. Ibid., 1056.

44. Ibid.

45. During the 1824 campaign, Jackson, in a letter to James W. Lanier (an old military associate), stated his principled approach to "internal improvements," noting, "Congress can constitutionaly [sic] apply their funds to such objects as may be deemed National," but "the general government in the prosecution of their objects cannot exercise an exclusive jurisdiction and invade the Soverignty [sic] of the States." Jackson to Lanier, [ca. May 15, 1824], in Moser, Hoth, and Hoemann, *Papers of Andrew Jackson*, 5:409.

46. Ellis and Kirk, "Jefferson, Jackson and the Origins of the Presidential Mandate," 44.

47. Jackson, "Maysville Road Veto Message," 8:279–300.

48. Campbell and Jamieson, *Presidents Creating the Presidency*, 165.

49. Ibid.

50. Ellis and Kirk, "Jefferson, Jackson, and the Origins of the Presidential Mandate," 45.

51. Cheathem, *Andrew Jackson and the Rise of the Democrats*, 150.

CHAPTER 5

1. Lincoln also consulted Daniel Webster's reply to Hayne over the issue of nullification, a speech he considered "the grandest specimen of American oratory." In William H. Herndon and Jesse W. Weik, *Herndon's Life of Lincoln*, with an introduction and notes by Paul M. Angle (original publication, 1889; repr., Cleveland: World Publishing, 1949), 386.

2. Richard E. Ellis, *The Union at Risk: Jacksonian Democracy, States' Rights, and the Nullification Crisis* (New York: Oxford University Press, 1987), viii.

3. Tulis, *Rhetorical Presidency*, 51–54, 73–75.

4. Ellis, *Union at Risk*, ix.

5. Remini, *Course of American Freedom*, 389–90.

6. Matthew S. Brogdon, "Defending the Union: Andrew Jackson's Nullification Proclamation and American Federalism," *Review of Politics* 73 (2011): 1–29.

7. *Exposition and Protest*, cited in Ellis, *Union at Risk*, 46.

8. Ibid., 9–12.

9. Van Buren was behind the Tariff of 1828, strategizing that higher tariffs would bring southern states to support Jackson. Together with states such as Pennsylvania, Indiana, Ohio, and New York, the South would win Jackson the election. See Cheathem, *Andrew Jackson and the Rise of the Democrats*, 109.

10. Ibid., 172.

11. Remini, *Course of American Democracy*, 9.

12. Sean Wilentz, *The Rise of American Democracy* (New York: Norton, 2005), 302.

13. Arthur M. Schlesinger Jr., *The Age of Jackson* (Boston: Little, Brown, 1945), 45.

14. Remini, *Course of American Freedom*, 136.

15. Parton, *Life of Andrew Jackson*. 3: 284.

16. Jackson wrote three different versions of the toast, and he asked Major Lewis and Andrew Donelson, separately, to pick their favorite. Both men made the same choice. Jackson was pleased, as their preference matched his own. See Remini, *Course of American Freedom*, 234.

17. Immediately after the toast, Haynes rushed to ask Jackson if by stating "Union" he meant the "Federal Union." Jackson replied that he indeed meant the "Federal" Union. See Martin Van Buren, *The Autobiography of Martin Van Buren* ed. John C. Fitzpatrick (Washington: Government Printing Office, 1920), 2:415.

18. The phrase is taken from Matthew 27:51, which describes the earthshaking moment Jesus died and the curtain in the Temple was torn. Van Buren, *Autobiography of Martin Van Buren*, 415.

19. Remini, *Course of American Freedom*, 233–35.

20. Marquis James, *Andrew Jackson: Portrait of a President* (New York: Grosset & Dunlap, 1937), 235.

21. Ellis, *Union at Risk*, 78.

22. Ibid., 79.

23. William W. Freehling, *Prelude to Civil War: The Nullification Controversy in South Carolina, 1816–1836* (New York: Harper & Row, 1965), 138–39.

24. "Speech of Mr. Daniel Webster of Massachusetts, January 26 and 27, 1830," in *The Webster-Hayne Debate on the Nature of the Union*, ed. Herman Belz (Indianapolis: Liberty Fund, 2000), 144.

25. Edward Livingston, "Speech of Mr. Livingston of Louisiana, March 9, 1830," in Belz, *Webster-Hayne Debate*, 480.

26. Ellis, *Union at Risk*, 193.

27. Given his position as John Quincy Adams's vice president, Calhoun initially concealed his authorship of the *South Carolina Exposition and Protest*. See H. Lee Cheek, ed., *John C. Calhoun: Selected Writing and Speeches* (Washington, DC: Regency, 2003), 295.

28. Merrill D. Peterson, *The Great Triumvirate: Webster, Clay and Calhoun* (New York: Oxford University Press, 1987), 170–212.

29. Jackson, "First Inaugural Address," March 4, 1829, in Richardson, *Compilation*, 3:999–1001.

30. Jackson, "First Annual Message to Congress," December 8, 1829, in Richardson, *Compilation*, 3:1013.

31. Andrew Jackson, "Second Annual Message to Congress," December 6, 1830, in Richardson, *Compilation*, 3:1063.

32. Ibid., 1075–76.

33. Ibid., 1076.

34. Ibid.

35. Ibid., 1080.

36. Ibid., 1086.

37. Ibid., 1088.

38. Jackson, "Third Annual Message to Congress," December 6, 1831, in Richardson, *Compilation*, 3:1118–19.

39. Andrew Jackson, "Fourth Annual Message to Congress," December 4, 1832, in Richardson, *Compilation*, 3:1162.

40. Andrew Jackson to Martin Van Buren, November 18, 1832, in *The Papers of Andrew Jackson,* vol. 10, *1832,* ed. Daniel Feller, Thomas Coens, and Laura-Eve Moss (Knoxville: University of Tennessee Press, 2016), 589.

41. Jackson, "Fourth Annual Message to Congress," 3:1169.

42. Ibid.

43. Ibid.

44. Remini, *Course of American Democracy,* 17.

45. Ibid., 19.

46. Parton, *Life of Andrew Jackson,* 3:466–67.

47. Jackson, "Proclamation," December 10, 1832, in Richardson, *Compilation,* 3:1217.

48. Ibid., 3:1203–4. Andrew Jackson's and Edward Livingston's signatures are affixed to the proclamation (an insert following p. 1203).

49. Ibid., 1204.

50. David Zarefsky and Victoria J. Gallagher, "From 'Conflict' to 'Constitutional Question': Transformation in Early American Public Discourse," *Quarterly Journal of Speech* 76, no. 3 (1990): 253.

51. Ibid., 253–55.

52. Jackson, "Proclamation," 3:1206. Italics in the original.

53. Ibid., 1211.

54. Ibid., 1212.

55. Ibid., 1211.

56. Ibid., 1213.

57. Remini, *Course of American Democracy,* 22.

58. Jackson, "Proclamation," 3:1215.

59. Ibid., 1215.

60. Ellis, *Union at Risk,* 85–96.

61. Remini, *Course of American Democracy,* 24.

62. Ellis suggests that in writing the proclamation, both Jackson and Edward Livingston were encouraged by Madison's rejection of the nullifiers' stance. The key issue was the men's denial that states' rights could include secession. Ellis, *Union at Risk,* 87. Brogdon argues that Livingston's and Jackson's different views prove the latter's direct construction of the Nullification Proclamation. See Matthew S. Brogdon, "Defending the Union: Andrew Jackson's Nullification Proclamation and American Federalism," *Review of Politics,* 73 (2011): 1–29.

63. Brogdon, "Defending the Union," 15, 25.

64. Remini, *Course of American Democracy,* 25.

65. Ibid., 28.

66. Andrew Jackson to Nathaniel Macon, September 2, 1833, cited in Ellis, *Union at Risk,* 184.

67. Ibid., 193.

68. Andrew Jackson to John Coffee, April 1833, cited in Remini, *Course of American Democracy,* 42–43.

69. Ellis, *Union at Risk,* 101.

70. Ibid., 158–59.

71. Major L. Wilson, "Andrew Jackson: The Great Compromiser," *Tennessee Historical Quarterly* 26 (1967): 74.

72. Ellis, *Union at Risk*, 75.

73. Tulis, *Rhetorical Presidency*, 53.

74. Wilson, "Andrew Jackson: The Great Compromiser," 64.

75. Ibid., 66.

76. In 1852, South Carolina would issue an ordinance stating that it had the right to secede. The state would leave the Union in 1860.

77. Wilson, "Andrew Jackson: The Great Compromiser," 75.

78. Abraham Lincoln cited in Sean Wilentz, "Abraham Lincoln and Jacksonian Democracy," in *Our Lincoln: New Perspectives on Lincoln and His World*, ed. Eric Foner (New York: W. W. Norton, 2008), 73.

CHAPTER 6

1. Notes, in Feller et al., Papers of Andrew Jackson, 7:71.

2. Ibid.

3. Andrew Jackson to James Gadsden, October 12, 1829, in ibid., 7:491.

4. Meacham, *American Lion,* 93.

5. Belohlavek, *Andrew Jackson: Principle and Prejudice,* 69.

6. William Blount to Andrew Jackson, December 28, 1809, in *Papers of Andrew Jackson*, vol. 2, *1804–1813*, ed. Harold D. Moser (Knoxville: University of Tennessee Press, 1985), 226–27.

7. James Monroe, "Sixth Annual Message to Congress, December 3, 1822," in Richardson, *Compilation*, 2:759.

8. Andrew Jackson to John Williams, May 18, 1814, in *Papers of Andrew Jackson*, vol. 3, *1814–1815*, ed., David R. Hoth, Sharon MacPherson, and John H. Reinbold (Knoxville: University of Tennessee Press, 1991), 73–75.

9. Andrew Jackson to Creek and Cherokee representatives, August 5, 1814, in ibid., 3:103.

10. Andrew Jackson to Rachel Jackson, August 10, 1814, in ibid., 3:114–15.

11. Andrew Jackson, "Exposition on the Seminole Controversy," [undated but written sometime in 1831, when Jackson assembled material to defend himself against accusations that he disobeyed orders], in *Papers of Andrew Jackson*, vol. 9, *1831*, ed. Daniel Feller, et al. (Knoxville: University of Tennessee Press, 2013), 805. The entire episode can be gleaned from pp. 805–26.

12. Belohlavek, *Andrew Jackson: Principle and Prejudice*, 39.

13. Freehling, *Prelude to Civil War*, 188.

14. Ibid.

15. Ibid., 234.

16. Ibid., 233.

17. Andrew Jackson, "First Inaugural Address," March 4, 1829, in Richardson, *Compilation*, 3:1001.

18. Andrew Jackson to the Creek Indians, March 23, 1829, in Feller et al., *Papers of Andrew Jackson*, 7:112.

19. Andrew Jackson, "Draft of the First Annual Message," [c. Dec. 7, 1829], Papers of Andrew Jackson, 7:609.

20. Ibid., 610.

21. Ibid.

22. Ibid. The draft ends here abruptly. John Eaton resumed it later.

23. "Draft by John Henry Eaton on Indian removal," [undated], in Feller et al., *Papers of Andrew Jackson*, 7:623.

24. Ibid., 624–25.

25. A dispute between the Creeks and the Cherokees further complicated the specific case of the Indian tribes of Georgia, where the state claimed possession of the tribes' land. See the following letter from the Georgia governor: George Rockingham Gilmer to Andrew Jackson, December 29, 1829, in ibid., 650–53.

26. Ibid., 1020–21.

27. Ibid., 1021.

28. Ibid.

29. Ibid., 1021–22.

30. Ibid., 1022. John Quincy Adams made a similar statement: "What is the right of huntsman to the forest of a thousand miles over which he has accidentally ranged in quest of prey." Cited in Stanley Lebergott, *The Americans: An Economic Record* (New York: Norton, 1984), 18.

31. Lebergott, *Americans: An Economic Record*, 19.

32. Andrew Jackson, "First Annual Message to Congress," December 8, 1829, in Richardson, *Compilation*, 3:1022.

33. Cheathem, *Andrew Jackson and the Rise of Democrats*, 162.

34. Andrew Jackson to the Chickasaw Indians, August 23, 1830, in Feller, Coens, and Moss, *Papers of Andrew Jackson*, 8:495–98. The amended draft with brackets became the official document. See note on p. 495.

35. Andrew Jackson to Maj. William B. Lewis, August 25, 1830, in ibid., 8:500–501. William Wirt was US attorney general from 1817 to 1829, and he was a counsel for the case the Cherokees brought against the United States.

36. Ibid., 501.

37. Ibid.

38. Ibid.

39. Andrew Jackson to Maj. William B. Lewis, August 31, 1830, in ibid., 8:516.

40. Brig. Gen. John Coffee to Andrew Jackson, September 29, 1830, in ibid., 8:531.

41. "Jackson's Outline of the Second Annual Message," [dated December 6, 1830, but likely drafted earlier], in ibid., 8:651.

42. Andrew Jackson, "Second Annual Message to Congress," December 6, 1830, in Richardson, *Compilation*, 3:1063–92.

43. Ibid., 1082–83.

44. Ibid., 1083.

45. Ibid.

46. Ibid.

47. Ibid.

48. Ibid., 1083–84.

49. Ibid., 1084.

50. Ibid.

51. Ibid., 1085–86.

52. Andrew Jackson to Brig. Gen. John Coffee, September 7, 1831, in Feller et al., *Papers of Andrew Jackson*, 9:561.

53. Andrew Jackson to the United States Senate (not sent), January 16, 1832, in Feller, Coens, and Moss, *Papers of Andrew Jackson*, 10:29.

54. Belohlavek, *Andrew Jackson: Principle and Prejudice*, 69–72.

55. Ibid.

56. Andrew Jackson to John Coffee, April 7, 1832, in Feller, Coens, and Moss, *Papers of Andrew Jackson*, 10:225.

57. Ibid., 226.

58. Andrew Jackson to John Coffee, November 6, 1832, in Feller, Coens, and Moss, *Papers of Andrew Jackson*, 10:554.

59. Jackson, "Fourth Annual Message to Congress," December 4, 1832, in Richardson, *Compilation*, 3:1167.

60. Andrew Jackson to Robert J. Chester, March 3, 1833, in Bassett, *Correspondence of Andrew Jackson*, 5:27.

61. Andrew Jackson, "Fifth Annual Message to Congress," December 3, 1833, in Richardson, *Compilation*, 3:1251–52.

62. Remini, *Course of American Democracy*, 121.

63. Andrew Jackson to B. F. Currey and H. Montgomery, September 3, 1834, in Bassett, *Correspondence of Andrew Jackson*, 5:288. Currey and Montgomery were the government emigration and enrolling agents for Cherokees. The Cherokees opted to move out of Georgia.

64. John Ross to Andrew Jackson, September 15, 1834, in ibid., 5:292.

65. John Ross and Others to Andrew Jackson, January 23, 1835, in ibid., 5:319–20. Capitalization in the original.

66. Andrew Jackson, "Sixth Annual Message to Congress," December 1, 1834, in Richardson, *Compilation*, 3:1332.

Query for endnote 66: Provide a date with source?

67. William A. Underwood to Andrew Jackson, May 25, 1835, in Bassett, *Correspondence of Andrew Jackson*, 5:352–53. Inconsistent capitalization in the original.

68. Gov. Wilson Lumpkin to Jackson, May 20, 1835, in ibid., 5:349–50.

69. Jackson, "Eighth Annual Message to Congress," December 5, 1836, in Richardson, *Compilation*, 4:1472–73.

70. Andrew Jackson to Joel R. Poinsett, August 27, 1837, Andrew Jackson Papers, 1775–1874, Series 6, Additional Correspondence, 1779–1855, Library of Congress, accessed June 13, 2017, www.loc.gov.

71. Jason Edwards Black, "Authoritarian Fatherhood: Andrew Jackson's Early Familiar Lectures to American's 'Red Children,'" *Journal of Family History* 30, no. 3 (2005): 247.

72. Ibid., 249.

73. Andrew Jackson to the Creek Chiefs, September 4, 1815, in Hoth, MacPherson, and Reinbold, *Papers of Andrew Jackson*, 3:382–83.

74. Cited in Black, "Authoritarian Fatherhood," 248.

75. Ibid., 257.

CHAPTER 7

1. Cited in Cheathem, *Andrew Jackson and the Rise of the Democrats*, 184.

2. "Jackson's Memorandum on Biddle's Letter," [ca. September 29, 1829], in Feller et al., *Papers of Andrew Jackson*, 7:459.

3. Amos Kendall to Andrew Jackson, November 20, 1829, in Feller et al., *Papers of Andrew Jackson*, 7:561.

4. Ibid., 7:561, 563.

5. Ibid., 7:562–63. Italics in the original.

6. "Draft by John Henry Eaton on the Bank of the United States," [ca. November 30, 1829], in Feller et al., *Papers of Andrew Jackson*, 7:587.

7. Ibid., 7:590–91.

8. "Draft by James Alexander Hamilton on the Bank of the United States," [ca. December 7, 1829]," in Feller et al., *Papers of Andrew Jackson*, 7:628. Col. James Alexander Hamilton was the son of Alexander Hamilton. He would serve as Jackson's aide and also as acting secretary of state for the first few days of the incoming administration.

9. Jackson, "First Annual Message to Congress," December 8, 1829, in Richardson, *Compilation*, 3:1025.

10. Ibid., 3:1025.

11. "From James Alexander Hamilton," January 4, 1830, in Feller, Coens, and Moss, *Papers of Andrew Jackson*, 8:14.

12. Ibid., 8:14.

13. Ibid., 8:14–15. Italics in the original. A note in Jackson's paper indicates that he copied Hamilton's outline in his memorandum book and used it when drafting his Second Annual Message. Ibid., 8:12.

14. Andrew Jackson, "Memorandum Book on the Bank of the United States, Message for 1830," in Feller, Coens, and Moss, *Papers of Andrew Jackson*, 8:602–5.

15. Ibid., 8:605. Inconsistent capitalization in the original.

16. Ibid.

17. Andrew Jackson, "Second Annual Message to Congress," December 6, 1830, in Richardson, *Compilation*, 3:1091.

18. Ibid., 3:1091–92.

19. Ibid., 3:1092.

20. Andrew Jackson, "Third Annual Message to Congress," December 6, 1831, in Richardson, *Compilation*, 3:1121.

21. "Draft by Amos Kendall," [ca. December 6, 1831], in Feller et al., *Papers of Andrew Jackson*, 9:750.

22. Andrew Jackson to Martin Van Buren, December 6, 1831, in Feller et al., *Papers of Andrew Jackson*, 9:731.

23. Ellis and Kirk, "Jefferson, Jackson, and the Origins of the Presidential Mandate," 47–48.

24. Worden Pope to Andrew Jackson, June 19, 1831, in Feller et al., *Papers of Andrew Jackson*, 9:316–19.

25. Andrew Jackson to James Alexander Hamilton, December 12, 1831, in Feller et al., *Papers of Andrew Jackson*, 9:768–69.

26. Andrew Jackson to John Randolph, December 22, 1831, in in Feller et al., *Papers of Andrew Jackson*, 9:782.

27. Ibid., 782.

28. Andrew Jackson to Martin Van Buren, December 17, 1831, in Feller et al., *Papers of Andrew Jackson*, 9:772.

29. James Alexander Hamilton to Andrew Jackson, January 12, 1832, in Feller, Coens, and Moss, *Papers of Andrew Jackson* 10:22.

30. Ibid.

31. James Alexander Hamilton, to Andrew Jackson, May 7, 1832, in Feller, Coens, and Moss, *Papers of Andrew Jackson* 10:266.

32. Ibid., 267.

33. Cheathem, *Andrew Jackson and the Rise of the Democrats*, 201.

34. Remini, *Course of American Freedom*, 361.

35. "Bank of the United States Veto Message," in Feller, Coens, and Moss, *Papers of Andrew Jackson*, 10:364–411.

36. Ibid., 10:367.

37. Ibid., 10:372.

38. Ibid.

39. Ibid., 3:372.

40. Ibid., 3:373.

41. Andrew Jackson, "Veto Message," July 10, 1832, in Richardson, *Compilation*, 3:1139–54.

42. Remini, *Course of American Freedom*, 369.

43. Jackson, "Veto Message," in Richardson, *Compilation*, 3:1139.

44. Ibid., 3:1139–40.

45. Ibid., 3:1141–42.

46. Ibid., 3:1143–44.

47. Ibid., 3:1144–45.

48. Ibid., 3:1145.

49. Ibid., 3:1146–47. Italics in the original.

50. Ibid.

51. Ibid., 3:1147.

52. Ibid., 3:1147–48.

53. Ibid., 3:1148–49.

54. Ibid., 3:1151–52.

55. Ibid., 3:1152.

56. After the bank veto, Clay was sure of his success in the next election that he wrote to a colleague, "The campaign is over, and I think we have won the Victory" (capitalization in the original). Henry Clay to Samuel C. Southard, July 21, 1832, in Seager, *Papers of Henry Clay*, 8:555.

57. Jackson, "Veto Message," 3:1152.

58. Ibid., 3:1153.

59. Ibid., 3:1153–54.

60. Ibid., 3:1154.

61. Ellis and Kirk, "Jefferson, Jackson and the Origins of the Presidential Mandate," 48–49.

62. John Randolph to Andrew Jackson, July 15, 1832, in Feller, Coens, and Moss, *Papers of Andrew Jackson*, 10:419.

63. Andrew Jackson to Amos Kendall, July 23, 1832, *in* Feller, Coens, and Moss, *Papers of Andrew Jackson*, 10:439.

64. "Views of Martin Van Buren on the Removal of the Deposits," March 1833 [no specific day indicated], in Bassett, *Correspondence of Andrew Jackson*, 5:25.

65. Andrew Jackson, "Fourth Annual Message to Congress," December 4, 1832, in Richardson, *Compilation*, 3:1163.

66. Andrew Jackson to Cabinet members, March 19, 1833, Andrew Jackson Papers, Series 1, General Correspondence and Related Items, 1775–1885, Library of Congress, accessed May 21, 2017, www.loc.gov.

67. Roger Taney to Andrew Jackson, March 1833 [no specific day indicated], in Bassett, *Correspondence of Andrew Jackson*, 5:34–39.

68. Amos Kendall to Andrew Jackson, March 20, 1833, in Bassett, *Correspondence*, 5:41–43.

69. Ibid., 5:44.

70. Andrew Jackson to Hugh L. White, March 24, 1833, in Bassett, *Correspondence*, 5:46.

71. Andrew Jackson to [addressee not indicated], March 24, 1833, in Bassett, *Correspondence*, 5:47.

72. Ibid., 5:48.

73. Andrew Jackson to Rev. Hardy M. Cryer, April 7, 1833, in Bassett, *Correspondence*, 5::53.

74. Marvin Meyers, "The Jacksonian Persuasion," *American Quarterly*, 5 (Spring 1953): 12-15.

75. Bray Hammond, "The Assault on the Federal Bank," in Sellers, *Andrew Jackson: A Profile*, 149–52.

76. Belohlavek, *Andrew Jackson: Principle and Prejudice*, 78.

CHAPTER 8

1. Heale, *Presidential Quest*, 83, 87–89.

2. Ibid., 90.

3. Campbell and Jamieson, *Presidents Creating the Presidency*, 187.

4. Remini, *Course of American Freedom*, 391.

5. Zarefsky, "Presidential Rhetoric," 614.

6. Schlesinger, "Impressive Mandate," 136–37.

7. Zarefsky, "Presidential Rhetoric," 614.

8. Andrew Jackson, "Draft of the Second Inaugural Address," March 1, 1833, Andrew Jackson Papers, Series 1, General Correspondence and Related Items, 1775–1885, Library of Congress, accessed June 4, 2017, www.loc.gov. A note preceding the draft indicates that the rough draft is in Jackson's handwriting. All references to this address are from this source.

9. Andrew Jackson, "Second Inaugural Address," March 4, 1833, in Richardson, *Compilation*, 3:1222.

10. Ibid.

11. Ibid.

12. Ibid.

13. Ibid., 3:1223.

14. Ibid.

15. Ibid.

16. Ibid.

17. Ibid., 3:1224.

18. Ibid.

19. Remini, *Course of American Democracy*, 47.

CHAPTER 9

1. Andrew Jackson, "Notes on Treasury Opinion," May 1833 [no specific day indicated], in Bassett, *Correspondence of Andrew Jackson*, 5:102. Italics in the original.

2. Andrew Jackson to William J. Duane, June 26, 1833, in Bassett, *Correspondence of Andrew Jackson*, 5:113–28.

3. Ibid., 5:113.

4. Ibid., 5:114–19.

5. Andrew Jackson to William J. Duane, July 17, 1833, in Bassett, *Correspondence of Andrew Jackson*, 5:137.

6. Andrew Jackson to James K. Polk, August 31, 1833, in Bassett, *Correspondence of Andrew Jackson*, 5:173.

7. Andrew Jackson to Martin Van Buren, September 8, 1833, in Bassett, *Correspondence of Andrew Jackson*, 5:182.

8. Van Buren to Jackson, September 14, 1833, in Bassett, *Correspondence of Andrew Jackson*, 5:185.

9. Andrew Jackson to Roger Taney, September 15, 1833, in Bassett, *Correspondence of Andrew Jackson*, 5:188.

10. Andrew Jackson, "Removal of the Public Deposits," September 18, 1833, in Richardson, *Compilation*, 3:1224.

11. Ibid.

12. Ibid., 3:1225.

13. Ibid.

14. Ibid., 3:1225–26.

15. Ibid., 3:1226.

16. Ibid., 3:1228.

17. Ibid., 3:1229.

18. Ibid.

19. Ibid., 3:1231

20. Ibid., 3:1235.

21. Andrew Jackson, "Draft of the Paper read to the Cabinet," in Bassett, *Correspondence of Andrew Jackson*, 5:193.

22. It is important to note that in two places, the draft is missing pages.

23. Jackson, "Draft of the Paper read to the Cabinet," 5:201.

24. Andrew Jackson informing the vice president of what he had been told, in Jackson to Van Buren, September 19, 1833, in Bassett, *Correspondence of Andrew Jackson*, 5:203.

25. Van Buren to Jackson, September 26, 1833, in Bassett, *Correspondence of Andrew Jackson*, 5:211.

26. Andrew Jackson, "Fifth Annual Message to Congress," December 3, 1833, in Richardson, *Compilation*, 3:1249. Jackson had learned his lesson the previous year, when his Annual Message was published earlier than its formal delivery day, and the opposition press found time to counter him. This time, Jackson instructed Blair to show his remarks to no one until their delivery. See Remini, *Course of American Democracy*, 119.

27. Jackson, "Fifth Annual Message," 3:1250.

28. Ibid.

29. Polk to Jackson, December 23, 1833, in Bassett, *Correspondence of Andrew Jackson*, 5:235.

30. Jackson's reply to Polk in Jackson's handwriting on the back of Polk's letter, December 23, 1833, in Bassett, *Correspondence of Andrew Jackson*, 5:236.

31. Henry Clay cited in Cheathem, *Andrew Jackson and the Rise of the Democrats*, 207.

32. Ibid., 207–8.

33. Andrew Jackson, "Jackson's notes on Clay's condemnatory Resolution," December 26, 1833, in Bassett, *Correspondence of Andrew Jackson*, 5:236.

34. Andrew Jackson to Amos Kendall, April 1836 [no specific day indicated], in Bassett, *Correspondence of Andrew Jackson*, 5:257.

35. Jackson would lose his fourth secretary of the Treasury, but he would appoint Taney chief justice of the Supreme Court in 1836. Taney would hold this position until his death in 1864, and he would be later known primarily for his infamous Dred Scott ruling.

36. Cheathem, *Andrew Jackson and the Rise of the Democrats*, 209.

37. Andrew Jackson, "Sixth Annual Message to Congress," December 1, 1834, in Richardson, *Compilation*, 3:1330.

38. Andrew Jackson, "Seventh Annual Message to Congress," December 7, 1835, in Richardson, *Compilation*, 4:1384–85.

39. Ibid., 3:1385–86.

40. Andrew Jackson, "Eighth Annual Message to Congress," December 5, 1836, in Richardson, *Compilation*, 4:1469.

41. Ibid., 4:1470.

42. Ibid., 4:1471.

43. Ibid., 4:1471–72.

44. Schlesinger, "Impressive Mandate," 139–40.

45. Andrew Jackson to Thomas H. Benton, January 17, 1837, in Bassett, *Correspondence of Andrew Jackson*, 5:450.

CHAPTER 10

1. Harold Holzer, "Visualizing Lincoln: Abraham Lincoln as Student, Subject, and Patron of the Visual Arts," in Foner, *Our Lincoln*, 102.

2. Franklin D. Roosevelt, "Address at the Jackson Day Dinner," January 8, 1936, in *The Public Papers and Addresses of Franklin D. Roosevelt*, ed. Samuel I. Rosenman (New York: Random House, 1938), 5:38–44, 39.

3. David McCullough, *Truman* (New York: Simon & Schuster Paperbacks, 1992), 606.

4. Cara A. Finnegan, "Recognizing Lincoln: Image Vernaculars in Nineteenth-Century Visual Culture," *Rhetoric and Public Affairs* 8, no. 1 (2005): 31–57.

5. Ibid., 41, 47.

6. James G. Barber, *Andrew Jackson: A Portrait Study* (Seattle: University of Washington Press, 1991), 6.

7. Ibid.

8. Cited in ibid., 26.

9. Ibid., 28–33.

10. Charles Henry Hart, "Life Portraits of Andrew Jackson," *McClure's Magazine* 9 (July 1897): 797.

11. Ward, *Andrew Jackson: Symbol for an Age*, 182–85.

12. Barber, *Andrew Jackson: A Portrait Study*, 53.

13. Ward, *Andrew Jackson: Symbol for an Age*, 57–58.

14. Sully would also be known for his portraits of Queen Victoria, which he completed a few years later. Jackson thus attracted some of the most prominent portraitists of the period, both in Europe and the United States. Thomas Sully, Portrait of Queen Victoria, www.royalcollection.org.uk. Accessed January 31, 2018.

15. *Nashville Gazette*, June 19, 1819, cited in Barber, *Andrew Jackson: A Portrait Study*, 57.

16. *National Advocate*, February 24, 1819, cited in ibid., 59.

17. Ibid., 42.

18. Ibid., 66.

19. *National Intelligencer*, February 13, 1828, cited in ibid., 67.

20. Ibid., 69.

21. Ibid., 75.

22. Ibid., 78.

23. Ibid., 80.

24. Ibid., 81–82.

25. *Cincinnati Advertiser*, May 4, 1825, cited in ibid., 87.

26. Ibid.

27. *Republican and Gazette* (Nashville), cited in ibid., 91.

28. *Whig and Banner* (Nashville), cited in ibid., 91.

29. Ward, *Andrew Jackson: Symbol for an Age*, 42–45.

30. Barber, *Andrew Jackson: A Portrait Study.*, 95–96.

31. *United States Telegraph*, (Washington, DC), May 25, 1829, cited in ibid., 96.

32. Ibid., 142–143.

33. Ibid., 152.

34. Kenneth Cohen, "'Sport for Grown Children': American Political Cartoons, 1790–1850," *International Journal of the History of Sport* 28, nos. 8–9 (May–June 2011): 1301.

35. Ibid., 1303.

36. John Sullivan, "Jackson Caricatured: Two Historical Errors," *Tennessee Historical Quarterly* 31, no. 1 (Spring 1972): 44.

37. Cohen, "'Sport for Grown Children,'" 1302–3.

38. Barber dates the cartoon to 1827 and suggests that it was issued following Clay's article refuting Jackson's charge as published by Carter Beverley. See Barber, *Andrew Jackson: A Portrait Study*, 161. Remini's volume on Henry Clay dates the cartoon to 1828.

See Robert V. Remini, *Henry Clay: Statesman for the Union* (New York: W. W. Norton, 1993), 320–21. Elsewhere, this cartoon has erroneously been attributed to the Bank War and dated 1834.

39. Sullivan, "Jackson Caricatured," 42. Sullivan provides a definitive assessment that this cartoon was issued in 1827 and may have been reissued in 1834.

40. Cheathem, *Andrew Jackson and the Rise of the Democrats*, 89.

41. William C. Cook, "The Coffin Handbills—America's First Smear Campaign," *Imprint* 27, no. 1 (Spring 2002): 23.

42. Ibid.

43. Ibid., 27–30

44. Sullivan, "Jackson Caricatured," 44.

45. Cook, "Coffin Handbills," 31.

46. Barber, *Andrew Jackson: A Portrait Study,* 157–58.

47. Ibid., 160–61.

48. Brandon Inabinet, "Democratic Circulation: Jacksonian Lithographs in U.S. Public Discourse," *Rhetoric and Public Affairs* 15 (2012): 663.

49. Barber, *Andrew Jackson: A Portrait Study*, 160–61.

50. Ibid., 153.

51. Ibid., 154.

52. Ibid., 156.

53. Remini, *Course of American Freedom*, 256–57.

54. Seeking to introduce "culture" to the Black Hawk, Jackson hosted Black Hawk, the tribal chief, during the tour, even taking him to a theatre show in Philadelphia. See Fletcher M. Green, "On Tour with President Andrew Jackson," *New England Quarterly* 36 (1963): 214.

55. Barber, *Andrew Jackson: A Portrait Study,* 164–65.

56. Ibid., 171–73.

57. Thomas Nast is credited with assigning the jackass as a symbol for the Democratic Party after the Civil War. However, John William Ward states that the image belongs more appropriately to Jackson's days, gradually evolving to the point that cartoonists began to employ it. See Ward, *Andrew Jackson: Symbol of an Age*, 88.

58. Inabinet, "Democratic Circulation," 659–60.

59. Ibid., 659.

60. John Sullivan, "The Case of 'A Late Student': Pictorial Satire in Jacksonian America," *American Antiquarian Society* 83, no. 2 (January 1, 1974): 285–86.

61. Ibid., 286.

62. Barber, *Andrew Jackson: A Portrait Study,* 208–9. In 1845, Sully would romanticize Jackson in a full-size portrait that returned to the 1815 battle scene. Jackson appears in uniform but lacks any distinct military insignia, and he is standing behind a cannon with a flume that indicates its firing position. Jackson's head is identical to the one Sully painted in 1824, and to the one that appears on the twenty-dollar note.

63. Jackson's image on the 1928 twenty-dollar bill replaced Grover Cleveland's. An earlier image of Jackson was issued in 1869 for the five-dollar bill, the first to use Sully's portrait.

64. Sullivan, "The Case of 'A Late Student,'" 285.

65. Inabinet, "Democratic Circulation," 659.

66. Sullivan, "Case of 'A Late Student,'" 285.

67. Ward, *Andrew Jackson: Symbol for an Age*, 192.

CHAPTER 11

1. Andrew Jackson to Roger Brooke Taney, October 13, 1836, Andrew Jackson Papers, Series 1, General Correspondence and Related Items, 1775–1885, Library of Congress, accessed May 19, 2017, www.loc.gov.

2. Ibid.

3. As practiced by Jefferson and Monroe. See Campbell and Jamieson, *Presidents Creating the Presidency*, 309.

4. Jackson to Taney, October 13, 1836.

5. Ibid.

6. Ibid.

7. Ibid.

8. Roger Brooke Taney to Andrew Jackson, October 15, 1836, Andrew Jackson Papers, Series 1, General Correspondence and Related Items, 1775–1885, Library of Congress, accessed May 19, 2017, www.loc.gov.

9. Roger Brooke Taney to Andrew Jackson, October 27, 1836, Andrew Jackson Papers, Series 1, General Correspondence and Related Items, 1775–1885, Library of Congress, accessed May 19, 2017, www.loc.gov.

10. Campbell and Jamieson, *Presidents Creating the Presidency*, 307–10.

11. Andrew Jackson, "Draft: Paper Read to the Cabinet," September 18, 1833, in Bassett, *Correspondence of Andrew Jackson*, 5:199. This passage, however, was not included in the final and formal statement of "Removal of the Public Deposits," in Richardson, *Compilation*, 3:1224–38.

12. Belohlavek, *Andrew Jackson: Principle and Prejudice*, 15.

13. Ibid., 56.

14. As major general and commander of the Division of the South, Jackson delivered a farewell address to the army upon his departure on May 31, 1821. See Andrew Jackson, "Farewell Address to the Army," *Niles' Weekly Register* (Baltimore), September New Series, no. 4, vol. 9, September 22, 1821, (accessed March 3, 2014), http://www.rarenewspapers.com

15. Remini, *Course of American Freedom*, 414.

16. Andrew Jackson, "Farewell Address," March 4, 1837, in Richardson, *Compilation*, 4:1512.

17. Ibid.

18. Ibid.

19. Ward, *Andrew Jackson: Symbol for an Age*, 41

20. Jackson, "Farewell Address," March 4, 1837, 4:1513.

21. Ibid.

22. Ibid.

23. Ibid., 4:1514.

24. Ibid.

25. Ibid.

26. Ibid., 4:1514–15.

27. Ibid., 4:1515.

28. Ibid.

29. Ibid., 4:1516–17.

30. Ibid., 4:1517.

31. Ibid., 4:1517–18.

32. Ibid., 4:1518.

33. Ibid., 4:1518–19.

34. Ibid., 4:1519.

35. Ibid., 4:1520.

36. Ibid., 4:1521.

37. Ibid.

38. Ibid.

39. Ibid., 4:1522.

40. Ibid., 4:1523.

41. Ibid.

42. Ibid., 4:1523–24.

43. Ibid., 4:1524.

44. Ibid., 4:1525.

45. Ibid., 4:1525–26.

46. Ibid., 4:1526.

47. Campbell and Jamieson, *Presidents Creating the Presidency*, 321–22.

48. Jackson, "Farewell Address," March 4, 1837, 4:1526–27.

49. Ibid., 1527.

50. Campbell and Jamieson, *Presidents Creating the Presidency*, 321.

51. Ibid.

52. Anson D. Morse, "The Political Influence of Andrew Jackson," *Political Science Quarterly* 1 (1886): 158.

53. Ibid., 162.

CHAPTER 12

1. Ward, *Andrew Jackson: Symbol for an Age*, 213.

2. Sellers, introduction to *Andrew Jackson: A Profile*, xiv.

3. Ibid., xvi.

4. Belohlavek, *Andrew Jackson: Principle and Prejudice*, 49.

5. Heale, *Presidential Quest*, 91.

6. Gerard Hauser, *Vernacular Voices: The Rhetoric of Publics and Public Spheres* (Columbia: University of South Carolina Press, 1999), 264.

7. Ellis and Kirk, "Jefferson, Jackson, and the Origins of the Presidential Mandate," 46.

8. *Alexis De Tocqueville: Democracy in America* (1835; repr., New York: Mentor, 1965), 10.

9. Meacham, *American Lion*, 87.

10. Andrew Jackson to the United States Congress (not sent), [ca. June 1832], in Feller, Coens, and Moss, *Papers of Andrew Jackson*, 10:354–57.

11. Belohlavek, *Andrew Jackson: Principle and Prejudice*, 52.

12. See Robert K. Murray and Tim H. Blessing, "The Presidential Performance Study: A Progress Report," *Journal of American History* 70 (1983): 535–55.

13. Jeffrey Scott Mio, Ronald E. Riggio, Shana Levin, and Redford Reese, "Presidential Leadership and Charisma: The Effects of Metaphor," *Leadership Quarterly* 16 (2005): 287–94.

14. Walter Fisher, "Romantic Democracy, Ronald Reagan, and Presidential Heroes," *Western Journal of Communication* 46 (1982): 299–301.

15. Perry M. Goldman, "Political Rhetoric in the Age of Jackson," *Tennessee Historical Quarterly* 29 (1970): 361–69.

16. Ibid., 369–70.

17. Jackson, "Seventh Annual Message," December 7, 1835, in Richardson, *Compilation*, 4:1383.

18. Ibid., 1384.

19. Remini, *Course of American Democracy*, 508. Jackson's nephew and longtime aide, Andrew Jackson Donelson, became the American diplomat in Texas after Jackson left the White House. Donelson implemented Jackson's long-standing desire to acquire Texas.

20. Remini, *Course of American Democracy*, 62–75.

21. Ibid., 63.

22. Green, "On Tour with President Andrew Jackson," 212.

23. *National Intelligencer*, July 2, 1833, cited in Remini, *Course of American Democracy*, 80.

24. Andrew Jackson to Andrew Jackson Jr., June 10, 1833, in Bassett, *Correspondence of Andrew Jackson*, 5:109.

25. Cheathem, *Andrew Jackson and the Rise of the Democrats*, 212.

26. Gerald J. Baldasty, "The Press and Politics in the Age of Jackson," *Journalism Monographs* 89 (1984): 2–3.

27. Baldasty, "Press and Politics in the Age of Jackson," 3–7, 19.

28. Meacham, *American Lion,* 218–19.

29. Ibid., 219.

30. Jennifer R. Mercieca, "The Culture of Honor; How Slaveholders Responded to the Abolitionist Mail Crisis of 1835," *Rhetoric and Public Affairs* 10 (2007): 66–67.

31. Henry Clay to Samuel Southard, July 21, 1832, in Seager, *Papers of Henry Clay*, 8:555.

32. John C. Calhoun, "Speech of Mr. Calhoun," January 13, 1834, in *The Works of John C. Calhoun*, vol. 2, ed. Richard K. Cralle (New York: D. Appleton, 1881), 320.

33. Andrew Jackson to John D. Coffee, April 6, 1834, in Bassett, *Correspondence of Andrew Jackson*, 5:260.

34. Andrew Jackson, "Protest," April 15, 1834, in Richardson, *Compilation*, 3:1289.

35. Ibid., 1309.

36. Remini, *Course of American Democracy*, 154.

37. Meacham, *American Lion*, 288.

38. Jackson, "Protest," 3:1289.

39. Ibid., 1291.

40. Ibid.

41. Ibid., 1298.

42. Ibid., 1299.

43. Ibid., 1309.

44. Ibid., 1310–11.

45. Ibid., 1312.

46. Thomas Benton, "Expunging Resolution," January 12, 1837, in *Abridgment of the Debates of Congress, from 1789 to 1856*, vol. 13 (New York: D. Appleton, 1860), 105–6.

47. Campbell and Jamieson, *Presidents Creating the Presidency*, 190.

48. Jennifer, Mercieca" The Irony of the Democratic Style," *Rhetoric and Public Affairs* 11, no. 3 (2008): 441–49.

49. Remini, *Course of American Democracy*, 413.

BIBLIOGRAPHY

Allen, Danielle. *Our Declaration: A Reading of the Declaration of Independence in Defense of Equality.* New York: Liveright, 2014.

Baldasty, Gerald J. "The Press and Politics in the Age of Jackson." *Journalism Monographs* 89 (1984): 1–29.

Barber, James G. *Andrew Jackson: A Portrait Study.* Seattle: University of Washington Press, 1991.

Bassett, John C., ed. *Correspondence of Andrew Jackson.* Vol. 5, *1833–1838.* Washington, DC: Carnegie Institution, 1931.

———. *Correspondence of Andrew Jackson.* Vol. 3, *1822–1828.* Washington, DC: Carnegie Institution of Washington, 1928.

Belohlavek, John M. *Andrew Jackson: Principle and Prejudice.* New York: Routledge, 2016.

Belz, Herman, ed. *The Webster-Hayne Debate on the Nature of the Union.* Indianapolis: Liberty Fund, 2000.

Benton, Thomas. "Expunging Resolution." January 12, 1837. *Abridgment of the Debates of Congress, from 1789 to 1856.* Vol. 13: 99-105. New York: D. Appleton, 1860.

Black, Jason Edwards. "Authoritarian Fatherhood: Andrew Jackson's Early Familiar Lectures to America's 'Red Children.'" *Journal of Family History* 30, no. 3 (2005): 247–64.

Brogdon, Matthew S. "Defending the Union: Andrew Jackson's Nullification Proclamation and American Federalism." *Review of Politics* 73 (2011): 1–29.

Calhoun, John C. *The Works of John C. Calhoun,* Vol. 2. Ed. Richard K. Cralle. New York: D. Appleton, 1881.

Calhoun, John C. *John C. Calhoun: Selected Writings and Speeches.* Ed. Lee H. Cheek. Washington, DC: Regency, 2003.

Campbell, Karlyn K., and Kathleen H. Jamieson. *Presidents Creating the Presidency: Deeds Done in Words.* Chicago: University of Chicago Press, 2008.

Carpenter, Ronald H. "America's Tragic Metaphor: Our Twentieth-Century Combatants as Frontiersmen." *Quarterly Journal of Speech* 76 (1990): 1–22.

Cheathem, Mark R. *Andrew Jackson and the Rise of the Democrats.* Santa Barbara: ABC-CLIO, 2015.

Cohen, Kenneth. "'Sport for Grown Children': American Political Cartoons, 1790–1850." *International Journal of the History of Sport* 28, nos. 8–9 (May–June 2011): 1301–18.

Cook, William C. "The Coffin Handbills—America's First Smear Campaign." *Imprint* 27, no. 1 (Spring 2002): 23–37.

De Tocqueville, Alexis. *Democracy in America*. Ed. Richard D. Heffner. New York: Mentor, 1965.

Depuy, Henry F. Ed. *Some Letters of Andrew Jackson*. Worcester: American Antiquarian Society, printed by Davis Press, 1922.

Ellis, Richard E. *The Union at Risk: Jacksonian Democracy, States' Rights, and the Nullification Crisis*. New York: Oxford University Press, 1987.

Ellis, Richard J. *Speaking to the People: The Rhetorical Presidency in Historical Perspective*. Amherst: University of Massachusetts Press, 1998.

Feller, Daniel, Harold D. Moser, Laura-Eve Moss, and Thomas Coen, eds. *The Papers of Andrew Jackson*. Vol. 7, *1829*. Knoxville: University of Tennessee Press, 2007.

Feller, Daniel, Thomas Coens, and Laura-Eve Moss, eds. *The Papers of Andrew Jackson*. Vol. 10, *1832*. Knoxville: University of Tennessee Press, 2016.

——, eds. *The Papers of Andrew Jackson*. Vol. 8, *1830*. Knoxville: University of Tennessee Press, 2010.

Feller, Daniel, Thomas Coens, Laura-Eve Moss, and Erik Alexander, eds. *The Papers of Andrew Jackson*. Vol. 9, *1831*. Knoxville: University of Tennessee Press, 2013.

Finnegan, Cara A. "Recognizing Lincoln: Image Vernaculars in Nineteenth Century Visual Culture." *Rhetoric and Public Affairs* 8, no. 1 (2005): 31–57.

Fisher, Walter. "Romantic Democracy, Ronald Reagan, and Presidential Heroes." *Western Journal of Communication* 46 (1982): 299–310.

Foner, Eric, ed. *Our Lincoln: New Perspectives on Lincoln and his World*. New York: W. W. Norton, 2008.

Freehling, William W. *Prelude to Civil War: The Nullification Controversy in South Carolina 1816–1836*. New York: Harper & Row, 1965.

Goldman, Perry M. "Political Rhetoric in the Age of Jackson." *Tennessee Historical Quarterly* 29 (1970): 360–72.

Green, Fletcher M. "On Tour with President Andrew Jackson." *New England Quarterly* 36 (1963): 209–29.

Hart, Charles H. "Life Portrait of Andrew Jackson." *McClure Magazine* 9 (July 1897): 795–804.

Hauser, Gerard. *Vernacular Voices: The Rhetoric of Publics and Public Spheres*. Columbia: University of South Carolina Press, 1999.

Hay, Robert P. "John Fitzgerald: Presidential Image Maker for Andrew Jackson in 1823." *Tennessee Historical Quarterly* 42 (1983): 138–50.

Heale, M. J. *The Presidential Quest: Candidates and Images in American Political Culture, 1787–1852*. London: Longman, 1982.

Herndon, William H., and Jesse W. Weik. Herndon's Life of Lincoln. Original publication, 1889. Reprinted with an introduction and notes by Paul. M. Angle. Cleveland: World Publishing, 1949.

Hoth, David. R., Sharon MacPherson, and John H. Reinbold, eds. *The Papers of Andrew Jackson*. Vol. 3, *1814–1815*. Knoxville: University of Tennessee Press, 1991.

Inabinet, Brandon. "Democratic Circulation: Jacksonian Lithographs in U.S. Public Discourse." *Rhetoric and Public Affairs* 15 (2012): 659–66.

Jackson, Andrew. "Farewell Address to the Army," May 31, 1821. Recorded in *Niles' Weekly Register* (Baltimore), September New Series, no. 4, vol. 9, September 22, 1821. www .rarenewspapers.com.

———. Papers. Series 1, General Correspondence and Related Items, 1775–1885. Library of Congress.

———. Papers, 1775–1874. Series 6, Additional Correspondence, 1779–1855. Library of Congress.

James, Marquis. *Andrew Jackson: Portrait of a President*. New York: Grosset & Dunlap, 1937.

Jasinski, James. "Liberty and Power in Nineteenth Century Public Argument: A Foucaultian Analysis." *Proceedings of the Fifth SCA/AFA Conference on Argumentation*. Ed. Joseph W. Wenzel. *Annandale VA: Speech Communication Association*, 1987): 513–21.

Latner, Richard, B. "The Kitchen Cabinet and Andrew Jackson's Advisory System." *Journal of American History* 65 (1978): 367–88.

Lebergott, Stanley. *The Americans: An Economic Record*. New York: Norton, 1984.

"Letter of Wyoming, to the People of the United States on the Presidential Election, and in Favour of Andrew Jackson." Philadelphia: S. Simpson & J. Conrad, 1824.

Letters of Wyoming. Accessed May 9, 2015. www.forgottenbooks.com

McCullough, David. *Truman*. New York: Simon & Schuster Paperbacks, 1992.

Meacham, Jon. *American Lion: Andrew Jackson in the White House*. New York: Random House, 2008.

Mercieca, Jennifer R. "The Culture of Honor; How Slaveholders Responded to the Abolitionist Mail Crisis of 1835." *Rhetoric and Public Affairs* 10 (2007): 51–76.

———. "The Irony of the Democratic Style." *Rhetoric and Public Affairs* 11, no. 3 (2008): 441–49.

Merry, Robert W. *A Country of Vast Designs: James K. Polk, the Mexican War and the Conquest of the American Continent*. New York: Simon & Schuster, 2009.

Meyers, Marvin. "The Jacksonian Persuasion." *American Quarterly* 5 (Spring 1953): 3–15.

———. *The Jacksonian Persuasion: Politics and Belief*. Stanford: Stanford University Press, 1957.

Mio, Jeffery Scott, Ronald E. Riggio, Shana Levin, and Redford Reese. "Presidential Leadership and Charisma: The Effects of Metaphor." *Leadership Quarterly* 16 (2005): 287–94.

Morse, Anson D. "The Political Influence of Andrew Jackson." *Political Science Quarterly* 1 (1886): 153–62.

Moser, Harold D., and J. Clint Clift, eds. *The Papers of Andrew Jackson*. Vol. 6, *1825–1828*. Knoxville: University of Tennessee Press, 2002.

Moser, Harold D., and David R. Hoth, and George H. Hoemann, eds. *The Papers of Andrew Jackson*. Vol. 5, *1821–1824*. Knoxville: University of Tennessee Press, 1996.

Moser, Harold D., ed. *Papers of Andrew Jackson*. Vol. 2, *1804–1813*. Knoxville: University of Tennessee Press, 1985.

Murray, Robert K., and Tim H. Blessing. "The Presidential Performance Study: A Progress Report." *Journal of American History* 70 (1983): 535–55.

Parton, James. *Life of Andrew Jackson*. 3 volumes. New York: Mason Brothers, 1961.

———. *Life of Andrew Jackson*. Vol. 3. New York: Mason Brothers, 1860.

Peterson, Merrill D. *The Great Triumvirate: Webster, Clay and Calhoun*. New York: Oxford University Press, 1987.

Ratcliffe, Donald. *The One-Party Presidential Contest: Adams, Jackson, and 1824's Five-Horse Race*. Lawrence: University Press of Kansas, 2015.

——. "The Right to Vote and the Rise of Democracy, 1778–1828." *Journal of the Early Republic* 33 (Summer 2013): 219–59.

Remini, Robert V. *The Course of American Democracy, 1833–1845*. Vol. 3 of *Andrew Jackson*. New York: Harper & Row, 1984.

——. *The Course of American Freedom, 1822–1832*. Vol. 2 of *Andrew Jackson*. New York: Harper & Row, 1981.

——. *Henry Clay: Statesman for the Union*. New York: W. W. Norton, 1993.

Richardson, James D., ed. *A Compilation of the Messages and Papers of the Presidents*. Vols. 2-4. New York: Bureau of National Literature, 1897.

Roosevelt, Franklin D. *The Public Papers and Addresses of Franklin D. Roosevelt*. Vol. 5.Ed. Samuel I. Rosenman. New York: Random House, 1938.

Schlesinger, Arthur M., Jr. *The Age of Jackson*. Boston: Little, Brown, 1945.

Seager, Robert, II, ed. *Papers of Henry Clay. Candidate, Compromiser, Whig*. Vol. 8, *March 5, 1829–December 31, 1836*. Lexington: University Press of Kentucky, 1984.

Sellers, Charles, ed. *Andrew Jackson: A Profile*. New York: Hill & Wang, 1971.

Sullivan, John. "The Case of 'A Late Student': Pictorial Satire in Jacksonian America." *Proceedings of the American Antiquarian Society* 83, no. 2 (January 1, 1974): 277–86.

——. "Jackson Caricatured: Two Historical Errors." *Tennessee Historical Quarterly* 31, no. 1 (Spring 1972): 39–44.

Sully, Thomas. Portrait of Queen Victoria. www.royalcollection.org.uk

Tulis, Jeffery K. *The Rhetorical Presidency*. Princeton: Princeton University Press, 1987.

Van Buren, Martin. *The Autobiography of Martin Van Buren*. Ed. John C. Fitzpatrick. Washington: Government Printing Office, 1920.

Ward, John William. *Andrew Jackson: Symbol for an Age*. London: Oxford University Press, 1955.

Wilentz, Sean. *The Rise of American Democracy*. New York: Norton, 2005.

Wilson, Major L. "Andrew Jackson: The Great Compromiser." *Tennessee Historical Quarterly* 26 (1967): 64–71.

Wise, Henry A. *Seven Decades of the Union*. Philadelphia: J. B. Lippincott, 1881.

Zarefsky, David. "Presidential Rhetoric and the Power of Definition." *Presidential Studies Quarterly* 34 (2004): 607–19.

Zarefsky, David, and Victoria J. Gallagher. "From 'Conflict' to 'Constitutional Question': Transformation in Early American Public Discourse." *Quarterly Journal of Speech* 76, no. 3 (1990): 247–61.

INDEX

Page numbers in **boldface** refer to illustrations.